TAKING ROOT

Recent Titles in

OXFORD STUDIES IN CULTURE AND POLITICS
Clifford Bob and James M. Jasper, General Editors

TAKING ROOT

*Human Rights and Public
Opinion in the Global South*

James Ron
Shannon Golden
David Crow
Archana Pandya

OXFORD
UNIVERSITY PRESS

OXFORD
UNIVERSITY PRESS

Oxford University Press is a department of the University of Oxford. It furthers
the University's objective of excellence in research, scholarship, and education
by publishing worldwide. Oxford is a registered trade mark of Oxford University
Press in the UK and certain other countries.

Published in the United States of America by Oxford University Press
198 Madison Avenue, New York, NY 10016, United States of America.

© Oxford University Press 2017

Library of Congress Cataloging-in-Publication Data
Names: Ron, James, editor.
Title: Taking root : human rights and public opinion in the global South /
James Ron, Shannon Golden, David Crow, Archana Pandya.
Description: New York, NY : Oxford University Press, 2017. |
Includes bibliographical references and index.
Identifiers: LCCN 2016045071 (print) | LCCN 2017006135 (ebook) |
ISBN 9780199975068 | ISBN 9780199975051 (paperback) |
ISBN 9780199975044 (hardcover) | ISBN 9780190677299
Subjects: LCSH: Human rights—Developing countries. |
Non-governmental organizations—Developing countries.
Classification: LCC JC599.D4 (ebook) | LCC JC599.D4 R66 2017 (print) |
DDC 323.09172/4—dc23
LC record available at https://lccn.loc.gov/2016045071

9 8 7 6 5 4 3 2 1

Paperback printed by Webcom, Inc., Canada

Hardback printed by Bridgeport National Bindery, Inc., United States of America

Contents

Preface

This book explores the popular reception of human rights ideas and organizations in the "global South," the name scholars often use to reference countries with lower or middling incomes. We focus on such countries for two reasons: First, the severity of human rights abuse is often correlated with poverty, inequality, and authoritarianism. Although countries in the "global North" have many of these problems, conditions are often more severe or pervasive in the global South.[1] Second, many scholars and even practitioners have argued that global North actors forced contemporary human rights perceptions, ideas, and methods on people and groups living in the global South.[2] Our study explores the evidence for these claims.

We began our research by interviewing hundreds of human rights experts and practitioners from countries throughout the global South. Next, we asked representative samples of global South publics what *they* actually know or think about human rights; we conducted large-scale surveys in all of Mexico and parts of India, Morocco, and Nigeria. We chose these case studies for their important *differences* in region, religion, and history, but also for their key *similarity* in that they all have vibrant human rights cultures. We wanted to know whether publics had similar attitudes toward human rights ideas and organizations, despite substantial differences between countries. Indeed, we found cross-national patterns in public human rights attitudes and ideas, and we argue that this provides an indication of global trends.

Until now, most researchers interested in the global spread of human rights norms have focused on their philosophical or historical origins; promotion by small groups of dedicated activists; embeddedness in international treaties, conferences, and organizations; and diffusion to political leaders and bureaucrats. Relatively few scholars, by contrast, have explored the public's varied *reception* of human rights ideas at the individual level, and most of those who have done so have used anthropological rather than survey methods.[3] International rights norms have cascaded globally, but most scholars still focus on their reception by national elites in analyzing "local" diffusion. Our investigation, by contrast, contributes to the growing call for systematic analyses of human rights attitudes from the "bottom up," across multiple regions and countries. We use survey methods, rather than ethnography, so as to better generalize. We acknowledge that this effort is nascent and modest, and that much work remains to be done; the "science" of human rights public opinion is just getting started.

This volume has been long in the making. In 2003, coauthor James Ron planned a multi-country ethnography of the global human rights movement, hoping to ask business, religious, and political leaders across world regions for their views of human rights ideas and organizations. Family considerations forced revisions to this plan. From 2006 to 2012, Ron and graduate students from McGill and Carleton universities in Canada interviewed about 240 human rights workers from the global

South. In 2012, Ron collaborated with David Crow at the Centro de Investigación y Docencia Económicas (CIDE), a leading public research institute in Mexico City, to initiate the *Human Rights Perceptions Polls*, a face-to-face survey about human rights, to eventually be administered in Mexico, Morocco, India, and Nigeria.

Although James Ron is the book's first author, this volume is the result of a genuinely collaborative effort. Shannon Golden worked closely with Ron in writing the manuscript, made many theoretical contributions, led the Nigerian field research, and played a key role in data analysis and visualization. David Crow supervised the surveys and data analysis, adding important theoretical insights throughout and contributing substantial portions of text. Archana Pandya led the Mumbai investigation and participated in the Mexico research, overseeing data collection throughout the project.

Many others helped along the way; their contributions refined our thinking and improved this manuscript, with any shortcomings remaining ours alone. Kathleen Rodgers was a key early collaborator, as were Ghita Bennesahroui, Maya Dafinova, Andrew Dawson, Maria Derks, Philippe Martin, Sarah Peek, Laura Sparling, and Sarah Wicks. Xiayoun Shen helped with data cleaning and merging, and Kassira Absar and Deanna Kolas helped with editing. At the University of Minnesota, the book benefited from the advice of Ragui Assaad, Bud Duvall, Ron Krebs, and Deborah Levinson. At CIDE, we received help from Guadalupe Gonzalez, Gerardo Maldonaldo, and Jorge Schiavon, as well as from Carlos Heredia, Lorena Ruano, Kim Nolan, and Brian Phillips. We received excellent feedback from scholars and practitioners during presentations at Arizona State University, Ben Gurion University, CIDE, the CUNY Graduate Center, Hebrew University, the International Human Rights Funders

Group, the Open Society Foundations, and Tel Aviv University. Oxford University Press series editors Clifford Bob and James Jasper were early supporters of the project, as was Oxford editor James Cook. We are grateful to them and to several anonymous reviewers for their thoughtful and detailed comments. We are also grateful to the many agencies and donors who supported our research, including the Harold E. Stassen Chair of International Affairs at the University of Minnesota, the Canada Research Chairs program, the Quebec government, Canada's International Development Research Centre, the U.S. National Science Foundation, and Canada's Social Science and Humanities Research Council.

TAKING ROOT

Public Opinion and Human Rights

Why Care?

Human rights have become a key language through which policymakers, scholars, and global activists articulate ideas of socioeconomic change, politics, and justice.[1] No matter where one turns, prominent authorities soon invoke "human rights" as policy critique or, increasingly, as policy justification.[2] Although human rights terminology began circulating internationally after World War II, it was only in the mid-1970s that leading global figures and agencies began using it regularly. According to historian Samuel Moyn, this growing popularity stemmed from human rights' status as the "last utopia" left standing once the luster had worn off the other big ideas for human improvement, including modernization, Marxism, anti-imperialism, and postcolonialism.[3] There are many other discourses and types of organizations today that promote social and political benefits; "human rights" is not the only or even perhaps the best discursive or organizational package. At this particular historical moment, however, it is one of the most globally prominent and thus is worthy of serious investigation.

Tracking this growth in the rhetorical usage of rights language to organize social action, social scientists began devoting more attention to human rights ideas, institutions, and policies in the 1990s.[4] Most scholars have focused on human rights' incorporation, or lack thereof, in the upper realms of international policymaking. This emphasis on elites has often made sense, as so much of the action surrounding human rights has occurred in transnational arenas. Of late, however, the focus has shifted to the way in which global human rights norms diffuse—top-down—to local contexts. Although individuals increasingly do figure in these accounts, the emphasis remains, typically, on elite "norm entrepreneurs" within or outside government, remarkable people who have blazed a human rights trail of some kind.[5] Ordinary members of the public and their views of human rights, by contrast, rarely figure in most of the relevant studies. Ironically, this lack of systematically gathered data about the views of ordinary people has not stopped legions of scholars from *claiming* that human rights principles and practice are *either* enthusiastically welcomed by the public *or* angrily rejected foreign, neocolonial impositions.

There is also an emerging scholarly consensus that domestic civil society is vital to human rights promotion efforts.[6] *International treaties* articulate the normative rules of the game; *transnational activists* monitor treaty compliance, protest violations, and lobby for reform; and *national political leaders* implement, or obstruct, human rights reforms. Without input, oversight, encouragement, protest, documentation, and advocacy from *local civil society*, however, not much will change over the long term.

Local human rights organizations are often the most immediate and concrete manifestations of international human rights norms. They are, moreover, physically and conceptually closest to the general public. Accordingly, this book asks questions about the interaction between these organizations and the public, and about the public's attitudes toward human rights ideas and groups. The next important turn in human rights scholarship, we believe, is to systematically consider perspectives from the public grassroots; we have obtained a relatively robust understanding of the global human rights landscape and mechanisms of top-down diffusion, but lack a comparable and systematic understanding of views "from below."

One of this book's central contributions is to explore nuance in definitions of "human rights" ideas and organizations. We want to understand how human rights are conceptualized and utilized by practitioners and the general public. Human rights are a tool that can have varied—even contradictory—meanings and uses by different actors, in different contexts. Different groups socially construct the phrase in different ways, in different times and places. To us, this does not mean human rights is an empty concept, but rather that it is a dynamic, contested, and evolving framework.

To avoid prejudging the public's definition of human rights, our surveys asked people for their views of "human rights organizations" in their own country, without specifying what precisely *we* thought this term meant. We also asked to what extent they associated the term "human rights" with a broad array of phrases, without limiting them to a single "textbook" definition of our own. Surveys will always be more constraining than open-ended interviews, but we made considerable efforts to give respondents the room to define "human rights" and "human rights organizations" in their own way.

Local Human Rights Organizations

Local human rights organizations (LHROs) are a major focus of our inquiry because they are situated at the intersection of the global and the local. Defining an LHRO involves complexity and ambiguity, as will be discussed in coming chapters. Although we did not provide a definition to respondents in our public surveys, we ourselves conceptualize LHROs as locally headquartered organizations that use "rights" in their mission, or in a description of their main activities. These groups regard individuals (and sometimes communities) as "rights holders," and regard states as "duty bearers." They take inspiration from international treaties and norms, but they also rely on domestic laws and constitutions. LHROs may incorporate religious messages into their work, but not to the exclusion of the secular "rights" component. To be sure, there are contradictions in any definition of human rights; for example, the interests of individuals and communities often diverge. Few complex ideologies are safe from such problems, however.

We picture the human rights-promoting structure in the global South as a pyramid, the upper tiers of which are inhabited by a relatively small numbers of influential actors headquartered in, and funded by, the global North. These include funders, such as official bilateral development assistance donors, intergovernmental organizations, private foundations, and the international nongovernmental organizations (INGOs) they fund. These INGOs are also headquartered in the global North, but maintain offices and operations in the global South, typically relying heavily on the work of highly professionalized staff.

The pyramid's lowest tiers include local groups and community-based organizations actively involved in the lives of individual people. Some of these work with an explicit human rights framework, others do not. There are few direct linkages between the top tiers and the pyramid's lowest levels, presenting a challenge for organizations at the top (how to have tangible impacts) and at the bottom (how to get funding, support, or attention for their work).

Structurally, the LHROs we are interested in inhabit the pyramid's middle levels, at the nexus of interaction between the global and the local. The base layers interact most closely with the general public in the global South (the "grassroots") and are therefore most responsive to and dependent upon public opinion. Top tiers, by contrast, are more attuned to and engaged with public opinion in the global North, or in transnational forums. Most of the human rights practitioners we interviewed worked in the middle, with the LHROs.

Local rights groups often supplement the work of less formally organized social movements, picking up the slack when these movements' energy wanes.[7] They may provide technical expertise in law, research, accounting, lobbying, communications, and public relations, complementing the raw power of citizen energy. They may also serve as intermediaries between domestic publics and international norms, literally and figuratively "translating" universal ideas into the local vernacular while highlighting their relevance to domestic challenges.[8] LHROs are also often conduits for international financial flows, which they may distribute with discretion. They also transmit information "from below" to international counterparts, furnishing them with the ammunition they need for their own publicity campaigns, reports, accountability, and strategizing. LHROs may also grant (or deny) international counterparts the physical access and political legitimacy they need to operate, fundraise, and flourish.[9]

In some cases, LHROs act as "brokers" in rights "markets," connecting the public's "demand" for rights observance with its potential "supply" by governments and others.[10] They intercede on behalf of aggrieved publics before those responsible for committing and/or righting wrongs, by centralizing information and documenting rights abuses; researching domestic laws and international norms; litigating cases for citizens in domestic courts; undertaking media campaigns to publicize abuses nationally and internationally; lobbying legislators to pass more stringent rights laws; pressuring prosecutors to initiate legal action against abusers; and trying to directly persuade abusers to change their behavior.

Like any broker, LHROs have their own interests, as well as those of their clients.[11] They seek money, influence, and status to perpetuate and grow their organizations and careers. As a result, there is always a possibility that the pyramid's lower tiers—the "grassroots"—will develop mistrust, dislike, and even enmity toward the broker class. We must never *assume* that ordinary people like and trust LHROs just because the latter say they want to help the former; we must always investigate empirically.

Public Opinion about Human Rights

Given this, our second major object of inquiry is public opinion. We argue that a systematic understanding of the public's attitudes toward human rights ideas and LHROs is essential to understanding the global human rights movement. For starters, public support for LHROs and their activities can dramatically upgrade their efficacy; if citizens dislike NGOs or simply doubt their capacity and intentions, they are unlikely to entrust these groups with cases to litigate, demands to aggregate into action programs, or information to document abuses. If the public does not trust LHRO reputations and intentions, moreover, international actors and governments are less likely to treat the groups' demands seriously.

In some cases, supportive public opinion can also protect LHROs from state repression. Recognizing the importance of domestic rights groups, governments worldwide are clamping down on their activities.[12] In response, domestic activists have urgently called on transnational allies in Geneva, Washington, New York, and London for help. These distant outsiders, however, can be of only limited assistance. To survive government repression and endure over the long term, local rights groups will have to mobilize the support of their co-citizens. Public opinion toward LHROs, in other words, is a vital force that can bolster LHRO success and defend against failure. As Scheindlin notes, "Public opinion shapes the overall environment in which human rights organizations operate"; supportive publics enable human rights work, and hostile publics create major obstacles.[13]

Understanding public opinion about human rights ideas and organizations also has implications for LHROs' claims to representation. Human rights practitioners and their financial donors often think of LHROs as representing the interests of "humanity," writ large, with special emphasis on the interests of particularly vulnerable sectors and populations. Funders and international NGOs in particular look to local rights groups to convey the needs and perspectives of local publics. This assumption of "representation" is problematic if public opinion polls reveal widespread negative ideas about LHROs, low public trust in these groups, or conceptualization of human rights that vary substantially from the views promulgated by LHROs and their donors.

Many scholars regard ordinary people as being on the "receiving end" of transnational norm diffusion, but publics do not passively accept ideas and norms handed down to them from above. Rather, they are actively engaged in shaping and reinterpreting human rights in light of their own contexts. Without a popular base for human rights ideas, it will be hard for even the most courageous and skilled local rights group to promote the human rights-respecting *societies* they seek.[14] Such societies "cannot be imposed from above or from the outside," Dicklitch and Lwanga note, but must instead "be cultivated from below," slowly and laboriously.[15]

Our concern with public opinion toward human rights ideas and organizations is not universally shared. Although most activists and scholars accept that local rights *groups* matter, some argue that the *general public's* support is either irrelevant, or tangential to broader human rights struggles. "Only a small percentage of the general population," one leading commentator argues, "will ever develop views about [human rights] issues." As a result, any focus on the general public's opinion is likely to "leave us overvaluing opinions that simply don't factor into the true political equation."[16] Others note that human rights groups tend to be "elite-centered, technical, and highly professionalized," and do not naturally seek allies among the general public.[17] Given this elite focus, any attempt by scholars to explore the public's feeling toward LHROs is ultimately misplaced; the public is simply not an important part of the human rights promoting process. Still others fear that focus on public sentiment can easily undermine human rights' transformative potential, leading message-obsessed, poll-following groups to circulate watered-down messages that appeal to the lowest common denominator, confusing the superficial support of the many with the more impassioned commitment of the few.[18] These concerns are valid, but we believe that the long-term impact, sustainability, and vitality of LHROs and their ideas is ultimately constrained, or enhanced, by the structure of public opinion. There is danger in obsessing about reputations, but rights scholars and LHRO practitioners cannot ignore public opinion either.

In social movement terms, our polls help us measure the extent to which local rights groups have successfully made public inroads. In international relations terms, we can gauge the extent to which one of the world's leading international norms—human rights—has been integrated into the lived experience of ordinary people.

Case Studies

We focus on four case studies: India, Mexico, Morocco, and Nigeria. We selected these countries because they are interesting and important cases in their own right, as major global and regional players politically, economically, and socially or culturally. They each have active, vibrant, and complex human rights histories and contemporary landscapes; understanding public opinion about human rights in these places is an important task. In Mumbai, the human rights community has been particularly known for activism on social and economic rights; in Mexico, for its focus on the disastrous fallout from the government's war on drugs; in Morocco, for its work on women's equality; and in Nigeria, for its focus on democratization. All four case studies are located in the global South, but this does not mean we are not interested in public opinion in the global North. There are no comparable data for publics in the United States, Canada, Western Europe, Australia, and other wealthy countries, but we are committed to extending our questionnaires to those areas. We chose to begin with countries in the global South for two reasons, as noted in the Preface: human rights abuses are often more severe in this part of the world, and both scholars and practitioners question the commitment of publics in the global South to liberal rights ideas.

Each of the countries we study here has developed a strong domestic human rights sector. Mexico, Morocco, India, and Nigeria have all made at least rhetorical commitments to international human rights standards. Each country has ratified at least half of the core international treaties, with pressure to do so often coming from domestic rights groups. In each of the six cities where we conducted NGO interviews, we identified dozens of active LHROs, one useful indicator of vibrant domestic human rights sectors. These groups count many successes in recent years. For example, activists in Mexico have brought national and international attention to disappearances and abuses committed by police and security forces; in Morocco, rights groups were instrumental in passing reforms to personal and family status laws to integrate women's rights; in India, rights groups have pushed national legislation that protects the right to education or food; and in Nigeria, LHROs have successfully framed domestic issues (such as abuses at the hand of multinational corporations or abductions by *Boko Haram*) as international human rights concerns.

A related necessary and pragmatic scope condition was that the context had to be politically open enough to permit LHROs to operate, to allow ordinary people to speak openly about human rights ideas, and to not present safety concerns to our team, partners, or respondents. Although there are certainly pockets of repression in each of these countries, the general political context is relatively free. Each of these countries typically scores at or better than the midpoint of *Freedom House* indices of civil or political liberties.

Our next consideration was to select cases with significant contrasts on characteristics likely to shape human rights organizing or public attitudes, approximating a "most different" case design.[19] These four countries diverge widely on characteristics that scholars and practitioners often regard as macro-level causal factors leading to differential political or human rights outcomes—such as world region,[20] religious composition,[21] colonial history,[22] "civilization,"[23] dominant language,[24] income, and rates of charitable donations.[25]

For example, *world regions* have very different historical and contemporary formulations of "human rights." Latin American countries might therefore have a stronger focus on civil and political rights, whereas African and South Asian countries may have a more developed socioeconomic approach. Religions also matter; *Catholicism* may have a greater affinity with human rights language, whereas Islam has a more awkward relationship. The potential importance of *colonial institutional legacies* is also clear: British colonial policies of indirect rule may have led to more diffuse relationships with the state, for example, and these may shape possibilities for legal recourse for human rights violations, and thus, the tactics of local rights groups.

Language similarly matters; if the population can speak or read UN languages, this may give them more connection to human rights discourse. *Urbanization* matters, because countries with more urban populations may have higher rates of exposure to human rights ideas, as global ideas are conveyed to cities more easily than rural hinterlands. *Per capita income* matters, because wealthier citizens may be less concerned with human rights issues in general, or with socioeconomic rights more specifically. *Higher rates of local charitable giving* may indicate a greater availability of domestic resources for LHROs, whereas in countries with *greater religious, ethnic, or cultural diversity* human rights discourse may be mobilized to protect the collective interests of subgroups or marginalized communities. The four cases we highlight in this book have substantial variation on these characteristics, as Table 1.1 illustrates.

In the following chapters, we find meaningful relationships among a range of key variables; for example, we find that people with higher education have more contact with human rights discourse and organizations, and that people who mistrust the US government trust LHROs more. When we identify relationships consistent across all four countries, our case selection strategy gives us greater confidence in the robustness of our findings. In observing similar findings across different cases, we argue that our findings may represent broader trends.

We do not claim that findings across four countries can or should be generalized to all settings, and we recognize that national NGO communities differ by their unique politics, institutions, and cultures.[26] However, we can speculate about in which types of countries or regions our findings will be more likely to hold true, as well as in which contexts our findings would not likely be applicable. Most generally, we feel at least some of the

TABLE 1.1 Case Attributes

	Mexico: Mexico City and San Cristobal	Morocco: Rabat and Casablanca	India: Mumbai	Nigeria: Lagos
LHRO Population in Locale of Study (total number identified)	74 in Mexico City and San Cristobal (2010–2012)	56 in Rabat and Casablanca (2011)	57 in Mumbai (2010–2011)	64 in Lagos (2014)
(Approximate) Urban Area Residents per LHRO	280,000	100,000	370,000	200,000
Civil Liberties (Freedom House, 1 = best, 7 = worst)	3 (2012)	4 (2012)	3 (2012)	4 (2014)
Ratification of Core International HR Treaties	16 of 18 (2012)	12 of 18 (2012)	10 of 18 (2012)	14 of 18 (2014)
World Region	Latin America	North Africa	South Asia	Sub-Saharan Africa
Major Religions	Christian, Catholicism	Islam	Hinduism, Islam, Buddhism, Christianity	Islam, Christianity

Colonial History	Spain	France	Britain	Britain
"Civilization"	Latin American	Islamic	Hindu	African, Islamic
Major Relevant Languages	Spanish	Arabic, French	Hindi, Marathi, English	English, Pidgin, Yoruba, Hausa, Igbo
Literacy Rate	95% (2015)	69% (2015)	71% (2015)	60% (2015)
Urbanization	79% (2015)	60% (2015)	33% (2015)	48% (2015)
GNI per capita, PPP (in international $)	$15,960 (2012)	$6,670 (2012)	$5,000 (2012)	$5,680 (2014)
Rate of Charitable Giving (% reporting donation to "a charity" in last month)	22% (2012)	6% (2012)	28% (2012)	29% (2013)
Sociocultural Diversity (religion and/or ethnicity)	Homogeneous	Homogeneous	Heterogeneous	Heterogeneous

findings we describe in the coming chapters will apply to countries in the global South where there is a well-developed human rights sector and at least moderate political freedom to discuss human rights ideas.

Public opinion might be drastically different in countries where there is not a vibrant domestic human rights sector, where the public is likely to be far less aware of human rights ideas, or where the public may have much stronger associations of "human rights" with foreign impositions. Our findings likely will also not apply to countries that have high levels of political repression, where people are afraid to talk and think about human rights activities and groups. In addition, some of our specific findings may not apply to certain contexts. For example, Chapter 5 explores the relationship between religion and human rights. Our four cases come from different religious traditions, but they all have highly religious publics. Thus, our findings would likely be very different in less openly religious countries, such as China.

Our Mixed-Methods Approach

We rely on both qualitative and quantitative data. Our hundreds of in-depth interviews with rights practitioners provide us with a deep, contextual understanding of the challenges and successes of local human rights work. Our thousands of face-to-face surveys with ordinary people, moreover, help us gauge the extent to which human rights ideas and organizations have permeated society.

We collected two types of in-depth, qualitative practitioner interviews: a purposive sample of key informants from 60 global South countries and representative samples of LHRO leaders from the four case study countries. More methodological details are available in Appendix A.

Purposively selected key informant interviews.[27] James Ron and his graduate students began the project with interviews at the International Human Rights Training Program (IHRTP), a three-week training course offered near Montreal by *Equitas*, a Canadian NGO. The course attracts some 140 mid-career human rights practitioners each year from the global South. From 2006 to 2010, they interviewed 128 attendees from 60 different countries, purposively sampling by organizational type, region, gender, and language to obtain a balanced, cross-regional view.[28]

Most (68 percent) interviewees worked for local NGOs in their home countries, and some worked in domestic branches of international organizations or in domestic government agencies. This sample does not represent local rights practitioners more broadly, as program participants enjoyed comparatively preferential access to transnational information and resources; instead, this was an "expert sampling" strategy, a variant of purposive selection.[29]

These interviews provide global breadth of insight about how domestically-based rights practitioners engage with, (re)interpret, and utilize global ideas and practices, as well as how domestic activists convey information to international audiences.

Interviews with representative LHRO samples. We then interviewed representative samples of domestic NGOs focused specifically on human rights. This data fill a significant gap in the field, which typically focuses on in-depth case studies and other types of non-representative data. Because there are no authoritative lists of domestic human rights organizations, it is very difficult to collect samples that represent the entire population of these organizations. To find organizations to interview, we conducted significant fieldwork from 2010 to 2014. To create comprehensive

lists—or "sampling frames"—of *all* active LHROs, we concentrated on specific, clearly bounded locations: Mexico City,
Mexico's political, economic, and cultural capital; San Cristóbal
de las Casas, a regional hub of rights-based organizing in the
Mexican state of Chiapas; Rabat and Casablanca, Morocco's adjacent political, cultural, and economic capitals; Mumbai, India's
cultural and financial capital; and Lagos, Nigeria's economic and
cultural (and formerly political) capital. Because of our sampling
techniques, these interview findings are generalizable to the
entire sector of LHROs in each city.

We constructed sampling frames using an iterative process
of Internet searches, key informant consultations, phone calls,
emails, and in-person office visits. The criteria for inclusion in
our list(s) were that organizations had to be active, legally registered, non-profit organizations, headquartered in the area
of interest, with "rights" in their mission statement, or in a
published description of their major activities. We identified
251 such groups in total, including 74 in Mexico City and San
Cristóbal, 56 in Rabat and Casablanca, 57 in Mumbai, and 64 in
Lagos.[30]

We interviewed representatives of 135, using stratified
random sampling to include an appropriate proportion of
organizations that were more central to their local network.
We operationalized this using a network analysis of Internet
links. We conducted most interviews in person, typically with a
senior LHRO representative.[31] We recorded the interviews fully,
and then selectively transcribed them. Interviews were a mix-
ture of open- and closed-ended questions, and lasted about an
hour. We completed 30 interviews each in Mexico City, Rabat
and Casablanca (combined), Mumbai, and Lagos, and 15 in San
Cristóbal.[32]

We asked these LHRO members to explain the workings
of their particular organizations, including their challenges

and successes in crafting a locally resonant human rights message, locating resources to support their work, and building relationships with relevant local and global stakeholders. In addition, we asked them—in their capacity as "experts"—to comment on the broader landscape of human rights work in their city or country.

The qualitative interviews revealed the extent to which the "development" and "human rights" discourses had merged. Only a minority of these LHROs were classic documentation and advocacy human rights groups. Instead, most were service delivery organizations (such as humanitarian aid or poverty alleviation) or broader civic advocacy groups (such as democracy promotion, civic education, or citizen empowerment). Expanding beyond the more narrowly-focused "classic" human rights groups, these organizations engage in all kinds of activities, using "human rights" as a tool to frame their work, articulate their justifications for action, and shape their strategies of intervention. These groups have decided that human rights principles, strategies, treaties, and norms, in one way or another, are important parts of their mission.[33] We thus label them "local human rights organizations," while urging readers not to associate this term exclusively with one organizational type. These groups are not local versions of Amnesty International, but are rather hybrids of multiple genres, all of which share an interest in human rights.

The Human Rights Perceptions Polls

Our second data source is public opinion from our *Human Rights Perceptions Polls*, which explore how ordinary people view human rights issues and groups. From 2012 to 2014, we surveyed 6,180 adults in our four countries: 2,400 in Mexico; 1,100 in Rabat,

Casablanca, and their rural surroundings; 1,680 in Mumbai and rural Maharashtra State; and 1,000 in Lagos and the rural areas of the nearby states of Ogun and Oyo.[34] Some of these questions were replicated by the *Americas and the World* surveys in Mexico (in 2014) and elsewhere in Latin America (2012–2014); these data are also available on our public website. In 2016 we launched a new survey in Mexico City with a special focus on fundraising, and use some of that data here as well.[35]

Sampling and representativeness. Due to random sampling procedures (multistage cluster sampling described in Appendix A), our findings are broadly representative of the entire populations from which the samples were drawn. The Mexico 2012 and 2014 surveys were carried out in collaboration with the *Americas and the World* project, and their samples are nationally representative. In India, Morocco, and Nigeria, we focused on major urban areas and their adjacent rural areas, a focus driven in part by cost, but also by logic: as global cities, major urban centers offer a "best case" scenario for human rights diffusion. If human rights ideas, organizations, and activists are not proliferating in these locales, they are even less likely to be influential elsewhere.

In each country, we worked with a respected and experienced local survey company. Due to our collaboration with an existing survey in Mexico, we faced limitations on the number of questions we could add to their existing questionnaire. To ensure high data quality, one or more author was present in each location, working intensively for multiple weeks with each survey company on questionnaire customization, sampling, interview technique, and data quality.[36]

The questionnaire. We developed our questionnaire based on interviews with key informants and LHRO leaders, the scholarly literature, and conversations with local colleagues. We asked about (1) attitudes toward and evaluations of domestic and international human rights ideas and organizations; (2) participation in and contact with the domestic human rights sector; and (3) respondents' demographic, economic, political, and religious characteristics. The full Nigerian version of the questionnaire is available online at www.jamesron.com; the other versions differ only slightly.

We placed human rights questions in comparative perspective. For example, we did not simply ask about "trust in local human rights organizations," one of our most crucial concepts; instead, we asked about trust in a broad range of social, political, and economic institutions and actors, including both local and international rights groups. This allowed us to situate respondent trust in LHROs within their broader trust spectrum. We used a similar comparative logic when asking about participation in, and donations to, human rights groups, asking also about participation/donation to political parties and neighborhood associations, among others.

We conducted the surveys in relevant local languages, working extensively to refine literal and conceptual translations of the questionnaire, and administering the surveys through face-to-face, household interviews. This was a necessarily complicated and fraught process, described in detail in Appendix A.

Key Findings

We find a level of grassroots diffusion of human rights language that is refreshingly encouraging and likely surprising to those who have worked to promote the development of human rights norms and ideas globally. The words "human rights" are relatively commonly heard among global South publics, suggesting the discourse has enjoyed some diffusion success. Less optimistically, we find the general public rarely has contact with human rights organizations themselves, certainly much more rarely than the idea they promote. Chapter 2 analyzes rates of exposure to human rights language and engagement with human rights organizations and activities. We find that people with comparatively higher socioeconomic status have more contact with human rights, whereas those in more disadvantaged positions are even less likely to report any form of exposure or engagement. The low level of personal connection between LHROs and the general public—particularly marginalized individuals—suggests that rights practitioners may be relying on shortcuts or alternatives to public outreach, avoiding or facing barriers to the slow and laborious work of grassroots mobilization.

Chapter 3 examines the reputations of human rights ideas and organizations by analyzing publics' definitions of "human rights" and trust in human rights organizations. Our most surprising poll finding is that people do *not* generally see "human rights" negatively. Seeing human rights as a foreign imposition, a tacit tool of US foreign policy, or as protections for "terrorists" or "criminals" are all clear minority opinions. This finding directly contradicts a wealth of scholarship arguing precisely the opposite—indeed, it contradicts our own expectations—and is directly opposed to the assumptions of many LHRO leaders themselves. The chapter also shows that ordinary people do *not* generally make strong distinctions between economic/social rights and civil/political rights. Although these different categories of rights are strongly distinguished in scholarly debates, ordinary people do not differentiate as sharply. Both types of human rights enjoy broad support, and many people support both.

Chapter 3 presents another surprising finding: the many people who trust local human rights organizations more strongly mistrust the US government, controlling for a plethora of other relevant factors. As students of international politics, we find this association intriguing, as it once again flies in the face of much scholarship and the fears of many human rights activists. Observers have long feared that the American government's rhetorical and financial support for LHROs and rights principles has tarnished these groups' reputations, transforming them into Trojan horses of the US foreign policy apparatus. In the countries we investigated, however, these fears seem largely unfounded; the public does not, for the most part, subscribe to these views.

Another key finding is the lack of a clear middle class constituency for human rights organizations. Although many scholars and activists believe that the growing global middle class is the human rights community's strongest source of support, our surveys do not find much support for these claims, controlling for other relevant factors. Nor do we find support for the notion that urban residents are more rights-supporting than rural citizens. Instead, we find that the best predictors of trust in human rights organizations are anti-power worldviews, illustrated through mistrust in domestic governments, in multinational corporations, and in the US government (and also mistrust in religious institutions, as shown in Chapter 5). These skeptical constituencies, who fundamentally mistrust organized authority of very different types, represent a key pocket of the public that could be mobilized by human rights groups, for human rights causes.

Chapter 4 discusses the shaky local resource foundation of domestic human rights sectors. We establish that LHROs rely heavily on international funds, a surprising finding given the breadth of popular support we find for human rights organizations and ideas. Ordinary people in the locales we investigated are not giving money to local human rights groups, but they do give money to other charitable causes. They have reasonably positive feelings toward human rights, trust human rights groups, perceive a need for human rights conditions to improve in their countries, and even have some degree of disposable income.

In this relatively favorable context, we argue that LHROs struggle to raise local funds because of deeply engrained philanthropic habits, both on the part of publics who give and LHROs who seek funding. We find that contact with human rights workers and groups is a key catalyst in moving individuals from the "likely to donate" category to actually making a donation. To more successfully cultivate a local support base that moves beyond ideological to actual resource support, LHROs need to develop more evidence-based strategies of reaching out to the general public. Donations to any public interest nongovernmental group are always subject to collective action problems; in the case of human rights, we believe that donors based in the global North have "solved" this problem by taking the public out of the equation altogether, and helping Southern groups survive financially without recourse to individual, local donations.

Chapter 5 explores the role of personal faith and organized religion in shaping human rights opinion. We present evidence for human rights conceptualizations that are unique to particularly religious traditions. Controlling for a wide range of factors, for example, Catholics are more likely to be supportive of human rights than non-Catholics, and Muslims tend to associate "human rights" with "women's rights" more than non-Muslims.

Additionally, contrary to much of the literature and many activist views, our opinion surveys suggest that different aspects of religiosity have divergent and often contradictory associations with human rights, defying simple categorizations. Regular attendance in a place of worship, for example, often has negative associations with human rights support. The personal aspects of religiosity, however, do not. The links between religion and human rights are complex and not easily generalized. We find a potentially strategic inroad to new constituents among religious publics; although the socially religious are more critical of human rights, interpersonal contact with human rights workers and groups is disproportionately more effective with these people and is associated with stronger support for human rights organizations. Based on this finding, we recommend that human rights practitioners engage with faith-based communities to a much greater extent.

Although this book is published by a university press and is in part aimed at scholars, we hope practitioners will find our work accessible and useful. Most importantly, we hope LHRO leaders and donors will take heart, as our data suggest the public is not as averse to their work as they fear. Government critics of LHROs and their ideas may be better organized and more vocal, but they do not appear to have fully persuaded the broader population. There *is* public support for human rights ideas and organizations in the global South, where publics do not consider LHROs as foreign implants foisted on them by powerful global North actors.

The second message for practitioners is that they must circulate more extensively within their own societies. Retail politics will not only encounter a half-opened door, given the public support we find, but may also yield important new streams of funding. As states crack down on foreign funding to local NGOs, domestic rights groups must learn how to raise more money from their co-citizens, rather than from overseas donors. Our research suggests these efforts may be more successful than most practitioners currently suspect.

Finally, our findings suggest that activists must work much harder to engage with organized religion. Although the people who attend mosque, church, or temple do tend to be more critical of rights groups, LHRO contact with these people has positive effects. Though the religious and international legal visions of human rights differ dramatically on the origin and content of rights, there is overlap that activists can leverage, if they approach faith communities with genuine respect.

2

Reach

Human Rights Exposure and Engagement

Most people know little about specific human rights declarations and treaties, and this "ignorance all but guarantees that uninformed victims won't benefit much from the [human rights] system."[1] Knowledge of individual legal instruments is not the same thing as knowledge of and exposure to "human rights" ideas or activism more generally, however. Although the ordinary person may not know the technicalities of the human rights system and the legal protections it affords, he or she may still be aware of human rights ideas and how they are mobilized in his or her community or country.

This chapter breaks down the notion of human rights consciousness into three components: (1) **Exposure**—How often do ordinary people *hear* the term "human rights"? (2) **Engagement**—What level of *contact* do they have with rights organizations? How many have *met* human rights practitioners, can *name* a specific rights organization, or have *participated* in an activity organized by a human rights group? (3) **Equity**—How do exposure and engagement vary by *socioeconomic status*? Together, these provide a measure of the extent to which publics are familiar and engaged with human rights ideas and organizations in their country.

We begin our study with the variable *Hear Human Rights*, which comes from responses to our question, *"In your daily life, how often do you hear the term 'human rights'?"*[2] These answers are important for at least two reasons. First, they tell us something about the penetration of "world culture" to the smallest unit of analysis, the individual. Since the 1990s, sociologists have tracked the spread of this alleged macro culture—of which human rights is a key part—through all manner of elite fora, texts, and institutions.[3] As transnational forces challenge the nation-state's supremacy, people may be increasingly prone to thinking of themselves as global citizens bound to one another as humans, rather than as citizens of specific states.[4] Exposure to the language of human rights is a basic but important indicator of the extent to which this process has even begun at the individual level.

Hear Human Rights also matters because the rights frame is a unique form of political discourse that protects individuals ("rights holders") and obliges states ("duty bearers") to take measures to uphold their rights. As a result, repeated exposure to the term may in theory influence an individual's interpretation of his or her surrounding political realities. Exposure to human rights language should be an initial step or necessary condition in a far longer and more complex process of individual-level internalization of the rights individuals should expect to have protected by states.

Our second variable is *Met Human Rights Worker*, a comparatively stronger measure of familiarity and engagement. It is based on our question, "*Have you ever met someone who works in a human rights organization?*"[5] We did not define "works" or "human rights organization," but rather let respondents answer based on their own understanding of the terms. This means our estimates are likely expansive, as some people with only a hazy sense of the organized human rights landscape might consider all manner of actors to be "human rights workers."[6] What matters for us, however, is whether people *think* they have met a human rights worker. If many report having done so, this suggests that LHROs are making broad local contact.

Next, we produced the variable, *Name Human Rights Organization*, using two questions. First, we asked respondents, *"Have you ever heard of organizations or associations working in the field of human rights in* [country]?"[7] Of those who answered "yes," we then asked, *"Can you tell me the names of all the human rights organizations or associations that you know?"*[8] An ability to name a specific group serves as a check on the variable, *Met Human Rights Worker*. If respondents reported having met a human rights worker but could not remember a specific organizational name, the contact was likely not particularly extensive or meaningful.

The theoretical and practical implications of interpersonal contact are broadly recognized. The business literature, for example, suggests that inter-firm contact breeds trust and cooperation,[9] the social movement literature says that successful activists develop personal ties with supporters,[10] and sociologists of knowledge say that personal "interaction rituals" transfer emotional energies and diffuse intellectual concepts.[11] Scholars of international law highlight the importance of conversations between members of the international legal community and representatives of individual states.[12] These studies all see meaningful interpersonal contact as necessary, though perhaps insufficient, for deeper impacts.

Freedom Summer, a classic sociological study of young Americans' decision to participate in high-risk civil rights activism, exemplifies the importance of personal contact.[13] Young people moved from the "potential" to "actual" participant list if they had experienced sustained interpersonal contact with *other* participants. Connection with like-minded others, in this case, was a precondition for serious engagement. When it comes to getting other people to do things—especially costly, time-consuming, or dangerous things—there is little substitute for personal contact.

Hearing, knowing, and contact are still relatively diluted measures of exposure and engagement. Individual *participation*, however, signals a personal investment in an issue or movement. To estimate *Participate in Human Rights*, we asked, *"Have you ever participated in the activities of a human rights organization?"*[14] Once again, we did not dictate the terms of either the "activities" or the "human rights organization," but simply recorded responses using the respondent's own understanding of these terms. As a result, some of those who replied "yes" may have been thinking of activities and organizations that we ourselves might not define as human rights. Our goal, however, was to estimate the extent to which members of the public believed they had participated in human rights-related activities, not in obtaining an estimate based on our own definition.

Theoretically, participation should matter for many reasons. First, collective action of any kind is rare and difficult, as ordinary people are often risk-averse or strapped for time, resources, and energy.[15] Given these limitations, it makes rational sense to let others participate in whatever needs to be done and reap the collective benefits later. Not all people are "free riders," however, and these problems can be overcome with coercion, incentives, or other solutions. Still, collective action is relatively rare and difficult, meaning that participation of any kind in a self-defined "human rights activity" is a notable achievement. Participation may also transform individuals into long-term change agents, empowering them to confront abusive or neglectful duty-holders in the future. "'Empowerment,'" two experts say, is a "state of confidence in one's ability to challenge existing relations of domination."[16]

Indeed, they note that the evidence suggests "collective action may engender experiences of empowerment, both for the individual participant and for the collective as a whole." *Freedom Summer*, for example, noted that years after the freedom rides were over, former participants remained more willing than others—controlling for other relevant factors—to join demanding social change efforts. Early participation had boosted these individuals' long-term propensity for collective action.

Participation in human rights actions can also have immediate political outcomes, of course, as the collective actions by the individually powerless can achieve great results. It may also boost the legitimacy of the LHROs involved; one of the main criteria distinguishing internationally prominent groups from their obscure counterparts is an ability to publicly mobilize large numbers of people.[17]

In short, getting the rights message out (*Hear Human Rights*), personally meeting potential constituents (*Met Human Rights Worker*), making enough of an impression so that ordinary people remember the name of your organization (*Name Human Rights Organization*), and coordinating public action (*Participate in Human Rights*) are all meaningful and successively difficult steps in a chain of human rights exposure, familiarity, engagement and, eventually, internalization and mobilization. These indicators are particularly important if we consider human rights as a social movement. If the goal of human rights workers and organizations is solely elite-level lobbying, public engagement indicators matter less. However, if one believes—as we do—that the human rights movement needs to sink deep social roots for reasons of political efficacy, fundraising, legitimacy, and survival, these indicators of public engagement are vital.

Findings

Most of the human rights practitioners we interviewed understood the importance of and desired to increase their levels of public contact, engagement, and participation. One practitioner in Morocco, for example, told us that LHROs in her country had worked hard to successfully "penetrate the grassroots" through determined organizational outreach, including efforts to use "mules to access mountainous rural areas and teach women about their rights."[18] The result of this hard-fought "proximity work," she said, was increased public support for human rights ideas and organizations. Indeed, even those practitioners who said their organizations were doing a poor job of reaching the public acknowledged the value of contact, engagement, and participation.

Our *Human Rights Perceptions Polls* offer rights practitioners cause for both celebration and concern. The public *does* frequently hear the term "human rights," but reports little contact with human rights workers, limited knowledge of specific LHROs, and rare participation in human rights activities. Organized human rights actors are regularly but vaguely heard, and they are seldom met, seen, or directly engaged. Figure 2.1 shows how often respondents in each country report hearing "human rights." With each country weighted equally to correct for their different sample sizes in the combined cross-national results, 36 percent of respondents reported hearing the term "frequently" or "daily," 35 percent heard it "sometimes," and only 28 percent reported hearing it "rarely" or "never." Publics are clearly heavily exposed to human rights language and discourse.

This optimistic assessment is tempered, however, by a comparison to elite public opinion. We asked the same question on a survey of 535 individuals holding high-level positions in

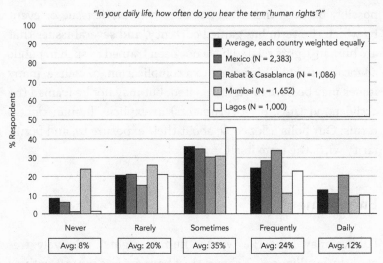

"In your daily life, how often do you hear the term 'human rights'?"

■ Average, each country weighted equally
■ Mexico (N = 2,383)
■ Rabat & Casablanca (N = 1,086)
■ Mumbai (N = 1,652)
□ Lagos (N = 1,000)

Never	Rarely	Sometimes	Frequently	Daily
Avg: 8%	Avg: 20%	Avg: 35%	Avg: 24%	Avg: 12%

FIGURE 2.1 Exposure to Human Rights Language Is High

government, politics, the private sector, mass media, academia, and civil society Mexico.[19] When we asked Mexican leaders how often they hear "human rights," fully 90 percent reported they hear it "daily" or "frequently," showing that human rights language circulates *much* more heavily in elite circles.

There is also substantial cross-country variation within the general pattern of exposure. In Morocco, a surprising 54 percent of adults living in and around Rabat and Casablanca reported hearing *droits de l'homme* (French) or *hukuk al insaan* (Arabic) daily or frequently, whereas in and around Mumbai, only 20 percent reported hearing *mānava adhikāra* (Hindi) or *mānavī adhikāra* (Marathi) with similar frequency. Why these differences? It is hard to know for sure, but Moroccan exposure rates are likely high because of LHROs' deep efforts over the last decade to push through constitutional reforms on women's rights issues[20] and the leading role of LHROs in Morocco's Arab Spring demonstrations.[21] By contrast, the Mumbai public's exposure is lower, possibly because there has not been a catalytic issue or event by which the term has gained currency, and several issues that are human-rights related have not been framed as such in public advocacy efforts. This points to a complication, of course; many issues may be human-rights related, but may not be framed (by activists, victims, or governments) in explicit "human rights" terms. Our polls ask people about their exposure to, and familiarity with, the term itself.[22]

Engagement

Publics may hear the words "human rights" relatively frequently, but Figure 2.2 shows they have *far less* contact with or participation in LHROs.[23] Human rights language may circulate in public discourse relatively commonly, likely due in part to public-awareness raising efforts of LHROs, but the organizations

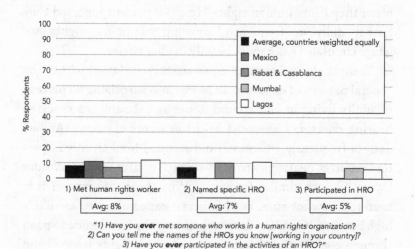

"1) Have you **ever** met someone who works in a human rights organization?
2) Can you tell me the names of the HROs you know [working in your country]?
3) Have you **ever** participated in the activities of an HRO?"

FIGURE 2.2 Public Engagement with Human Rights Organizations Is Low

themselves are much less frequently encountered. Only 8 percent of the individuals we polled, on average, reported having "met a human rights worker," and only 5 percent reported ever having "participated in the activities of a human rights organization," however they defined the terms. Even these low figures may be too expansive, as some respondents likely had very broad definitions of "human rights" or were thinking of "workers" or "organizations" of a different sort.[24] As a point of reference, elites in Mexico have much higher rates of contact with rights groups than the general public: 86 and 32 percent of Mexican leaders, respectively, reported having met a human rights worker and participating in organized human rights activities. When we asked them to identify any specific domestic human rights group, only 7 percent of the public, on average (across the three cases for which we have data; we did not ask the question in Mexico), could name a specific human rights organization in their country. In Morocco, 29 percent of respondents said they had heard of at least one such group, but only 10 percent could offer a specific name when asked.

When we overlap *Hear Human Rights, Met Human Rights Worker, Name Human Rights Organization,* and *Participate in Human Rights*, we find that virtually *no one* in our sample fit all measures of exposure and engagement. Indeed, only *eight individuals out of our entire three-country sample* of 3,780 persons, or 0.002 percent, reported that they hear "human rights" often, had met a human rights worker, could name a specific human rights organization, *and* had participated in the activity of a human rights organization.[25]

The public is thus vastly more likely to *hear* the global language of human rights than to have any kind of concrete experience with its representatives. This may be because rights groups focus on media messaging, rather than other forms of engagement. In Lagos, we asked respondents *where* they most

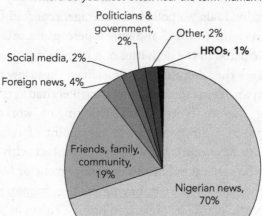

FIGURE 2.3 Lagos Respondents Overwhelmingly Hear the Words "Human Rights" from Domestic News

frequently hear "human rights," and, as Figure 2.3 indicates, a majority (70 percent) reported encountering the term primarily through domestic news sources, with interpersonal contact lagging far behind.

Equity

We know that elites (in Mexico, but very likely elsewhere as well) are more familiar with human rights, but how do a broader range of socioeconomic factors relate to human rights exposure and engagement across multiple countries? One argument suggests that human rights familiarity should *increase* as we descend the socioeconomic spectrum.[26] After all, the demand for human rights "products"—for the mobilization of human rights terminologies, workers, ideas, and strategies—should be highest among the most materially or socially disadvantaged, as they tend to suffer the most from human rights abuse.[27] The "wretched of the earth" should be the human rights movement's natural constituency, and human rights "suppliers"—practitioners, activists, and professionals—should be motivated to prioritize contact with them. With highly motivated rights "suppliers" energetically engaging eager rights "consumers," rates of human rights exposure, contact, familiarity, and participation should increase among the socioeconomically disadvantaged.

Sociological theory, however, predicts the opposite. People in higher socioeconomic brackets have more access to technology and information, and are often more drawn to abstract or cosmopolitan ideas.[28] Historically, the urban, middle, and highly organized working classes have been most supportive of the liberal ideologies undergirding notions of individual rights. Social elites may also see human rights as a status symbol or luxury good, an upper-class belief system that distinguishes them from the masses.[29] Thus, although human rights activists may *hope* they are in higher demand and more heavily prevalent among the poor, sociological logic leads us to expect otherwise.

To empirically test these opposing predictions, we statistically examined the relationship between socioeconomic status (SES) and our indicators of human rights exposure and engagement. We assessed a respondent's SES through: **education**, measured through our question "*What is the highest level of education you completed?*";[30] **place of residence**, based on urban/rural country-specific census classifications;[31] **income**, measured through responses to our question "*Considering your family's total income, which statement best describes your status?*," which allowed respondents to subjectively rank the ability of their income to cover their expenses;[32] and **Internet use**, measured by the simple query, *"Do you use the Internet?"*[33]

We use multivariate regression to assess the link between these four explanatory variables and our four outcome measures of human rights exposure and engagement; we also statistically control for gender, age, and country.[34] Table B.1 (in Appendix B) presents the full statistical results, and Table 2.1 below summarizes the statistically significant relationships. The socioeconomic (independent or explanatory) variables are on the left hand side of the table, and the (dependent or outcome) variables of exposure and engagement are listed across the top.[35]

Table 2.1 demonstrates that socioeconomic status is indeed a meaningful predictor of human rights familiarity. *Education* is positively associated with all four of our outcome measures, revealing that more highly educated people have greater exposure to human rights language and engagement with the human rights movement. *Residence* is nearly uniformly significant across all models, with urban dwellers hearing "human rights" more often, being more likely to know a human rights worker, and being more likely to participate in HRO activities than rural residents (nationwide in Mexico, and those close to the urban areas of Lagos, Mumbai, and Rabat/Casablanca). *Internet*, similarly, is nearly universally significant, indicating individuals with online resources have greater human rights exposure. *Subjective Income Squared*, however, introduces greater nuance. Both poorer *and* richer respondents reported more frequent exposure to human rights language, whereas middle class individuals hear "human rights" comparatively less. The relationship between income and hearing "human rights" is thus U-shaped, offering evidence for *both* sides of the debate. Being male and older is also associated with greater human rights familiarity.

TABLE 2.1 Predicting Exposure to Human Rights Language and Engagement with HROs

	1 Hear HR Discourse (N = 5,829)	2 Met HR Worker (N = 5,730)	3 Named Specific HRO (N = 3,543)	4 Participated in HRO (N = 5,621)	5 Participated in HRO: Expanded Model (N = 3,155)
Education	More frequent	More likely	More likely	More likely	More likely
Subjective income (squared)	U-shaped	—		—	—
Urban residence	More frequent	More likely		More likely	More likely
Internet user	More frequent	More likely		More likely	More likely
Woman	Less frequent	Less likely		—	—
Age	More frequent	More likely	More likely	More likely	More likely
Expanded model					
Hear HR discourse					More likely
Met HR worker					More likely
Named specific HRO					—

Relationships shown are statistically significant at the 0.10-level or higher. All models control for country and weight countries equally, Model 1 is ordinal logistic regression; models 2–5 are logistic regression, Models 3 and 5 do not include Mexico.

Overall, Table 2.1 suggests that the higher respondents are on the socioeconomic scale, the more likely they are to *hear* about human rights, *have met* human rights workers, *know the names* of specific human rights organizations, and *have participated* in human rights activities, as defined by their own understanding of those terms. To get a sense of how important these effects really are, consider the relationship between education and human rights engagement, holding all other variables constant at their means. Our pooled models predict that, on average, only 4 of every 100 persons with no formal education will have met someone whom they define as being a human rights worker. For people with 20+ years of education, however, we predict that, on average, 19 of every 100 people will have met someone whom they define as being a human rights worker. The predicted probability of interpersonal contact between the public and the organized human rights movement, in other words, increases by 375 percent over the educational spectrum. Similarly, our models predict only 5 of every 100 respondents with no education can name a specific human rights group, but 26 of every 100 people with 20+ years can do so, an increase of 420 percent. Higher socioeconomic status is clearly associated with much higher likelihood of human rights exposure and engagement.

Finally, we ran another statistical model predicting *Participate in Human Rights* (Model 5 in Table 2.1), adding this time, as additional independent variables, the three other indicators of familiarity with the human rights movement (*Hear Human Rights, Met Human Rights Worker,* and *Name Human Rights Organization*).[36] Before, we used these measures as dependent variables (Models 1–4 in Table 2.1); here, we treat them as explanatory factors to examine whether they are statistically associated with a higher likelihood of participation. Participation, after all, is a more intense form of engagement and a vital outcome for practitioners interested in the "human rights as a social movement" model. Not surprisingly, we find that hearing "human rights" more often and having met a human rights work do predict *participation* in human rights activities. As social movement theorists would expect, face-to-face contact and exposure to the language are indeed associated with an individual's direct engagement in action.

Implications

As world culture theorists would anticipate, human rights language has diffused widely among ordinary people in the global South. If exposure to discourse is a necessary (though insufficient) condition for the eventual internalization of human rights ideas, this finding provides cause for celebration. Publics are exposed to the idiom of "human rights" and may have therefore begun building a political reality in which they are the ultimate possessors of rights and states are the ultimate "duty-bearers." (They may well be engaged in other framings of social justice and political mobilization, but our polls do not measure those.)

There is far less cause for optimism when it comes to more direct or intense human rights engagement, however. Ordinary people rarely meet rights workers, and few can name a specific group or recall having participated in a human rights activity. This should trouble rights practitioners, because interpersonal contact often helps engage and mobilize publics, which can enhance strength and efficacy of a movement. Of even greater concern, the socioeconomically disadvantaged have substantially less human rights exposure and engagement, suggesting that rights language and practice cluster *most* among those who need human rights reforms or protections *least*.

Certainly, however, our measures are static snapshots in time. We recognize that public engagement with human rights ideas and organizations is likely to shift dramatically depending on current political, social, or economic developments, and how human rights sectors respond to current issues and events with media, advocacy, or other outreach campaigns. Ongoing studies of shifts in publics' levels of contact with human rights ideas and groups is sorely needed.

Low public engagement with human rights, and the disproportionately lower rates of engagement among people of lower socioeconomic status, undermine LHRO claims to represent the poorest and most needy sectors. It is difficult to claim representation of people you have never met, who have never heard of you, who cannot recollect the name of organizations in your field, and who have never participated in an activity you organized.

Arguably, the more that ordinary people are actively engaged with the organized human rights movement, the more likely societies are to become rights respecting. Broad domestic constituencies for human rights ideas and activities make it much more difficult for governments to ignore human rights issues, claims, or advocacy. Public exposure and engagement are only the beginning in this process, however. As local rights groups themselves know, they must urgently find ways to expand their reach. In the next chapter, we turn to our study of the meanings that people ascribe to human rights, and the extent to which they trust the organized, nongovernmental, and most physically proximate carriers of an explicit "human rights" message, their country's national LHROs.

3

Reputation

Human Rights Meanings and Trust

People often hear "human rights," but what do the words really *mean* to them? Do publics associate the phrase with political and civil liberties, such as freedom from state repression, or with socioeconomic protections, such as access to clean water?[1] Do more troubling associations come to mind, such as that of foreign domination, US imperialism, or undue protections for criminals and terrorists?[2] What are the connections, moreover, between these meanings and the public's trust—or mistrust, as the case may be—in local human rights organizations (LHROs)?

The publics we sampled define "human rights" as protecting people from all manner of abuse; they do not make strong distinctions between economic/social and political/civil rights. Most do *not* conceive of human rights as a foreign imposition, and most do *not* associate human rights with excessive protections for suspected criminals and terrorists. Instead, human rights are most often defined positively, and trust in LHROs corresponds with *mistrust* in concentrated power at both global and local levels. In addition, we find no evidence of a singular socioeconomic support base for human rights; we find no consistently pro-human rights middle class across countries.[3]

These findings can help practitioners more clearly identify constituents, know what makes the public more or less likely to support which definitions of rights, and investigate the extent

of LHROs' public credibility. For human rights activists protest-
ing government abuse, for example, knowing that significant
segments of the public trust and support their work should be
enormously empowering. For scholars, moreover, there is clear
value in knowing that publics do not view human rights as a
neo-imperialist tool and in identifying fundamental drivers
of pro-human rights sentiment. We recognize, of course, that
other factors shape human rights reform, and that our survey
questions did not explore the compromises people might make
between human rights and other values. Still, our findings are
a crucial first step. At this point in history, global human rights
actors and institutions have been actively working for decades
to promote diffusion and "vernacularization" of human rights
ideas. In the previous chapter, we found that the language of
human rights has, in fact, spread relatively widely. Now, we turn
toward tracking the public's stance toward human rights ideas
and organizations. They hear the words, but what meaning do
they have? Do they resonate with their life experiences? They
are (rarely, but sometimes) interacting with human rights organizations, but are these interactions positive? Do publics trust
LHROs to represent their interests?

Afraid of Public Opinion?

Many of the practitioners we interviewed pessimistically feared
that human rights ideas and groups enjoy little public support,
or even attract negative sentiments. As Figure 3.1 shows, half
of the human-rights workers we interviewed told us they either
"agreed strongly" or "agreed" that *"Human rights is hard for the
average person in [my country] to understand and use."*

One common challenge, practitioners said, was that ordinary people often found "human rights" too abstract or vague,
and thus meaningless or not particularly useful. As one Bolivian

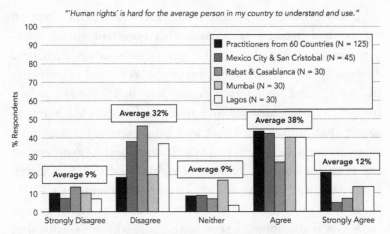

"'Human rights' is hard for the average person in my country to understand and use."

The 60-country practitioner sample is a purposive sample;
the other samples are representative of LHROs in each city.
The average is the mean across samples, with all five samples weighted equally.

FIGURE 3.1 Human Rights Practitioners Think "Human Rights" Is Difficult for People to Understand

practitioner explained, "Human rights are everything, [but] at the same time, [they] are nothing."[4] Or as a Filipino practitioner noted, the concept "is [so] very broad . . . sometimes you get lost."[5] Scholars echo these fears, saying "human rights" are a "catchall," fitting willy-nilly "into whatever worldview you have, without any anchors or attachments."[6] Human rights can be the ideological equivalents of tofu, taking on whatever political flavors surround them.

Still others worried that people viewed human rights as something available to or of interest only to the privileged. According to one Cameroonian practitioner, "When you talk to a poor person about human rights, she is under the impression that you are good and you live well, so it is easy for you to talk about such things."[7] Many informants emphasized rural-urban socioeconomic differences; in Pakistan, for example, one said that rural "people are very poor, very illiterate and they don't know what's going on."[8]

Other practitioners more ominously feared that "human rights" had become associated with powerful global interests, including those of the US government or multinational corporations. Scholars share these concerns; the prominence of "rights" and "democracy promotion" in US foreign policy, including in military aid and intervention, has led many to assert that human rights act as a smokescreen for American machinations. As one Yemeni practitioner told us, "People often say that 'the concept [of human rights] is directly imported from America, because America wants to colonize us.'"[9] Do those with pro-American attitudes trust human rights groups more? Or is the opposite true, with those who are skeptical of global powers turning to human rights more readily, to provide a critical lens?

Many practitioners also feared the public viewed them as supporters of criminals and terrorists. In Mexico, one said the public believes "that human rights defenders help to release murderers and rapists."[10] These perceptions may spring, in part, from human rights practitioners' concern for accountability and due process or from office-seekers' eagerness to exploit potential connections. The slogan of one ultimately successful gubernatorial campaign in Mexico, for example, was that "human rights are for humans, not *ratas* ["rats," Mexican slang for criminals]."[11] Many practitioners, in other words, feared their co-citizens understood human rights in ways they did not intend. We investigate these and other reputational fears in our polls.

We also test for cynicism emerging from "over-saturation" of human rights discourse in contexts where human rights violations continue to occur, which is certainly the case in each of these four countries. Does the rising tide of human rights verbiage breed more or *less* trust in LHROs? In the Communist era, torrents of Marxist-Leninist propaganda eventually backfired, making citizens more cynical of state socialism.[12] Is the same happening for human rights? In Mexico, a state-funded agency vigorously promotes human rights through public service announcements, leading one expert to write that in 2014, "No matter what radio station I had on, I was assured at least three times an hour that *I* had human rights, *you* had human rights, and that *we all* had human rights."[13] This overexposure, she said, could easily "suck the idea [of human rights] of its very lifeblood." Practitioners we interviewed voiced similar concerns, saying the gap between ideals and reality was so vast that people often responded with derision to the very mention of "human rights."

We also wanted to know whether greater familiarity with the rights sector was indeed correlated with greater support, as hypothesized in the previous chapter. According to one US study, citizens with more knowledge of Congress tended to hold the body in *lower,* rather than higher, esteem.[14] Might better knowledge of the rights sector produce similarly negative results? In Malawi, according to one ethnographer, this process is already underway, as LHROs roam the countryside sparking public resentment with their overweening arrogance.[15] Infected, perhaps, by a neocolonial disposition, practitioners could be provoking public *resistance* to human rights ideas and organizations.[16]

This chapter explores the drivers of trust in LHROs. First, we explore the relationship between *different definitions of human rights* and trust, and then explore the role of *trust in other actors and institutions*, controlling for a wide range of factors. We probe the effects of *human rights familiarity and engagement* and the impact of *socioeconomic factors*. Our objective is to begin building a profile of human rights supporters in Mexico, Morocco, India, and Nigeria, identifying patterns that may hold throughout other portions of the global South as well. We want to show how nuanced understandings of public opinion can actually be a resource for rights groups, rather than a black box of uncertainty and hostility.

What the Polls Show

Our *Human Rights Perceptions Polls* reveal a largely encouraging picture. We first asked people to what extent they associate "human rights" (in local languages) with a range of phrases or definitions.[17] We did this to find out what ordinary people *themselves* think when they hear "human rights." We did not want to impose our own definition or one supplied by an international text, as that is often a key critique of the global human rights-promoting sector. Instead, we simply listed alternative phrases, many of which were contradictory, and asked respondents to tell us which best fit their own interpretation of "human rights."

Some phrases we offered to the public are positive-sounding, such as "protecting people from torture and murder," whereas others have more negative connotations, such as "protecting criminals" or "protecting terrorists." Others imply foreign maneuverings, such as "promoting foreign ideas and values" and "promoting US interests." We asked respondents to rate how strongly they associated "human rights" with each phrase, using a scale of 1 ("not at all") to 7 ("a lot"). Anything higher than the midpoint of "4" indicates that respondents *did* relatively strongly associate the phrase with human rights, whereas lower numbers indicate very little or no association. As seen in Figure 3.2, publics were far more likely to associate "human rights" with positive phrases.

Defining human rights as "not protecting or promoting anyone's interests" corresponds to practitioner fears that publics view these rights as useless, arguably one of the most negative phrases we included. Across all samples, the average strength

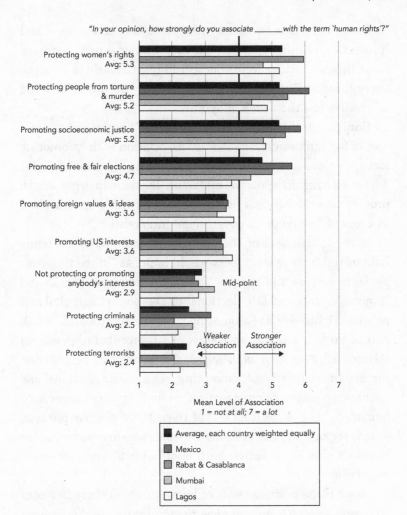

"In your opinion, how strongly do you associate _____ with the term 'human rights'?"

FIGURE 3.2 Publics Have Largely Positive Associations with "Human Rights"

of this association was 2.9, demonstrating that most respondents did *not* perceive "human rights" as a waste of time or as a purely empty concept. Overall, just 25 percent of our samples scored this definition at a 5, 6, or 7 on the scale. The same holds for associating human rights with "protecting terrorists"[18] and "protecting criminals." Although practitioners strongly feared these interpretations were widespread (particularly in Mexico), survey respondents scored them at only an average of 2.4 and 2.5, well below the scale's midpoint.

Contrary to fears that publics viewed "human rights" as a tool of foreign powers, the average association with "promoting foreign values and interests" or "promoting US interests" was 3.6 for each, again below the midpoint. The data, in other words, provide no evidence that publics readily regard "human rights" as a tool of foreign or US government intervention.

Instead, members of the public were more likely to define human rights as practitioners would hope, as "protecting people from torture and murder" (average association of 5.2) and "promoting free and fair elections" (4.7)—both classic civil and political rights—or as "promoting socioeconomic justice" (5.2). Across our four samples, an average of 40 percent of respondents selected a 5, 6, or 7 for *all three* phrases: "protecting people from torture and murder" *and* "promoting free and fair elections" *and* "promoting socioeconomic justice." Fully 85 percent associated human rights with at least one of these three positive phrases. Across regions and cultures, many people we surveyed regarded human rights as including both civil/political and economic/social dimensions.

These three positive views of human rights cohere in a constellation in which no one view predominates, as the associations were heavily (but not fully) correlated. The associations with civil and political rights ("protecting people from torture and murder" and "promoting free and fair elections") were correlated at 0.51; the correlation between the civil and socioeconomic definitions of rights was nearly as high (.49); that between the political and socioeconomic associations was only slightly lower (.43). In theory, these figures are at the middle of the 0 (no correlation) to 1 (full correlation) range. In practice, correlations between attitudinal items rarely approach the theoretical maximum of 1; they rarely top .60 or .70. This means that the correlations we observed here are nearer the upper end of the *feasible* range.

The data also suggest that much (though not all) of the public views human rights as part of an all-inclusive package. Factor analysis points unambiguously to a one-factor solution, suggesting that a unified, latent concept—"human rights" writ large—thus undergirds and unifies these individual associations.[19] This public reluctance to differentiate between "first" and "second" generation rights should be of particular interest to today's human rights practitioners and scholars, many of whom have long assumed a significant divide between generations of rights. In 1993, the UN Vienna World Conference on Human Rights made the "indivisibility of human rights" into an article of faith in intergovernmental rhetoric; our polls suggest ordinary people have internalized this interpretation. Conflicts may rage in scholarly and practitioner circles, but the debate is less acute among ordinary people.

Even more intriguingly, respondents in three countries frequently *and strongly* associated human rights with women's rights (we did not ask this in Mexico), an interpretation transcending the civil-political/social-economic divide. Across samples, this association's mean strength was 5.3, with an average of 68 percent of respondents choosing a 5, 6, or 7 on the scale. This association was particularly salient in Morocco, where 85 percent of respondents ranked this association at 5, 6, or 7. Clearly, the strong Moroccan mobilizations around women's rights over the last 15 years have deeply shaped the public's definition of human rights.[20] Globally, issues related to gender and sexuality have often been framed in terms of human rights. We see strong evidence of the grassroots diffusion of this frame. Of course, an evaluative question remains: for ordinary people, does this association with women's issues make them perceive human rights ideas and groups more positively or more negatively? We address this later in the chapter.

Thus, although many practitioners fear human rights ideas are viewed negatively, our polls paint a different picture. Across countries and world regions, respondents had more positive than negative associations with "human rights" and rarely considered the idea to be a foreign imposition. These results could be overly optimistic; in some cases, respondents may have offered "socially desirable" answers, rather than their true feelings, a widely recognized problem in polling circles.[21] However, the odds of over 6,000 randomly selected respondents doing this in remarkably consistent ways across four different countries seem low.

In addition, our results resemble those obtained by several other surveys. A 2007–2008 poll by WorldOpinion.org at the University of Maryland asked 47,241 people in 28 countries and territories (only six of which were in the global North) for their views on the principles in the Universal Declaration of Human Rights (UDHR).[22] The results showed that "the norms of the UDHR receive robust support throughout the world . . . [and] are endorsed by majorities in every country." A nationally representative survey of 1,500 Korean citizens found that 44 percent expressed "support" for human rights principles.[23] A series of polls in Russia, conducted from 2001 to 2012, found consistently high support for economic rights, along with dramatically increasing support for basic civil liberties.[24] The latter is particularly noteworthy, given the country's escalating political crackdown. There are not many representative surveys of the public's human rights opinions, but there is cause for cautious optimism among those that do exist.

Trusting LHROs

Publics could have positive attitudes toward human rights *ideas* while mistrusting local human rights *organizations*. As revelations of Stalin's abuses mounted, for example, many leftists continued to support Marxist-Leninist concepts while adamantly opposing the Soviet regime. More recently, following revelations of sex scandals, many Catholics remain deeply attached to their faith while expressing intense dislike of the Church hierarchy. It is possible for people to remain committed to values, but grow disillusioned with the organizations that claim to uphold those principles.

To learn how respondents felt about human rights groups in their country, we asked if they trust LHROs. To contextualize their responses, we asked about trust in over a dozen additional international and domestic institutions, including (in three of the four countries) domestic NGOs. We inserted the option, "[country] *human rights organizations*," into the mix at different points, using systematic rotation to avoid order bias or result contamination.[25] For the most part, we asked respondents to score their trust in each institution on a scale of 1 to 4, but in Mexico we asked half our sample to use a 1–7 range as part of a broader survey experiment conducted by the poll's directors. To standardize the two scales, we have rescaled all responses from 0 ("no trust") to 1 ("a lot of trust").

Why did we decide to ask about "trust" as a barometer of feelings toward LHROs? What does "trust in LHROs" really mean? Given the diversity of local rights groups and policy areas, can we say anything meaningful about such an abstract concept, particularly without defining "LHRO" for respondents? We believe so. Survey researchers have long grappled with analogous questions in other fields, and have typically concluded that generalizing about abstractions such as "trust" is indeed useful. For example, in the field of comparative democratization, scholars have debated the utility of measuring the concept of "satisfaction with democracy."[26] Because democracy can encompass so many potential elements—including politicians, policies, institutions, and democratic principles—what are survey respondents thinking of when they respond to researchers' questions? One prominent interpretation argues that the concept "satisfaction with democracy" is best thought of as a "summary measure" that expresses the respondent's overall judgment about democracy, into which different subcomponents enter with greater or lesser proportion.[27] Satisfaction with democracy is also both conceptually and empirically useful because it often predicts important forms of political participation, including voting and protest. Similar arguments apply to other intriguing measures, including "feeling thermometers" and "presidential approval" ratings in US electoral studies.[28] Although both are highly polyvalent concepts, they have empirically definable content and meaningful statistical associations—including causal ones—with a variety of important outcomes, including electoral choices and legislative outcomes.

Similarly, our *Trust in LHROs* variable is a summary measure, a respondent's cumulative judgment about the national human rights sector as a whole; it can also be considered a weighted average with different components. One component is the type of organization that an individual respondent is thinking about, and another is the particular policy domain within which a given organization operates. Our research does not measure these specific components, but rather summarizes and encapsulates the respondents' overall judgment of their country's organized, nongovernmental rights sector.

Another concern is that we may be measuring an individual's proclivity to trust *in general*, rather than her particular trust in local rights groups. This concern is amplified if we use trust in other institutions to predict *Trust in LHROs*; later in this chapter, for example, we consider how trust in the US government is related to trust in local rights groups. In such cases, are we analyzing the relationship between these two ideas, or are we just showing that trust predicts trust? To account for this, our statistical analyses include a control variable, *Average Trust*, a calculation of each individual's average trust in *all* the institutions we asked about.[29]

Relatedly, *Trust in LHROs* may actually be capturing an individual's proclivity to trust non-state charitable or altruistic actors more broadly. One way to test this is to compare *Trust in LHROs* to public trust in domestic NGOs, which includes a much larger range of organizations. We explicitly make this comparison; our trust questions included a query about "*trust in* [country] *NGOs*" (everywhere but Mexico). Statistical analysis shows that *Trust in LHROs* is actually higher than trust in domestic NGOs. Average trust in domestic NGOs in our pooled Mumbai, Rabat/Casablanca, and Lagos samples was 0.44 (where 1 = "a lot of trust"), whereas average *Trust in LHROs* in only those three samples was 0.49, a statistically significant difference (note that Figure 3.3 below shows average *Trust in LHROs* for all four samples, which is higher than 0.49).[30]

Figure 3.3 summarizes results for six of the institutions we asked about, including one actor that was highly trusted across samples—"religious institutions"—and one that was consistently and deeply mistrusted: domestic "politicians." It also includes trust in multinational corporations and the US government, two pillars of global economic and political/military power.[31] For comparison's sake, we include a measure of respondents' trust in their co-citizens, as well as their trust in domestic NGOs.

The four-sample average for *Trust in LHROs* was 0.52, higher than trust in the general population (0.51) and domestic NGOs (0.44) but lower than trust in religious institutions (0.64). *Trust in LHROs* was also *higher* than in the US government (0.44), multinationals (0.43), and domestic politicians (0.31). Mexicans trusted LHROs the most, whereas Moroccans in and around Rabat/Casablanca reported the least trust in LHROs (although

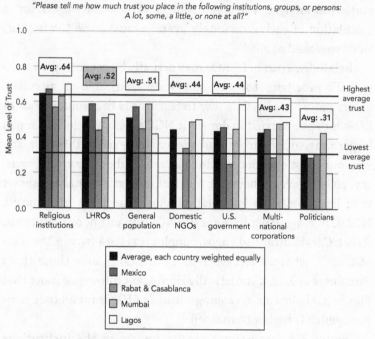

"*Please tell me how much trust you place in the following institutions, groups, or persons: A lot, some, a little, or none at all?*"

FIGURE 3.3 Publics Moderately Trust Local Human Rights Organizations (LHROs)

Moroccans were generally less trusting than respondents from the other countries).[32]

Overall, this suggests human rights groups occupy a reasonably strong reputational position, closer to the upper than the lower bound of the public's trust spectrum. This is true despite the previous chapter's finding that most citizens rarely encounter "human rights workers," are incapable of naming specific LHROs, and seldom participate in LHRO activities. (Later in the chapter we test whether those who have more contact are more critical of LHROs, or if there is truth to the idiom "to know is to love.") The public often hears "human rights" and moderately trusts its organized flag-bearers, despite limited engagement with or in-depth knowledge of LHROs. Importantly, when NGOs have a human rights focus, publics actually trust them more readily than NGOs in general, suggesting particularly strong reputations for domestic rights groups.

Linking Meaning and Trust

Based on our practitioner interviews, we had conceived of some definitions of human rights as "negative" (promoting foreign values and US interests, protecting criminals) and others as "positive" (protecting people from torture and murder, promoting socioeconomic justice). These practitioner assumptions, however, may not be empirically supported. After all, to advocates of criminal justice reform, protecting those accused of crimes from abuse is a *good* thing. Similarly, those who see local social or cultural systems as unjust and corrupt might welcome an infusion of foreign values. To investigate whether the "negative" associations really are negative and if the "positive" associations really are positive, we use simple statistical regressions to analyze the relationship between each of our definitions and *Trust in LHROs*. Trust is an unambiguously positive concept: it might be abused or misplaced, but the sentiment of trust itself connotes inherently positive feelings toward the thing or person trusted. Therefore, we consider positive associations between trust in LHROs and a specific definition of human rights as a sign that the association is positive; conversely, a negative statistical relationship means the association is negative.

Table 3.1 below summarizes our findings. The results for the pooled data across all samples confirm our assumptions: the phrases originally classified as negative—"protecting criminals," "not promoting or protecting anything," "promoting

foreign values," and "promoting US interests"—are indeed statistically associated with lower *Trust in LHROs*.[33] In contrast,
the three phrases originally classified as positive—"protecting
people from torture and murder," "promoting socioeconomic
justice," and "promoting free and fair elections"—are associated
with higher *Trust in LHROs*.

We conducted the same analysis on individual country data,
and these do not contradict the general findings from the pooled
sample, although there were contradictory findings on women's
rights. In Mumbai, defining "human rights" as "women's rights"
is associated with less *Trust in LHROs*, whereas in Rabat and
Casablanca and Lagos it is associated with *more* trust (we did not
ask the question in Mexico, unfortunately). Thus although publics strongly associate human rights with women's rights across
countries, they differ on whether this is "good" or "bad." There
was a similar lack of consensus on "protecting terrorists."

This analysis allows us to group together the positive associations and high trust into a combined category: *Human Rights
Inclined*. To join this conceptual group, a respondent needs to
trust local rights groups above the midpoint (at least 0.51 on
the 0-to-1 scale) and associate "human rights" with at least one
of the three positive definitions (choosing a 5, 6, or 7). Across
the four countries, the average proportion of respondents who
are *Human Rights Inclined* is 40 percent, with per-sample estimates ranging from 29 percent (in Mumbai) to 49 percent (in
Mexico).[34] In other words, there is a cross-national constituency
for human rights ideas and groups, regardless of world region or
cultural factors. The smallest constituency is in Mumbai and the
largest is in Mexico, but in none of our four cases does this pro-
human rights constituency drop below a fourth of the sample.
We consider how rights groups might mobilize the *Human Rights
Inclined* in the next chapter, where we investigate the potential
for LHRO fundraising.

TABLE 3.1 Relationships between Respondents' Definitions of "Human Rights" and Trust in Local Human Rights Organizations (LHROs)

		4-Country Pooled	Mexico	Rabat and Casablanca	Mumbai	Lagos
Public sees as positive	"Protecting people from torture and murder"	More trust	More trust	More trust	No finding	No finding
	"Promoting socioeconomic justice"	More trust	No finding	More trust	No finding	No finding
	"Promoting free and fair elections"	More trust	More trust	More trust	No finding	Less trust
Mixed	"Protecting women's rights"	No finding	N/A	More trust	Less trust	More trust
	"Protecting terrorists"	No finding	N/A	No finding	No finding	Less trust
Public sees as negative	"Promoting foreign values and ideas"	Less trust	Less trust	Less trust	Less trust	Less trust
	"Promoting US interests"	Less trust	Less trust	Less trust	Less trust	Less trust
	"Not protecting or promoting anybody's interests"	Less trust	No finding	Less trust	Less trust	Less trust
	"Protecting criminals"	Less trust	Less trust	No finding	No finding	Less trust

Relationships shown are statistically significant at the 0.10-level or higher. All models are OLS regressions, controlling for average trust. The pooled model controls for country and weights countries equally.

Critiques and Fears: What Drives Trust in LHROs?

Is there a middle class constituency for human rights groups, as some experts believe? Or do the socioeconomically marginalized publics see LHROs most favorably, as many activists might hope? We shed light on this debate, but we more fundamentally question whether support for local rights groups is driven by socioeconomics at all. We also investigate whether contact with the human rights sector is associated with more or less trust in LHROs ... or whether this is inconsequential in either direction. Our analysis ultimately suggests *Trust in LHROs* is shaped by values and worldviews that cut *across* socioeconomic lines and levels of engagement with the human rights sector.[35]

This discussion maps onto broader debates about the sources of ideology and political attitudes. One widely held view, influenced by materialist strands of social science, suggests that socioeconomic positions, interests, and processes drive public attitudes. By contrast, more culturally-oriented social scientists—"constructivists"—suggest worldviews have ideational rather than socioeconomic origins, such as political or national culture. Worldviews, in this perspective, are driven by other worldviews; as ideologies mutate, norms are contested, renegotiated, and reworked by ideational entrepreneurs. From this perspective, material interests still matter, but not as much or as directly as socioeconomic materialists would argue.

A classic study of American public opinions toward foreign policy argued that distinct "postures" toward international affairs, including "militarism, isolationism, and anticommunism," shape individual preferences.[36] These postures are ideational in nature and exist independently of socioeconomic location. More recently, scholars argue that US foreign policy "hawks" and "liberals" are motivated by different worldviews, not economic interests. Liberals respond to an underlying respect for individual rights regardless of national identity, whereas hawks respond to norms of community self-preservation.[37] Similarly, studies of global anti-American sentiment find socioeconomic status is an inconsistent predictor and that other ideational factors shape views of the United States.[38] Even popular attitudes toward globalization—a largely economic phenomenon—are driven by a combination of economic *and* ideational forces.[39]

Ideational analyses of this sort give ample room for agency and change. If worldviews are independent of narrow material interests, then individuals and nongovernmental organizations that traffic in symbols, information, and ideas—the "norm entrepreneurs" of transnational activist networks—can, in theory, reform the world.[40] Material considerations within and among states are not hardwired; instead, creative agents make change by working with, around, and through ideas. Human rights practitioners generate new ways of thinking and behaving at international and national levels; their entire raison d'etre is to persuade the socioeconomically weak *and* powerful to change their attitudes and actions.

Across our four samples, we find that *Trust in LHROs* is driven by three "dispositions" toward political and economic power: mistrust in the US government, multinational corporations, and domestic authorities. Each leg of this anti-power worldview has a somewhat different socioeconomic base; the constituency for local human rights organizations cuts *across* social groups, not limited to the middle class or any other socioeconomic group.

Anti-Power = Pro-Human Rights

Human rights supporters mistrust the US government, multinationals, and their own governments. This finding may seem logical to human rights activists themselves, who often have a critical, anti-establishment orientation; however, human rights are often invoked—or perceived to be—to promote interests of these powerful actors. As such, it is essential to map out where human rights supporters are actually found within global South publics. Figure 3.4 shows that each of the three anti-power stances are strongly held by over half of the people we surveyed, though just 36 percent of people across the four samples hold *all three* perspectives.

Trust in powerful actors is significantly related to *Trust in LHROs*, though not in ways anticipated by some critiques of the human rights movement. We find that greater *mistrust* in

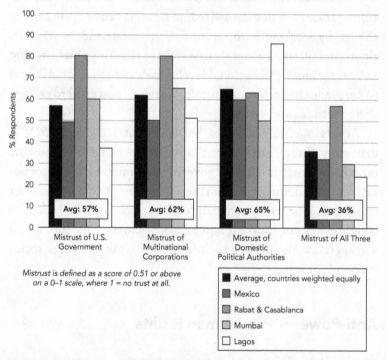

Mistrust is defined as a score of 0.51 or above on a 0–1 scale, where 1 = no trust at all.

Legend:
- Average, countries weighted equally
- Mexico
- Rabat & Casablanca
- Mumbai
- Lagos

Categories: Mistrust of U.S. Government (Avg: 57%); Mistrust of Multinational Corporations (Avg: 62%); Mistrust of Domestic Political Authorities (Avg: 65%); Mistrust of All Three (Avg: 36%)

FIGURE 3.4 Mistrust of Powerful Actors

political and economic authority is a consistent predictor of greater *trust* in LHROs. We discuss each in turn.

Mistrust in the US Government: As discussed above, some scholars, governments, and activists have criticized human rights ideas and organizations as Trojan horses for US foreign policy. If this critique holds sway in the court of public opinion, we would expect anti-American respondents to also *distrust* human rights organizations, whom they would see as unwitting dupes of empire at best and as its active agents at worst. Conversely, pro-US respondents are more likely to trust LHROs if they perceive rights groups as promoting a US agenda. If we find a positive relationship between trust in the US government and *Trust in LHROs*—more trust in the former means more in the latter—it would give credence to the anti-imperialist critique of rights.

There clearly are significant pockets of mistrust toward the US government worldwide, and these deepened from 2002 to 2009, particularly in the Middle East and among Muslim populations. The US-led invasion of Iraq and the abuses associated with the "war on terror" are obvious causes, as well as public criticism by governments opposed to or fearful of US foreign policy, including China, Russia, Venezuela, and Ecuador.[41] We might expect this view to be most prevalent in Morocco, a nearly uniformly Muslim country, or in Nigeria, where war-on-terror rhetoric has been activated in the fight against *Boko Haram* in the northeast.

In many cases, such governments have focused their criticisms on local NGOs, including human rights groups, many of which are financially supported by US or other northern agencies, a topic we explore in the next chapter. In Venezuela, for example, former president Hugo Chavez complained that liberal NGOs are "financed with millions and millions of dollars from the Yankee empire," whereas in Ecuador, President Rafael Correa has "repeatedly accused domestic NGOs" of "being agents of US influence."[42] The Russian leadership makes similar arguments, as have rulers in Egypt, Pakistan, Hungary, India, and more.[43]

Allegations of this sort are not restricted to authoritarian governments or democratic backsliders; human rights groups have come under "friendly fire" from pro-rights constituencies as well. In spring 2014, for example, a group of high-profile liberal elites publicly slammed Human Rights Watch for maintaining a de facto "revolving door" with US officialdom, saying this made the New York-based group appear as an appendage of the government.[44] Given "the impact of global perceptions on HRW's ability to carry out its work," they wrote, even "the appearance of impropriety" would cause reputational harm.[45] HRW's leaders rejected the charges, but acknowledged "the stigma of 'western imposition'" often impedes their efforts and those of other rights groups.[46]

Scholars also accuse rights groups of jumping on the US foreign policy bandwagon. One leading British scholar, for example, argued that the international human rights movement became a de facto US foreign policy ally in the early 1990s. Washington realized "the utility of human rights rhetoric for legitimating foreign policy," and leading human rights strategists seized "the chance to use a liberal hegemon to enshrine global norms ..."[47] Others have suggested that US (and other Western countries') rhetorical support for international human rights is a calculated maneuver aimed at papering over domestic inequalities or justifying global military interventions.[48]

Some scholars, commentators, and activists view links between human rights promotion and US foreign policy with *approval,* not opprobrium. One international relations scholar, for example, calls the US, European Union, and other liberal democracies "stewards" of human rights, or countries "willing to invest substantial resources in protecting human rights abroad."[49] US engagement with rights groups at home and abroad, scholars suggest, belongs to a long tradition of collaboration with liberal, private, voluntary groups.[50] Although American rights groups criticize US policy, they also enjoy warm relations and regular access to official policymakers. "Promoting freedom and democracy and protecting human rights ... are central to US foreign policy," according to the State Department.[51] Radical critics view such statements as rank hypocrisy, but many US liberals view them as honest, well-meaning declarations of intent. Regardless, both see a close and self-reinforcing link between international human rights promotion and the official US policy apparatus. And although most such commentary refers to *international* rather than local rights groups, evaluations of the former can easily spill on to the latter. Local groups are tightly linked to their international counterparts through information exchanges, training efforts, and the all-important funding mechanisms described in the next chapter. If *international* rights groups are stalking horses for US imperialism, local groups could easily be (or be seen as) the same.

Our *Human Rights Perceptions Polls* find that some people in these four countries *do* share these fears. As Table 3.1 above indicated, associating human rights with "promoting US interests" is indeed associated with lower *Trust in LHROs*. And yet, perceptions that the United States and other foreign actors have hijacked the global human rights movement were by no means dominant. Just 33 percent of respondents, on average, associate human rights with "promoting US interests" (ranking a 5, 6, or 7). Roughly one third of respondents have some concern that the human rights movement is a proxy for US political interests (and trust rights groups less because of this), but roughly 67 percent do *not* believe that rights are tied to US policy.

To investigate the relationship between perceptions of the United States and *Trust in LHROs*, we use *Mistrust in US Government.* We asked, *"How much trust do you place in the U.S. government?"* and flipped the 0–1 scale so that 1 equals greatest "mistrust." The percentage of each country sample who mistrust the US government (above 0.51 on the 0–1 scale)[52] ranges from a low of 37 percent in Lagos to a whopping 80 percent in Rabat and Casablanca, where the population was highly mistrusting of Washington. On average 57 percent of respondents mistrusted the US government. Rural residents and supporters of the ruling political party were more mistrustful of the US government overall, as were respondents in Mumbai and Rabat/Casablanca.

Our multivariate regression, discussed in detail below, reveals that *Mistrust in US Government* is significantly related to more *Trust in LHROs.* This is good news for rights practitioners concerned that citizens may see them as American stooges. If most people thought the United States had successfully hijacked the human rights agenda, mistrust in the one would be *positively* correlated with mistrust in the other. Our finding is the opposite: most respondents likely view local rights groups rather as bulwarks against US power. In the public eye, local rights groups are more likely "counter-hegemonic" than "hegemonic."[53]

Before detailing the full multivariate analysis, we discuss the two other anti-power worldviews: mistrust in multinationals and mistrust in domestic political authorities.

Mistrust in Multinational Corporations: As was true for anti-Americanism, critical scholars and activists have argued for an unholy alliance between the global human rights movement and the economic powers that be. If our data support this perspective, we would expect to see those who view economic powers favorably also supporting human rights groups; respondents who view LHROs as conduits for international economic interests *and* approve of these interests would trust LHROs more.

Part of this concern over the influences of global economic powerhouses stems from traditional Marxist ideas, which associate individual rights with private property and exploitation.[54] In this critique of classical liberalism, "rights" and the institutions charged with enforcing them merely hide the naked interests of the wealthy and powerful. Associating global economic forces with human rights is partly an extension of this logic to the international arena. Links between major rights groups and wealthy private donors have also attracted substantial concern. For instance, according to one activist, global financier George Soros "has built a global empire of networked nongovernmental organizations (NGOs) allegedly promoting 'human rights.'" The critique is that these groups "constitute a modern day network of imperial administrators undermining national governments . . . and replacing them with a homogeneous 'civil society' that interlocks with 'international institutions' run from and on behalf of Wall Street and London."[55] Global opinion leaders often package economic policies promoting free trade, financial liberalization, and structural adjustment together with human rights promotions; these ideas are then used together to batter down protectionist walls, promote private industry, and make the world safe for global finance.

Another strand of this critique is more concerned by reformist collaborations between human rights groups and private businesses, including efforts to generate global human rights standards for transnational corporations. According to an article in the left-wing *New Internationalist*, "Many a campaign to hold transnationals to account has petered out into 'working with business' and corporate social responsibility projects." In some cases, liberal NGOs "actively seek corporate 'partners' with the promise to make the latter look good by association."[56] The critique is that human rights groups offer political or social cover for rapacious businesses seeking to hide their misdeeds.

In return, presumably, those companies make direct or indirect financial contributions to the human rights sector.

To statistically test the public's views of these critiques, we use the variable *Mistrust in Multinationals*.[57] Here we also flipped the scale so that 0 denotes maximum *trust* in multinationals and 1 is maximum *mistrust*. Across all four samples, an average of 62 percent of respondents mistrusted multinational corporations (0.51 and above): 50 percent in Mexico, 51 percent in Lagos, 65 percent in Mumbai, and 80 percent in Rabat and Casablanca (see Figure 3.4). Overall, rural residents and women are more mistrustful of multinationals. Mexicans are more trusting of multinationals than respondents in either Mumbai or Lagos.

Our statistical analysis demonstrates most respondents do not believe local human rights groups are working for global capitalists. Instead, more *Mistrust in Multinationals* is reliably associated with more *Trust in LHROs*. This does not tell us about the actual pattern of human rights organizations' engagement with global economic actors (those critiques may well be valid), but we provide a reading of how *the public* assesses this critique. The publics in our samples do not believe that LHROs are in cahoots with international business.

Mistrust in Domestic Political Authorities: Finally, we expect that publics who are critical of their domestic governments will also look to rights groups to press for accountability and change. Indeed, we find that those who are skeptical about their own political and governing authorities are supporters of local rights groups.

Mistrust in political authorities, a sentiment called the "democratic deficit," is produced by poor government service provision and performance set in stark contrast to rising popular aspirations for democracy and an increasingly critical media.[58] In 2014, Pew reported that 76 percent of respondents across 34 developing countries complained that "corrupt political leaders" were one of their chief concerns.[59] In many respects, mistrust in one's own government is the attitude we would expect to be most closely aligned with positive views of human rights organizations, whose primary function is often seen to be criticizing domestic political authorities.

And yet, a handful of leading rights practitioners have begun worrying that disaffected citizens *do* view LHROs as part of the political status quo. According to a leading Brazilian practitioner, "The mass protests spreading from Cairo to Istanbul, Madrid to Santiago, and from Tunis to São Paulo, all demonstrate that millions worldwide seek more just, dignified, and humane societies." And as publics "are deeply disillusioned with state authorities," she fears that increasing numbers "may [also] regard [human rights] NGOs with similar distrust."[60] Publics may have begun to view rights groups as part of the same corrupt, state-public-service-bureaucratic complex that has so badly disappointed.

To investigate the empirical basis for these fears, we created an index variable, *Mistrust in Domestic Political Authorities*, by averaging responses to three separate queries about the respondent's trust in domestic politicians, national executive, and national legislature.[61] Once again, we flipped the scale so that 1 denotes maximum *mistrust*. Overall, 65 percent of respondents scored 0.51 and above on *Mistrust in Domestic Political Authorities*, ranging from a low of 50 percent in Mumbai to a high of 86 percent in Lagos (see Figure 3.4). If critics' fears are correct, *Mistrust in Domestic Political Authorities* should be inversely associated with *Trust in LHROs*; if people mistrust their own government, they should also mistrust the human rights groups they see as sharing the same social background and ideological orientations as government officials.

We find precisely the opposite, however, suggesting publics view human rights groups as holding their governments to account, rather than as government partners in a corrupt status quo. Across four samples, greater *Mistrust in Domestic Political Authorities* is associated with greater *Trust in LHROs*. This relationship is substantively more important in the statistical models than either *Mistrust in the US Government* or *Mistrust in Multinationals*. Overall, greater mistrust in domestic authorities is associated with urban residence, middle-income groups, non-voters, younger people, and men.

Figure 3.4 (above) shows that 36 percent of respondents, on average, strongly hold *all three* perspectives. In other words, just over one-third of respondents are simultaneously mistrustful of the global hegemon (the US government), global economic powerhouses (multinationals), and their own domestic political authorities.

Testing the Anti-Power = Pro-Human Rights Thesis

We bring these factors together (with relevant controls) into a single set of statistical models to estimate the unique impact of each anti-power worldview on the public's trust in local human rights organizations.[62] We summarize our main findings below in Table 3.2 (Table B.2 in Appendix B presents full statistical models). Model 1 shows the impact of our explanatory variables for all four countries pooled, whereas Models 2–5 show each country sample individually.[63] In the first column we list our explanatory variables. *Anti-Power Worldviews* includes the three indicators already discussed: *Mistrust in US Government, Mistrust in Multinationals,* and *Mistrust in Domestic Political Authorities.* If anti-power respondents are more trusting of local rights groups, the relationship will be *statistically significant* and *positive.* These three variables are "ideational," socially constructed worldviews, not socioeconomic or demographic factors.

TABLE 3.2 Predicting Trust in LHROs (OLS Regression)

	1 4-Country Pooled (N = 3,956)	2 Mexico (N = 1,909)	3 Rabat and Casablanca (N = 416)	4 Mumbai (N = 863)	5 Lagos (N = 768)
Anti-Power Worldviews					
Mistrust in the US Government	More trust	More trust	More trust	More trust	No finding
Mistrust in Multinational Corporations	More trust	More trust	More trust	More trust	More trust
Mistrust in Domestic Political Authorities	More trust	More trust	No finding	More trust	More trust
(trust in domestic politicians, trust in legislature, trust in president or prime minister)					
Contact with Human Rights					
Index of hearing, knowing, naming, and participating	More trust	No finding	No finding	No finding	No finding

(continued)

TABLE 3.2 Continued

	1 4-Country Pooled (N = 3,956)	2 Mexico (N = 1,909)	3 Rabat and Casablanca (N = 416)	4 Mumbai (N = 863)	5 Lagos (N = 768)
Socioeconomic Factors					
Education	No finding	No finding	No finding	No finding	No finding
Urban residence	No finding	No finding	No finding	No finding	No finding
Subjective income (squared)	No finding	No finding	No finding	U-shaped association	No finding
Internet user	No finding	No finding	No finding	No finding	No finding

Relationships shown are statistically significant at the 0.10-level or higher. All models also control for support for the ruling party, voting in the last election, age, gender, and average trust. The pooled model controls for country and weights countries equally.

Next, we include *Contact with Human Rights,* an index aver-aging responses to our four questions from Chapter 2 on human rights exposure and engagement: hearing "human rights" daily or frequently, having met with a human rights worker, know-ing the name of a specific rights organization, and having par-ticipated in the activities of a human rights organization. In that chapter, we treated measures of human rights contact as dependent variables to be explained, finding people with higher socioeconomic status had more human rights contact. Here we include *Contact with Human Rights* as an explanatory variable for *Trust in LHROs.* We scale *Contact with Human Rights* from 0 to 1, where 0 denotes minimal contact with the human rights movement—someone who does not hear "human rights" fre-quently, has never met a human rights worker, cannot name a human rights group, and has never participated in human rights activities—and 1 denotes maximum contact.[64]

We include *Contact with Human Rights* in our analysis to help us investigate the quality of citizen interactions with the human rights movement. If hearing "human rights" and meeting human rights workers is a positive experience for most respondents, the coefficient for this variable will be statistically significant and positive; more contact means more trust. If the relationship between *Contact with Human Rights* and *Trust in LHROs* is sig-nificant and negative, conversely, this means that more contact means less trust in local rights groups.

Does it make sense to consider a respondent's *Trust in LHROs* absent any meaningful contact with human rights organizations and discourse? It does, we believe, just as it makes sense to ask US voters for their views of politicians even if they have never personally met one or participated in a political rally. By includ-ing *Contact with Human Rights* in our analysis, we are able to test the hypothesis that greater familiarity and engagement impacts *Trust in LHROs,* in one direction or another.

Our third group of explanatory variables is socioeconomic factors. Just as *Contact with Human Rights* describes a set of concrete behaviors or experiences, socioeconomic factors are tangible, material indicators. We introduced all of these in the previous chapter, including *Subjective Income* perceptions relative to expenditures, urban or rural *Residence*, years of *Education*, and *Internet Use*. Once again, we square our subjective income measure to investigate whether its relationship with trust is curvilinear. If the middle classes are indeed more trusting of local rights groups, as some scholars expect, the relationship will be statistically significant and take the form of an inverted "U," signifying that the rich and the poor—the two extremities of the "U"—have lower trust in local rights groups.

Finally, we include political control variables in the models, the findings for which we report in Table B.2 in Appendix B. This accounts for other factors that might influence *Trust in LHROs*. *Support Ruling Party* denotes respondents who identified with the political party in executive power at the time of the survey, and *Voted* denotes respondents who reported voting in the most recent national election. These variables help control for the political dynamics of each country, which are likely to impact trust in local human rights groups. As we did in the previous chapter, we include *Age* and *Gender*, standard demographic controls, as well as *Average Trust*, the individual means of trust scores across all institutions and actors on our questionnaire.[65]

Finally, we include *Country* in the pooled model to control for country-specific fixed effects.

Evidence from Public Opinion: What Drives Trust in LHROs?

Contrary to critics who argue that publics view rights groups as allied with US interests, global business, or ruling domestic authorities, Table 3.2 shows that greater citizen mistrust in all three power sources is significantly associated with greater *Trust in LHROs* in the four-country sample and in at least three of the four individual country samples. For example, respondents in Mexico, Mumbai, and Lagos who mistrust their own government are more trusting of local human rights groups. The evidence consistently shows that people with anti-power worldviews have more *Trust in LHROs*. These results are remarkably stable across countries, persisting above and beyond variation in many other factors, including *Contact with Human Rights*, socioeconomic status, political variables, and demographic characteristics.

Figure 3.5 demonstrates the magnitude of these relationships. The three lines represent the effects of each anti-power

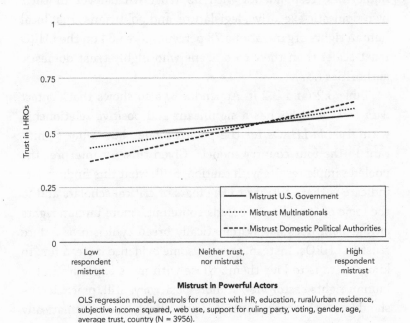

Mistrust in Powerful Actors

OLS regression model, controls for contact with HR, education, rural/urban residence, subjective income squared, web use, support for ruling party, voting, gender, age, average trust, country (N = 3956).

FIGURE 3.5 Mistrust in Powerful Actors Associated with More Trust in Local Human Rights Organizations (LHROs)

worldview: *Mistrust in US Government* (the solid black line), *Mistrust in Multinationals* (the dotted black line), and *Mistrust in Domestic Political Authorities* (the black dashed line). Each line pools effects across the four countries. Respondents with no trust whatsoever in the US government (located on average at .58 of the LHRO trust scale) will trust human groups, on average, 21 percent more than those who trust the US government a lot (.48 on the scale), all else being held constant. The same is true for respondents mistrustful of global economic power. Respondents who utterly mistrust multinationals trust LHROs 42 percent more than those who trust multinationals the most (an increase from .43 to .61—again, holding all other variables at their means). The largest substantive impact on *Trust in LHROs* is associated with *Mistrust in Domestic Political Authorities*; respondents with no trust whatsoever in their own domestic executive, legislature, and politicians trust local human rights organizations 73 percent more (.64 on the LHRO trust scale) than their co-citizens who highly trust domestic authorities (.37).

Table 3.2 (and B.2 in Appendix B) also shows that *Contact with Human Rights* has a significant and positive relationship with *Trust in LHROs* for the pooled model, but is not significant in the four country models. Given this, we interpret the pooled sample results with caution. Still, what this finding *does* indicate is that contrary to the fears of critical scholars and to the logic of "familiarity breeds contempt," more human rights engagement does *not* systematically breed cynicism or reduce trust in LHROs. Instead, there is some evidence instead for "to know them is to love them": those with more exposure to the human rights sector view it more positively. Still, practitioners should note that more contact is not reliably and systematically associated with major *increases* in trust; although contact is not necessarily *hurting* reputations, it is not associated with clear and consistent positive impacts either.

None of our socioeconomic factors are statistically significant in the pooled model, and only one, *Subjective Income Squared*, is significant in any of the four country models (Mumbai). The relationship there is U-shaped, suggesting that Mumbai's middle class is *less* trusting of local rights groups than the city's very poor or very wealthy. There is no evidence in our data for a global middle class that is supportive of local human rights groups— at least not after accounting for differences in worldviews. As none of our measures of socioeconomic status shows any consistent impact, we conclude these tangible factors are less useful in predicting trust in local rights groups than the intangibles (though we are reluctant on the basis of only four countries to dismiss them as completely inconsequential). Rather, *Trust in LHROs* emerges from a set of attitudes toward the political and economic world at large, the bases for which are drawn across socioeconomic strata. (For the socioeconomic predictors of *Anti-Power Worldviews*, see Table B.3 in Appendix B.)

Few of our control variables were statistically significant (see Table B.2 in Appendix B). After accounting for anti-power worldviews, political variables—*Support for Ruling Party* and *Voted*—have no statistically significant association with *Trust in LHROs*. It is the anti-power attitude that matters, and these views cut across party identification and voter turnout. Women are more likely to *Trust in LHROs* in the pooled model but not in the country models, suggesting that substantive impact is not consistently strong. *Average Trust* matters, as expected, because individuals with a general propensity to trust will also trust local rights groups more. Finally, the fixed effects (country dummy variables) show Mumbai respondents are less trusting overall than those in Mexico.

Human Rights Resonates with "Anti-Power" Publics

Political and economic worldviews shape citizen trust in their local rights groups. Mistrust in the US government and multinationals is consistently associated with greater trust in local rights groups, but the largest effect by far is citizens' mistrust in their own domestic political authorities. Across our four samples, respondents who strongly mistrust their governing institutions are much more likely to trust their local human rights organizations.

These findings may surprise those who allege that the human rights movement has become too cozy with political and economic power. Public perceptions are to the contrary (whether or not these critiques have a basis in reality is another matter); pro-human rights publics mistrust Washington, multinationals, and their own governments. If rights groups want to grow local constituencies, they should account for these "anti-power" attitudes and shape messages that resonate with these worldviews.

Where are anti-power constituencies to be found? Interestingly, these worldviews are not as widespread as one might assume. Just over a third of respondents strongly held all three views simultaneously, though taken singly any of the three anti-power worldviews has a greater number of adherents.

Critics of the US Government. Surveys suggest that many people distinguish between US citizens and government and hold contradictory attitudes, strongly admiring some aspects of the United States while deeply detesting others.[66] "Anti-Americanism" takes many forms,[67] even though popular attitudes toward the United States remain reasonably positive. In 2015, 69 percent of respondents polled by Pew across 39 countries indicated "favorability" toward the United States.[68]

Given substantial country variation, the consistent link we find between *Mistrust US Government* and *Trust in LHROs* is all the more remarkable.

Each of these four countries has a very different relationship with the US government. Mexico has by far the most intense connection, and its political class, one expert says, is prone to "an almost reflexive bristle" when discussing US policy. Still, Mexico is also tightly connected to its wealthier neighbor through trade, migration, tourism, investment, and shared security concerns.[69] In 2008, Mexico began receiving US military and economic aid through the Merida Initiative, aimed at combating drug traffickers; in 2012, the year of our survey, Mexico's annual US aid package was almost $210 million.[70]

Neither India, Morocco, nor Nigeria has the same overwhelmingly close relationship with the United States, but none are indifferent. Until the Cold War's end, the Indian government's stance toward Washington was frosty.[71] Ties have warmed since then, and in 2008 the two countries struck a landmark nuclear agreement and now collaborate on multiple initiatives.[72] In 2012 (the year of our poll), however, the United States extended only $175 million in aid to India, a modest sum given the country's vast size.

Historically the Moroccan government (though not its public) has been a more consistent US ally. During and after the Cold War, the monarchy viewed itself as a staunch US ally in the fight against Communism and later against radical Islam.[73] Morocco's monarchs have often supported US attempts to broker an Israeli-Arab or Israeli-Palestinian peace deal. In return, Washington has offered Morocco diplomatic support, including backing for its position on the disputed Western Sahara. In 2012, US aid to the North African kingdom was $52.2 million, far higher per capita than aid to India. The Moroccan public, however, has been heavily influenced by the criticisms of America that pervade Arab and Muslim worlds; the number of US government supporters in our Rabat and Casablanca sample is lower than elsewhere.

US-Nigeria government relations were particularly strained during the 1990s, when Nigeria was ruled militarily. Since the 1999 political transition, Abuja has become one of the largest African recipients of US aid, totaling $336 million in 2012. And although US officials often criticize Nigerian government behavior, they are ultimately clear supporters, collaborating with the Nigerian government and military against the Islamist *Boko Haram* insurgency. The Nigerian public, perhaps cognizant of the role of US aid, holds Washington in relatively high favor; Lagos respondents reported significantly greater trust in the US government than did respondents in any of the other three samples.

These four countries represent great diversity in types and intensities of US relations, so the consistent relationship between more *Mistrust in US Government* and greater *Trust in LHROs* is extraordinary. Pockets of anti-American sentiment may shift over time and space, but US government skeptics remain reliable supporters of domestic human rights sectors.

Critics of Multinationals. Concern over the negative impacts of globalization escalated in the 1990s following the demise of the Soviet Union, trade and financial liberalization, and successive financial crises in Asia (1997), Russia (1998), Argentina (1998–1999), and then, globally (2008).[74] Although "anti-globalization" is a broad tent, most proponents are concerned with the negative impacts of global trade, finance, privatization, and externally imposed reforms.[75] These sentiments occasionally erupt in popular protests at economic summits, such as the 1998 World Trade Organization meeting in Seattle, or are debated in alternative political gatherings, such as the World Social Forum. Although this sentiment is strongly felt in some quarters, its global prevalence—as was true for anti-Americanism—should not be overstated. According to a 2014 Pew study, most respondents in a 44-country sample expressed support, in principle, for global trade and business development.[76]

Scholars have identified several socioeconomic drivers of antiglobalization dispositions, including unskilled workers who are more likely to be harmed by foreign direct investment and marginalized communities likely to be displaced by new development projects. Ideational orientations also matter; concerns about consumerism, the pace of modern life, and dwindling national political autonomy also fuel anti-globalization ideas.[77] Many of those concerned with economic globalization are also mistrustful of the US government, as Washington and the economic interests it represents are often globalization's beneficiaries or enforcers. The size of America's economy, global footprint, political influence over international institutions, and control of the world's reserve currency all contribute to shared fears of the US government *and* of economic globalizers.[78]

Critics of the State. Criticism of national political authorities is globally widespread and is the most prevalent anti-power frame in our samples, with 65 percent of respondents ranking *Mistrust in Domestic Political Authorities* above the midpoint. Other global polls also suggest this sentiment may be more widespread than either anti-Americanism or antiglobalization. More people worldwide are unsatisfied with their own governments than with either the US government or global economic actors. This makes sense, of course, as most people have regular and direct contact with national authorities, but only indirect and intermittent contact with the US government or multinationals.

Human rights groups already are actively engaged in holding governments to account in each of these countries. In Mexico, as the government attempts to downplay abuses its own security forces commit (or are complicit in) in the war against the drug cartels, human rights groups have pushed for investigations and accountability. The Mexican government has actively promoted human rights rhetoric, but LHROs have used these rhetorical commitments to expose where the government is falling short of its claims. In Morocco, activists are critical of the government's attempts to limit freedom of speech or association, particularly for politically sensitive groups that may be seen as undermining Islam or the monarchy in some way. In each of these countries, human rights groups find themselves needing to walk a line between cooperation with their governments and being critical of abuses committed by those same authorities. In their search for potential supporters, human rights groups should not have far to travel to find those who criticize their own governments and look to human rights as a way to bring domestic or international heat to the political status quo.

Our analysis suggests that LHRO allies are to be found among people opposed to internationally and nationally powerful actors. For practitioners to construct frames that resonate well with these publics, successful human rights messages should include overtones critical of the United States, global economic power, and—above all—domestic authorities. Of course, this is an approach that is a natural fit with how many human rights organizations already do craft their message and organize their activities.

Contrary to much scholarly and practitioner opinion, we do not find that socioeconomic or political variables have direct and consistent impacts; allies of the human rights movement are located in multiple social spaces and levels, including both the countryside and the city, and among both the rich and the poor. Certainly material factors matter, but the mechanism through which they matter is by the development of worldviews, which then become more powerful than the socioeconomic characteristics that gave rise to them.

Our findings suggest that pro-human rights publics—in these countries and perhaps more broadly—likely favor a social movement approach that uses human rights principles "from below" for the purposes of counter-hegemonic mobilization.[79] The public sees LHROs as allies of this counter-hegemonic subaltern community, rather than as opponents in the struggle against concentration of power. This is good news for those who want human rights to be a social movement for the oppressed. Across our four samples, publics view human rights as part of a struggle to improve their domestic governance and control negative effects of globalization and US primacy.[80]

In our interviews with human rights workers, many practitioners were more pessimistic than our polls warrant. In Mexico, practitioners thought the public disliked them because of their allegedly greater efforts on behalf of criminals, rather than victims of crime. And yet our polls showed that this view was not widespread in Mexico, and that much of the public trusted LHROs. What explains this gap in practitioner and public perceptions?

The misperception may be due to the difference between elite and mass opinion. Human rights practitioners are more embedded in elite discussions, and Chapter 2 showed they have greater contact with people of higher socioeconomic backgrounds. If the general public is more supportive of LHROs than either the media or elites, human rights practitioners may not know this because they do not come into sufficient contact with this "silent majority." Human rights practitioners, engaged as they are in daily politics, may not recognize the extent to which the public appreciates them. In part this disconnect between the sector's self-perceptions and public opinion may be due to LHROs' lack of significant face-to-face contact with ordinary people. In part, however, it also comes from human rights scholars, donors, and researchers lack of systematic investigation of what the general public actually thinks about human rights ideas and organizations. Scholars and other critics have accused rights groups of serving this or that interest, and made claims about how the public likely views LHROs. Until our *Human Rights Perceptions Polls*, however, no research group had systematically investigated whether ordinary people thought "human rights" was associated with foreign or US interests, to what extent they trust LHROs, and how trust is associated with trust in other actors.

Much work remains to be done; public opinion surveys must be improved and replicated across time and space. Still, the initial signs are reasonably positive and promising for human rights practitioners.

4

Resources

Universal Values, Foreign Money

In the pyramid-like structure of the global human rights sector, resources flow top-down from funders in the global North to LHROs. This current configuration (described in our opening chapter) is almost taken for granted. Our practitioner interviews show that most domestic rights groups depend heavily on foreign aid, whereas fundraising from individual citizens in their own countries is extremely rare.[1]

Fundraising from institutional sources in the global North is comparatively easier, but it may involve long-term risk. Governments worldwide are cracking down on foreign aid to domestic civil society, fighting the wave of external support for liberal NGOs that began in the 1980s and accelerated mightily after the Cold War.[2] Research on other NGO sectors suggests that reliance on foreign aid often weakens and divides civil society. When non-profits raise more resources locally, by contrast, it strengthens their ties to local constituents, develops more local accountability, and ultimately better reflects local priorities. Today, systematic LHRO dependence on foreign aid is rapidly becoming the sector's Achilles heel.

Given the support we have identified for human rights ideas and organizations, the *potential* for LHRO fundraising among the general public seems high. Additionally, publics in these countries *do* give to other charitable causes, most notably religious organizations. Nearly 70 percent of the 6,180 people we surveyed across four countries said they believed LHROs in their country raised most of their funds locally, when of course this is not the case. The door to local fundraising for LHROs sits at least moderately ajar.

This chapter describes and seeks to explain the persistence of the *foreign* funding resource pattern for *domestic* human rights sectors. In particular, we note the high cost for LHROs of raising money locally, given that long-established individual philanthropic routines prioritize donations to "tangible" charities, while routine support for policy, advocacy, and legal work has become well established in international donor circles. As a result, LHROs pursue international resources, rather than engage in costly domestic fundraising efforts. This paucity of local fundraising and low rates of direct LHRO-public engagement (analyzed in Chapter 2) have become caught in a mutually reinforcing cycle.

If local rights groups do not begin to capitalize on the public support documented in Chapter 3, they face an uncertain future. Of course, we recognize that local funding for human rights is far from a panacea, and there can be significant problems associated with raising money in deeply unequal societies.[3] Still, we argue that it is reasonable to suggest that LHROs should—and can—develop a more diverse domestic resource base. Amnesty International and Human Rights Watch raise substantial funds from individual citizens in the countries where they are based; in theory, LHROs could do the same, given the public support we have found for their work.[4]

Foreign-Funded LHROs

Our interviews confirmed a perhaps unsurprising fact: LHROs in Mexico, Morocco, India, and Nigeria rely heavily on foreign

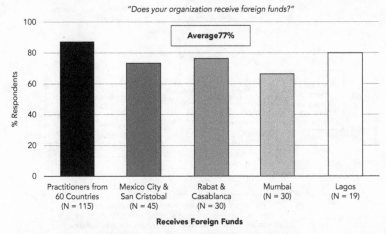

"Does your organization receive foreign funds?"

FIGURE 4.1 Most Practitioners' Organizations Receive Foreign Funds

funds. Most (77 percent) of the human rights practitioners we interviewed said their organization receives foreign aid (Figure 4.1).[5] In a Mexico City study we conducted in 2016, 85 percent of LHRO representatives said their organizations receive foreign money, comprising 74 percent of their budgets.[6] In Lagos, 68 percent of those reporting foreign aid told us that external money covered half or more of their expenses.

We asked practitioners about funding conditions for LHROs more generally in their country. We asked, *"What percentage of human rights organizations in* [your country] *receive substantial funding from foreign donors?"* The average estimate across samples was roughly 71 percent (Figure 4.2).

Next we asked, *"How many human rights organizations in* [your country] *raise substantial local funds,"* and the most common response was "very few" (Figure 4.3).

Finally, we asked practitioners to speculate what might happen *"If foreign funding for human rights work in* [your country]

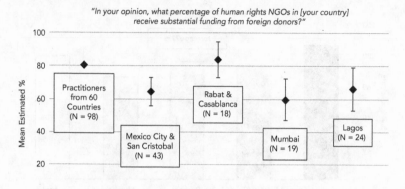

"In your opinion, what percentage of human rights NGOs in [your country] receive substantial funding from foreign donors?"

The 60-country practitioners sample is a purposive sample.
The other four samples are representative of LHROs in each city;
95% confidence intervals shown for the representative samples.

FIGURE 4.2 Practitioners Estimate High Percentage of LHROs Receive "Substantial" Foreign Support

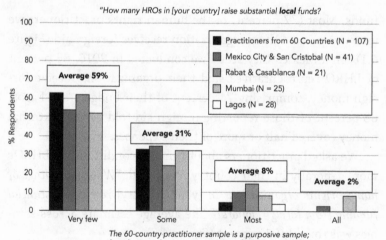

"How many HROs in [your country] raise substantial **local** funds?

The 60-country practitioner sample is a purposive sample;
the other samples are representative of LHROs in each city.
Average is the mean across samples, with each of the five
samples weighted equally.

FIGURE 4.3 Practitioners Estimate Very Few Rights Groups Are Locally Funded

was cut off." Most predicted worst-case scenarios: that the sector would "collapse somewhat" or "collapse entirely" (Figure 4.4).

Although "collapse" may sound alarmist, the scenario is not farfetched. By 2012, one quarter of low- and middle-income countries had recently placed legal restrictions on external aid to domestic civil society; many others are considering doing so. For LHROs, the results can be catastrophic. For example, in 2010 the Ethiopian government passed new restrictions on foreign aid to human rights (and other politically sensitive) groups, and within a year the country's LHRO sector had shrunk from 125 to 12 organizations.[7] Domestic donors might have helped soften the impact, but few Ethiopians reached into their own pockets, even though Ethiopians do donate money to some causes; according to a 2013 Gallup poll, 14 percent reported donating to a local charity in the previous month.[8] If global South publics could support LHROs with levels of financial support commensurate with the high levels of trust and ideological support

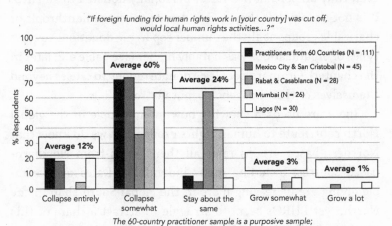

"If foreign funding for human rights work in [your country] was cut off, would local human rights activities...?"

- Practitioners from 60 Countries (N = 111)
- Mexico City & San Cristobal (N = 45)
- Rabat & Casablanca (N = 28)
- Mumbai (N = 26)
- Lagos (N = 30)

Average 12% — Collapse entirely
Average 60% — Collapse somewhat
Average 24% — Stay about the same
Average 3% — Grow somewhat
Average 1% — Grow a lot

The 60-country practitioner sample is a purposive sample; the other samples are representative of LHROs in each city. Average is the mean across samples, with each of the five samples weighted equally.

FIGURE 4.4 Most Practitioners Said LHROs Would "Collapse" without Foreign Funding

we have already found, this could be a substantial benefit for domestic rights groups.

Why Citizens Do Not Donate to LHROs

Our *Human Rights Perceptions Polls* confirm what practitioners said: few people in global South publics donate to LHROs. This is actually somewhat surprising. In Morocco, India, and Nigeria (the samples for which we have the most complete data on giving), 56 percent thought human rights conditions in their country were poor, saying there was "not much" or "no respect at all" for individual human rights. This indicates that they perceive a need for human rights work in their country. Forty-two percent thought LHROs in their country were primarily funded by their co-citizens, showing there is a perceived local base to support human rights work. Of those who thought *both these things*, however, fully 98 percent had never personally donated to an HRO. It is not simply that they do not donate to any philanthropic or charitable groups at all; the number reporting donations to *other* types of organizations was notably higher (see Table 4.2, later in the chapter). Ordinary people *do* donate money to causes beyond themselves or their households, but not to LHROs.

There are no data showing how many people in the global North contribute to human rights groups, but we do know that Northern-based groups raise all their funds from Northern-based sources, including many individuals. Rates of charitable giving are increasing more in the global South than in the North,[9] yet LHROs seem to struggle to attract a share of this fiscal goodwill. Why do LHROs in the global South not raise substantial funds in their own countries? We turn to several alternative explanations.

Fear of political reprisal is a commonly cited and logical reason that citizens of the global South might not donate to LHROs. After all, repression is the main reason local rights activists go transnational in the first place. And yet, rights groups in *less* repressive contexts *also* rely heavily on external aid. Neither India, Mexico, Morocco, nor Nigeria were so fearsomely governed at the time of our research to deter citizens from donating to local rights groups. Although the ghosts of past repression may linger, the practitioners we spoke with in those countries did not cite fear as a key reason that co-citizens did not donate money.

A rigorous test of this explanation would require tracking of giving patterns over time, as repression eases or intensifies; however, even a brief consideration of contemporary political contexts does not strongly support the repression argument, at least in these four cases. In Morocco, the monarchy began liberalizing in the 1990s, and conditions improved further when Mohammed VI assumed the throne in 1999. Serious human rights concerns remain, but political repression has eased substantially since the infamous "Years of Lead" of the 1970s and 1980s.[10] The country now has a vibrant civil society and an outspoken and self-confident domestic rights sector. None of the practitioners we interviewed in Rabat and Casablanca said citizens feared contributing financially, yet they acknowledged that few rights groups raised local funds. Morocco's current political conditions do not explain this pattern.

The same is true for Mexico. In 2010–2011, the years we conducted interviews in Mexico City and San Cristóbal, the country was entering its second decade of electoral democracy. Certainly, criminal violence was high and abuses by non-state and state actors were all too common. Still, none of the LHRO leaders we interviewed said citizens were too scared to donate, although one expert did explain that fear (largely of criminals, but also of corrupt officials) *might* inhibit donations in specific, high-violence areas of the country. There is little reason to believe that in Mexico, ordinary citizens across the country do not donate to LHROs because they fear retaliation from the government, or from criminals.

India has a longer and more established democratic tradition, but also contends with internal violence, repression, and insurgency. In some parts of the country, government-allied militias target critical civil society groups, typically from the political left. The government often pressures civil society groups to curb their tongues, using the draconian Foreign Contribution Regulation Act to enforce discipline. The Ford Foundation and Greenpeace are among several groups that have been prohibited from giving or receiving contributions under the law.[11] These pressures make some local donors too nervous to contribute, especially to groups working on sensitive national security issues. And yet, even though LHROs working on less controversial issues are subject to less scrutiny,[12] they also struggle to raise domestic money. Fear of political retaliation may explain a portion of non-donations to LHROs in India, but it certainly does not explain it all.

Nigeria transitioned from military to democratic rule in 1999, in part due to pressures from LHROs. When the last military government promised a transition to civilian rule, a schism materialized among LHROs, with some advocating working with the government through the transition, and others maintaining a more radical anti-establishment stance. Over a decade later, these two strands are still apparent, and many LHROs do work with government.[13] After military rule, Nigeria entered an era of official support for human rights, bringing a new role for LHROs as recognized civil society actors, rather than as agitators and activists.[14] Still, local Nigerian rights groups have not raised substantial local financial support.

Political repression may explain this pattern in some author-itarian countries, but in more politically favorable environ-ments, it is less persuasive.

A second possible explanation for the dearth of local funding is low public "demand" for LHRO services. Ordinary people may not donate because they do not perceive a strong need for the pol-icy, legal, and advocacy services LHROs provide because: (1) their assessments of existing human rights conditions are relatively favorable, or (2) their opinions of rights groups—or the concept of rights itself—are relatively *un*favorable.

Chapter 3, however, demonstrated that publics do trust LHROs and do have positive associations with human rights ideas. Table 4.1 (below) shows that 40 percent of respondents, on average across samples, are *Human Rights Inclined* in that they trust LHROs *and* associate "human rights" with at least one positive phrase ("promoting free and fair elections," "promot-ing socioeconomic justice," or "protecting people from torture and murder").[15] If citizens are not forthcoming with donations, it is not because they distrust LHROs or have low opinions of "human rights."

What about the *perceived need* for the advocacy work of domestic rights groups? To assess this, we asked, *"In your opin-ion, how much respect is there for individual human rights nowadays in* [country]?"[16] Table 4.1 shows that across the four countries an average of 56 percent of respondents *Perceive Poor Human Rights Conditions*, believing there is either "no respect at all" or "not much respect" for human rights in their country. The per-sample estimates range from 41 percent in Lagos to 80 per-cent in Mumbai. This signals that there is moderate-to-strong demand for the work of groups explicitly dedicated to improv-ing local human rights conditions; large portions of the pub-lics perceive significant work to be done to improve domestic human rights.[17]

TABLE 4.1 Locating "High Probability Donors"

	4-Country Pooled	Mexico	Rabat & Casablanca	Mumbai	Lagos
Human Rights Inclined	40%	49%	36%	29%	45%
Trust LHROs and associate "human rights" with at least one positive definition (5, 6, or 7)					
Perceive Poor Human Rights Conditions	56%	55%	47%	80%	41%
Report little or no respect for human rights in their country					
Have Self-Reported Disposable Income	42%	38%	38%	37%	53%
Report having enough money to cover their monthly expenses without difficulty					
High Probability Donors	10%	9%	7%	13%	10%
Combination of all three above categories					
% of High Probability Donors who report ever donating to an HRO	5%	NA	7%	1%	6%

Mexico data come from the 2014 survey; because not all questions were asked in 2012; however, the 2014 survey did not ask about actual donations. All data have sampling weights applied; the pooled data weight countries equally. Response rates for the individual questions range from 70% to 99%.

TABLE 4.2 Patterns of Giving

	4-Country Pooled	Mexico (N = 2,400)	Rabat & Casablanca (N = 1,000)	Mumbai (N = 1,680)	Lagos (N = 1,000)	Lagos "voluntary" donations only
Religious organizations	34.8	12.6	0.3	38.0	88.2	80.8
Parents associations	16.7	12.5	0.8	6.1	47.3	32.6
Neighborhood associations	13.9	NA	1.1	7.3	33.4	16.6
Environmental organizations	10.8	3.5	0.5	7.9	31.3	15.6
Professional associations	6.3	NA	0.5	0.8	17.6	8.9
Political parties	4.5	4.0	0.3	7.0	6.5	5.8
Unions	3.2	3.0	0.3	1.7	7.6	3.1

(continued)

TABLE 4.2 Continued

	4-Country Pooled	Mexico (N = 2,400)	Rabat & Casablanca (N = 1,000)	Mumbai (N = 1,680)	Lagos (N = 1,000)	Lagos "voluntary" donations only
Human rights organizations	2.9	1.4	1.1	4.2	4.9	4.0
Nongovernmental organizations	2.7	NA	0.5	2.6	4.9	4.5
Ever donated to at least one of these	42.0	22.8	4.7	44.4	95.9	88.9

In Mexico, donation questions were only asked of respondents who said yes to participating in a given organization; the Mexico percentages have been calculated using the full sample as a base, thus likely underestimating the donations to each type of organization. The table indicates the total number of respondents for each survey (N); response rates for these questions in Rabat and Casablanca, Mumbai, and Lagos were all above 98 percent. All data have sampling weights applied; the pooled data weight countries equally.

When we overlap the people who are *Human Rights Inclined* with those who also *Perceive Poor Human Rights Conditions,* we find that 24 percent of respondents across countries hold both perspectives. Thus, roughly one-quarter of the population simultaneously: (1) believes that their country needs human rights remedies, (2) trusts LHROs, and (3) has positive associations with "human rights." In theory, this group should be financial supporters of LHROs, willing to contribute money to organizations they trust to help make a difference. Why are local rights groups not raising more money from these citizens—especially in these democratic (or liberalizing, in the case of Morocco) countries?

A third alternative and logical explanation is that ordinary people in the global South are simply too poor to contribute to perceived "luxuries" such as LHROs. This argument seems particularly salient for Nigeria and India, where Purchasing Power Parity (PPP)-adjusted per capita income in 2012 was roughly $5,000 (in current USD),[18] near the global bottom. However, as Figure 4.2 noted above, LHRO leaders in Rabat and Casablanca estimated a *higher* proportion of LHROs receive substantial foreign support than their counterparts in Mumbai or Lagos, even though Morocco's per capita income was higher than both.[19] LHRO leaders in Mexico, moreover, offered statistically *similar* estimates to India and Nigeria, even though Mexico's per capita income was over three times larger.[20] And, as Figure 4.3 above notes, practitioners across *all* samples believed that "very few" LHROs in their countries raised funds domestically, regardless of their country's income. Indeed, in analyzing the 60-country practitioner interviews, we find no statistical association between practitioner estimates of the number of LHROs in their country receiving "substantial" funds and their countries' per capita income.[21]

Indeed, broader research suggests aggregate development levels are generally poor predictors of citizen donation to non-profits.[22] According to 2012 Gallup polls cited by the Charities Aid Foundation, an average of 22 percent of the population in our four countries of interest reported donating money to a charity *in the last 30 days*, with per sample estimates ranging from a low of 6 percent in Morocco to a high of 30 percent in Nigeria.[23] These figures, however, likely exclude Islamic tithing, or *zakat*.[24] According to a different Pew survey with more specific wording, 92 percent of Moroccans and 80 percent of Nigerian Muslims voluntarily and annually fulfill their *zakat* obligation by donating as much as 2.5 percent of their income to mosques and/or religious foundations.[25] Overall, in other words, people in the global South do donate money.

A more significant problem may be that acute poverty is concentrated precisely among those *most supportive* of human rights ideas and groups. To investigate, we identified which survey respondents *Have Disposable Income*, by selecting those who reported their monthly income allowed them to either *"cover expenses and save"* or *"just cover expenses, without major difficulties."*[26] This is a subjective measure of income representing what respondents themselves feel about their income versus expenses, rather than an "objective" analysis based on an estimation of household assets. As such, it is a better measure of those who might *feel* able to contribute, at least in theory. Table 4.2 below demonstrates that the per-sample percentage who *Have Disposable Income* ranges from 37 percent in Mumbai to 53 percent in Lagos, with a cross-sample average of 42 percent. Across survey respondents, who are representative of the entire populations of these areas, we find significant numbers of people are in fact able to comfortably cover their expenses, thus potentially freeing some of their resources for charitable causes.

Next, we overlap respondents who report that they *Have Disposable Income* with those who are also *Human Rights Inclined* and *Perceive Poor Human Rights Conditions*. The group at the intersection of this Venn diagram is theoretically the most likely to donate to LHROs: they are *High Probability Donors*. These people trust LHROs, associate human rights with positive ideas, view human rights conditions in their country as poor, and have at least a modicum of self-identified disposable income. As Table 4.1 shows, 10 percent of respondents are *High Probability Donors*, with per country estimates ranging from 7 percent in Rabat and Casablanca to 13 percent in Mumbai.

This definition of *High Probability Donor* may be too restrictive, as people with low incomes often do donate to charitable causes.[27] In fact, the Charities Aid Foundation tells us that the world's most charitable societies in 2012 included Myanmar, where 85 percent of the population reported donating money to a charity in the last 30 days, and Thailand, where 70 percent had donated that month.[28] Myanmar and Thailand are, of course, relatively poor countries, with per capita GDPs of $1,100 and $5,700, respectively, placing them toward the very bottom of the global income scale.[29] At a minimum, though, the *High Probability Donor* category is conceptually useful, representing the "most likely" LHRO donors. And yet—vexingly—very few of these "best case" individuals had ever opened their pocketbooks to LHROs; just about 5 percent of *High Probability Donors* reported ever donating money to a human rights organization.[30]

Each of the most common explanations we have considered fall somewhat short of explaining why there is little local money for local rights. Political repression is salient in some countries, but not particularly constrictive in others, including the four studied here. Public demand for human rights remedies also seems high, as people are critical of conditions in their countries and see LHROs and their messages positively. Many individuals also report some disposable income, suggesting high levels of poverty cannot account for low donations. Nevertheless, only a tiny percentage of *High Probability Donors* report ever donating to a human rights organization.

Philanthropic Habits

Socially constructed, habitual routines of charitable giving may contribute part of the answer. Philanthropy is an inherently routinized activity.[31] As one anthropologist notes, the human impulse to share with others is "cultivated and articulated in ritual practice"; another observes that extra-household giving is subject to "culturally specific" routines, norms, and styles.[32] Individuals, groups, and organizations generally give in accordance with accepted local norms. In Muslim societies, people often donate to religious institutions that administer *zakat*, the alms giving required of every believer.[33] In Jewish-American communities, charity focuses on highly celebrated and legitimate organizations (such as the United Jewish Appeal), accepted activities (such as education), and the right kind of beneficiaries (typically, Jews in need).[34] In many Christian traditions, believers are expected to tithe a set percentage of their income to the church or other charitable causes. Philanthropy certainly can exist outside these socially accepted parameters, but is less common and more open to contestation.

Seeing philanthropy through this lens of socially-constructed and culturally-rooted practices helps explain LHROs' reliance on foreign funders, despite the perils of doing so and the theoretical potential for domestic fundraising. On the donor or "supply" side, these routines prompt Northern-based institutions (and some individuals) to give to LHROs, while simultaneously disincentivizing individuals and institutions in the global South from doing the same. In the global South, philanthropic routines lead would-be donors to concentrate almost exclusively on organizations providing material social assistance, often of a religious nature. On the "demand" side, most LHROs rationally decide there is too steep a hill to climb to solicit local funds successfully, focusing instead on Northern sources, most of which are institutional. These choices become path-dependent and routinized, as switching to local fundraising strategies can be prohibitively difficult when systems are oriented outward. As a result, rational calculations become ingrained conventional wisdom, a habit that takes on a life of its own as it becomes taken-for-granted business as usual.

People all around the world have long donated to faith-based charities seeking to relieve pressing material needs. It is far less common to donate money to secular advocacy groups focused on structural or policy change, such as LHROs.[35] In Asia, for example, a multi-country study found that although people give generously to religious charities, they rarely donate to social change NGOs.[36] Similarly, in Palestine, another report argues, people regularly donate to local *zakat* committees, but rarely give to what the authors call "strategic" NGOs, most of which rely on foreign aid.[37] In Nigeria, one rights practitioner explained that his organization was considering dropping "human rights" from their title so as to better appeal to the local donors who would be interested in charitable causes.[38]

Although philanthropic habits are powerful, they can shift as social movements and change agents reinterpret existing routines. In nineteenth century India, for example, social innovator Swami Vivekananda reworked traditional Hindu doctrines of social service to create the radically egalitarian Ramakrishna Mission, which disavowed entrenched caste and religious differences.[39] Gandhi did the same a few decades later, reworking traditional Hindu concepts of *dan* (gift-giving) and *seva* (service) to create a new philanthropic synthesis focused on land reform, Hindu-Muslim unity, curbing Untouchability, and more.[40] In countries with large Islamic populations, similarly, philanthropic innovators have repeatedly reworked interpretations of *zakat*, taking traditional alms giving in all manner of new directions, such as building new universities in Turkey.[41]

These reinterpretations require sustained effort, deep cultural fluency, and strong alliances with more traditional charities. To change local giving patterns, LHROs would have to invest heavily in redefining themselves and their work as socially legitimate targets of local philanthropic largesse. For example, LHROs would have to convince at least some religious opinion leaders that good Muslims could satisfy their *zakat* obligation by donating to rights groups. Below, we provide evidence that key informants and LHRO leaders realize how challenging this transformation would be and have instead chosen to focus their energies elsewhere, at least for now.

As global South publics remain entrenched in philanthropic routines that prioritize giving to other types of groups, in parts of the global North both public and private agencies have grown increasingly interested in supporting international human rights.[42] In some cases, individual citizens in the global North may also be more willing to give than those in the global South, as implied by research on Amnesty International's struggle to build membership-based organizations in the global South.[43] Most Northern funds for Southern civil society groups are donated by public sector institutions such as development agencies or private foundations.

Among these institutions, philanthropic routines have changed so that donating to human rights groups in the global South is a socially accepted practice.[44] Tracking the rise of the "rights-based approach to development" helps illustrate how this happened.

As a form of publicly organized philanthropy, international development assistance is heavily subjected to the pressures of habit, routine, and legitimacy.[45] Northern-based international aid agencies spend enormous time, effort, and money identifying the processes, recipients, activities, and evaluation methods that are most "appropriate" in the eyes of significant stakeholders, including donors and governments. Indeed, the critical development literature often castigates the sector for its preoccupation with passing "fads."[46]

Cognizant of this, change agents constantly seek to modify aid routines of Northern agencies, hoping to redirect the sector's $130 billion-plus budget toward the issues they most believe in. The international assistance arena is constantly abuzz with these debates, leading to the often chastised cycle of development fads. One such shift occurred in the mid-late 1990s in the wake of the Rwandan genocide. Until then, international development and human rights had inhabited distinct policy and funding worlds.[47] Development actors had access to large annual Official Development Assistance (ODA) disbursements, but human rights activists struggled to survive on more meager support from a handful of private donors.[48] All this changed after 1994, when critics noted that Rwanda's vast array of internationally supported development agencies had failed to anticipate or prevent mass killings.[49] If development groups had been more attuned to mounting human rights abuses, critics said, they would have alerted the world. A number of development groups began incorporating human rights ideas, concerns, and principles into their operating procedures and strategies, and eventually a new "routine" emerged. In 2003, the United Nations put an official stamp of legitimacy on this new approach, integrating human rights into all its activities.[50] By 2014, according to a former USAID director, development and human rights had become "partners at last," with roughly 6 percent out of a total $135 billion[51] in official development assistance focused on human rights work.[52]

In this context, and as most private philanthropy in the global South (and elsewhere) is still oriented toward traditional charitable activities, LHROs have come to see external fundraising as the easiest option. This decision is also path-dependent; once a sector starts down the road of international funding, switching to local funding becomes increasingly costly.[53] LHROs have ample practice appealing and applying to international donors, but cultivating new local sources would entail substantial effort, recruiting or retraining staff, investing in targeting local donors, figuring out how local donors could safely transfer money, and more.[54]

Where Individuals Give Instead

We asked the 6,180 people who participated in our survey whether they had ever donated money to a range of groups—religious organizations, political parties, parents associations, environmental organizations, unions, and human rights organizations. In Nigeria, Morocco, and India we also asked about neighborhood associations, professional associations, and nongovernmental organizations. Unlike the above-mentioned Gallup polls reported annually by the Charities Aid Foundation, we asked respondents whether they had *ever* donated, rather than if they donated *in the last 30 days*. Table 4.2 summarizes the relatively high frequency of giving reported by these individuals.

Like Gallup, we find that people in our countries of interest *do* donate to charity, with faith-based entities by far the most frequent recipients.[55] For example, 38 percent of our Mumbai sample reported donating to "religious organizations," as did a remarkable 88 percent of Lagos respondents. (The way our survey team asked the question in Morocco likely did not capture religious giving, which would explain the low figure for Rabat and Casablanca. Unfortunately, variation crept into the way the survey companies asked this question in different countries, complicating direct cross-sample comparisons on giving.[56]) Contributions to parents associations were also common, up to 47 percent in Lagos and its environs. We find an average of 42 percent of respondents reported donating at least once to at least one of the groups we named.

To try to provide a more stringent measure of altruistic giving, in Nigeria, we added a follow-up question to distinguish between a "compulsory levy" (such as membership fees or required neighborhood dues) and a "voluntary donation." We still found high rates of voluntary giving across organizational types, demonstrating that the majority of donors consider their contributions freely given. Even accounting for the possibility · that some "donations" may not be entirely voluntary, the willingness to give seems strong.

The table above actually shows rather remarkable rates of giving among ordinary people in these four countries—just not to human rights organizations. Across samples, just 1 to 5 percent of the publics are HRO donors.[57] Even more concerning, human rights donations are also extremely unlikely among those we would most *expect* to make donations. Recall Table 4.1, which showed just 5 percent of *High Probability Donors* report having donated to HROs at any point. Charitable giving is not uncommon, but donations to rights activities are comparatively rare, even from those most supportive and trusting of human rights ideas and organizations, who perceive human rights conditions in their country to be poor, and who have some disposable income.

Our practitioner interviews confirmed the tendency to give to anything *except* human rights. In India, one LHRO worker said her family donates generously to "the school, infrastructure and . . . temple" in their village, but would never consider donating to a rights group, including her own; it would seem entirely unnatural.[58] In Mexico, average people regularly "give to religious foundations,"[59] and in Morocco, "[I]f we [the LHRO] had a charity approach, as opposed to [a human rights] approach, we would have a lot more [local] financing."[60]

Indeed, many of the practitioners we interviewed said there was, in theory, local money for local human rights. Figure 4.5 reports the percentage of practitioners who replied affirmatively to our question, *"Is substantial local funding for human rights organizations a possibility in your country?"* Between 43 and 93 percent in each sample believed substantial local funds were available.

We carried out a survey experiment in Lagos to further gauge the feasibility of local individual donations, asking, *"Taking into account your ability to donate, would you give [x] naira to a human rights organization of your choice?"* We split the sample randomly into four groups, asking about progressively larger hypothetical

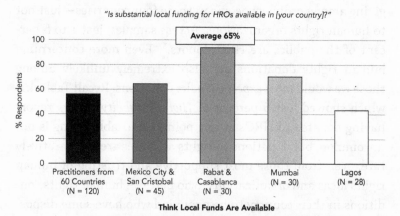

"Is substantial local funding for HROs available in [your country]?"

Average 65%

% Respondents

Practitioners from 60 Countries (N = 120)	Mexico City & San Cristobal (N = 45)	Rabat & Casablanca (N = 30)	Mumbai (N = 30)	Lagos (N = 28)

Think Local Funds Are Available

The 60-country practitioner sample is a purposive sample;
the other samples are representative of LHROs in each city.
Average is the mean across samples, with each of the samples weighted equally.

FIGURE 4.5 Practitioners Are Optimistic about Local Funding for Human Rights

donations; 250 people each were asked about donating 500, 1000, 3000, and 5000 Nigerian naira, about $2.50–$25.00 USD. Respondents were remarkably willing to give, as 87 percent said they would give about $2.50, 75 percent would give $5, 53 percent would give $15, and 51 percent said they would give $25. To put that in perspective, $25 USD is about 5 percent of the average monthly income in Nigeria; a comparable donation in the United States would be roughly $233.[61] Although asking a hypothetical question like this surely finds people *overestimating* their willingness to give, it is suggestive that over half of respondents said they would give at any of these amounts, even at a level that would seem to require substantial personal sacrifice.[62] This charitable proclivity could be a crucial resource for LHROs, but it is currently diverted nearly exclusively to other recipients.

In 2016, we returned to Mexico to conduct another person survey of adults living in Mexico City and its urban environs.[63] Among other things, we handed out packets of 50 pesos to each respondent (roughly 3 USD at the time of the survey), and assured them that the money was entirely theirs to keep. Later, we read out a narrative to each respondent about a "human rights organization" in Mexico that was seeking donations, and asked them if they might be willing to donate some or all of the 50 pesos to that group. The point of our experiment was to vary the narrative and see which one garnered more donations. For our purposes here, however, we note that the median donation was 20 pesos; 80 percent of respondents donated something. To us, these data cumulatively suggest that donations from members of the public are a potentially useful resource for LHROs.

Despite evidence that people *do* donate to charitable causes, practitioners' perceptions that substantial local funding *is* available, and the high *willingness* of Lagos and Mexico City respondents to give to rights groups, global South publics remain untapped donors for human rights causes. Recently, a handful of private groups, including the Open Society Foundations, have been exploring the possibilities for local funding. The issue has re-emerged in the context of Amnesty's attempt to decentralize from London to regions in the global South.[64] For example, the Indian section of Amnesty has begun to raise money locally with media advertisements; according to the AI secretary general, the section may eventually become self-sustaining.[65] Similarly, Action Aid, a hybrid development/human rights organization that relocated its headquarters from London to Johannesburg, says it too is making great efforts to raise money in the global South.[66]

Preserving Philanthropic Routines

Beyond such efforts, why have most donors not made local fundraising efforts a condition of their grants to human rights groups? It may be, as some have suggested for the humanitarian sector, that Northern donors implicitly prefer to keep LHROs dependent on them for funding and leadership.[67] It could be the case that donors are guided by a bureaucratic instinct for self-preservation. It may also be, as one African activist recently suggested, that Northern donors inherently mistrust LHROs' ability to spend money wisely.[68] Finally, donors might accept the notion that human rights activity is a form of "emergency work" that must not be delayed or held hostage by long-term, risky local fundraising efforts. Northern donors often perceive human rights promotion, like humanitarian aid, as something urgently needed to stave off imminent harm. Given this mindset, it may seem churlish to require local rights groups to begin extensive efforts at local fundraising. Whatever the reason, the donor side of this story requires further investigation.

For their part, most LHROs seem similarly disinterested in cultivating local donors; when asked about engaging local citizens as potential *donors*, most rights practitioners drew a blank. Although they recognize vulnerabilities from heavy dependence on foreign funds, reaching out to their co-citizens for the purposes of fundraising is not part of their existing repertoire, and it is not something their international supporters mention or require. Among practitioners, it is clear that existing incentives and the organizational structures established as a result push LHROs toward international fundraising. In Nigeria, one told us, local funding "doesn't come as quickly as when you go to a [foreign] donor that deals with ... human rights;"[69] in Indonesia, "it's easier to get big money from international sources;"[70] and in Bangladesh, LHROs "are ... getting the funds from the [international] donors [and] ... not giving much ... time" to explorations of local funding.[71] In 2016, we conducted a survey of 34 Mexico City LHROs; once again, most reported that their funding was heavily dependent on foreign sources. Only three groups reported engaging in door-to-door fundraising with the general public, and only one had dues-paying members. In Mexico City, human rights groups do not regularly and systematically ask the public for donations. Yet our data show that these efforts could potentially bear fruit.

Changing gears in this way would require a costly conceptual and organizational investment, however. In India, one LHRO leader explained, stewarding potential local donors would require "a lot of effort," "human resources," and new "skills,"[72] and in Mexico, another said, groups simply lack the "know-how" to raise funds locally.[73] In Morocco, another practitioner explained, "[W]e do not know how to get to [local funding]" or "who to go to."[74] Fundraising for human rights has become something done looking outward, not locally. It is a routine that is hard to dislodge; to overcome deeply engrained and self-sustaining habits would be costly, time-consuming, and fraught with uncertainty.

Approaching international donors requires substantially less cost. Transnational rights activists paved the road in the 1990s and early 2000s, inserting human rights considerations into standard grant templates and sector-wide protocols, as discussed above. In the 1980s, defining oneself as a "human rights" group would not have helped gain funding from multilateral or bilateral donors. However, by the late 1990s and 2000s, groups that branded themselves as "rights promoting" had become legitimate and desired recipients of international aid, entitled to access specific categories of funding devised for human rights or other similar activities, including "rule of law," "freedom of information," "good governance," "civil society promotion," or "democratization." Human rights grant giving had been mainstreamed through all these categories. As a result, pursuing international rather than local money has become the most rational option for harried, hard-working, and hard-pressed LHRO leaders.

Contact as a Catalyst

We have argued that there is strong potential for local funding for local rights, and now offer a strategic suggestion on how to transform potential to actual currency. We end with a brief discussion of the link between LHRO public engagement and donations. In Chapter 2, we showed that few people had met human rights workers, could name specific rights organizations, or had ever participated in a rights-related activity. Evidence from our "willingness to give" survey experiment in Lagos suggests making contact with potential donors is extremely valuable. We used a logistic regression model to predict what factors are associated with respondents being willing to donate to an HRO. Supporting our theoretical expectations, people who were

Human Rights Inclined were more willing to give, as were wealthier and older people. However, even when controlling for support for human rights, the level of the hypothetical donation, and socioeconomic factors, we found a strong positive association with our index variable, *Contact with Human Rights*.[75] Those who had a higher score on the index of hearing, meeting, naming, and participating were more likely to be willing to donate to rights organizations. People measuring 0 on the *Contact Human Rights* scale have a predicted 63 percent chance of being willing to donate, whereas those with maximum contact have a predicted 87 percent chance, controlling for a range of other explanatory factors.[76]

Figure 4.6 shows that, across cases, *High Probability Donors* are no more likely to have met a human rights worker than respondents who are not high probability donors; on average, 9 percent of *High Probability Donors* could recall ever meeting a

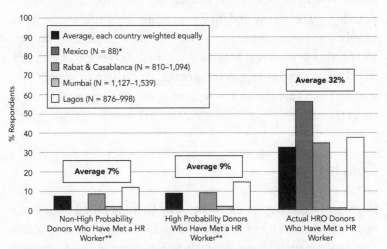

FIGURE 4.6 Contact with Human Rights Workers Matters in Attracting Donations

HRO worker, a figure statistically indistinguishable to the average for the rest of the sample (7 percent).

Empirically, personal contact seems crucial for moving people from "potential" to "actual" donors. Figure 4.6 demonstrates that 32 percent of those who report actually donating to HROs say they have met a human rights worker, much more than either *High Probability Donors* or their non-high-probability counterparts.

Correlation is not causation, of course; human rights supporters may have first decided to contribute, which then led to occasions to meet human rights workers. Still, the broader point remains: contact and donations are logically and empirically correlated. The rate of HRO contact with ordinary citizens is low, even among those most likely to support their work, whereas the rate of contact among those who actually donate is much higher. Increasing personal contact with *High Probability Donors*—who in fact did very often say they would be *willing* to donate to HROs—would likely provide a significant impetus to move someone into the "actual donor" category. To do this, local rights groups will have to do a much better job of identifying their potential supporters, contacting them, and soliciting money from them with the help of appropriately modified cultural frames.

Conclusion

We began this chapter exploring why there is broad public support for human rights ideas and organizations, but only a slim domestic financial base. Even though publics in the four countries where we collected data face relatively low rates of political repression, support human rights ideas and groups, see a need for rights-promoting activities, and have some measure of disposable income, local citizens do not give to LHROs. Instead, these groups rely heavily on outside sources, while local citizens make donations to other philanthropic organizations.

One explanation is that LHROs are not personally connecting with the *High Probability Donors* in their country. Over half these publics perceive poor human rights conditions in their country, roughly 4 in 10 are *Human Rights Inclined,* and a similar number have disposable income. Taken together, *High Probability Donors* make up 10 percent of the population, yet only a very small number of these have ever donated money to a human rights group or have ever had personal contact with an LHRO or a rights practitioner—although one of the correlates of donations is precisely this kind of contact. LHROs have not successfully managed to make strategic contact with those who would be the most likely to donate to their cause.

The reason, we argue, is that it is far easier in the contemporary structure of the global human rights movement to raise money internationally than locally, whereas the benefits to the movement of raising greater local support are more long-term or intangible. In the same way, to potential donors in the global South, human rights work may seem too long-term or intangible. Charitable giving by individuals in these countries is widespread but focused heavily on faith-based charities that offer immediate material relief. Giving money to non-profit organizations focused on structural or policy change, by contrast, is rare and socially unpopular. People may be *Human Rights Inclined*, but their long-standing, deeply engrained habits of philanthropic giving point their pocketbooks away from LHROs.

In the global North, however, activists successfully shifted the standard philanthropic operating routines of donor agencies, pushing them to incorporate human rights ideas and organizations into their funding practices, reversing earlier practices that had relegated human rights to fringe funding. Once human rights and development discourses merged into the "rights-based approach to development," human rights activists worldwide gained access to significant pools of Northern funds, de-incentivizing LHRO efforts to raise money domestically. Although obtaining funding from Northern-based agencies is always a "scramble" and never easy,[77] these agencies have created standard operating procedures and templates for processing human rights funding proposals. As a result, it is far easier for LHROs to appeal to agencies based in the global North, where they are not required to persuade anyone that human rights promotion is a legitimate activity worthy of donations. That work of shifting philanthropic routines toward human rights work has already been done in the global North, whereas it has not yet made much progress in the South.

In a sense, we are describing a collective problem of enormous proportions. The publics in these countries are critical of human rights conditions, trust domestic rights groups, and support human rights ideas. Moreover, most think that human rights groups in their country are already raising money from citizens like themselves. The problem, it seems, may be that human rights groups are not aggressively asking for the money in culturally appropriate ways. It is always hard to raise money for collective causes, because each individual has an incentive to "free ride"; groups can overcome this barrier with hard work, but in the case of human rights fundraising, donors in the global North have short-circuited this process. Donors in Geneva, London, Brussels, and New York have "solved" the collective action problem by taking the "collective" out of the equation, replacing small donations from human rights-inclined publics with larger blocks of money for individual projects and organizations.

To boost their autonomy, create stronger relations with their constituents, and avoid being targeted by the government as "foreign agents," LHROs should be strategically prioritizing expanding their domestic funding base. To do so, they could make use of the kind of strategic analysis offered here to identify potential citizen supporters and determine effective means of reaching them. Person-to-person interactions may help move individuals from high probability to *actual* donors. In the long run, this may transform philanthropic routines and habits so that LHROs become legitimate, taken-for-granted recipients of local financial giving.

5

Religion

Human Rights Ally and Rival

Our final task is to offer analysis of the complicated relationship between religiosity and human rights. We set out asking about relationships between human rights organizations and other types of social actors, organizations, or groups, such as political parties, and organized religion emerged as one of the most significant. The human rights practitioners we interviewed told us that organized religion was *either* their biggest challenge *or* their most important potential partner in disseminating human rights ideas. They were highly cognizant of how powerfully religious worldviews shape people's lives, decisions, values, and actions. Prompted by these strong opinions from practitioners, we asked ordinary people about religion in our *Human Rights Perceptions Polls*. Results confirmed that faith was so central to peoples' lives that to *not* ask about it would have been akin to overlooking income, education, or gender. The more we investigated the rights-religion connection, the more we realized just how fraught it can be; as the *Economist* notes, religion and human rights are "awkward, but necessary, bedfellows."[1]

Religious teachings and their proponents offer codes of conduct and basic principles to live by, and human rights ideas and activists do the same. This creates dynamic potential for either conflict or collaboration. Our previous chapters provided several hints about the current balance of conflict/collaboration between the two. Human rights groups have far less regular contact with the public than do religious actors. The public generally trusts religious institutions more highly than they do LHROs, and they make donations by far the most frequently to religious groups. By these measures, it might behoove rights groups to identify ways to shape a message that resonates with religious worldviews or to strategically collaborate with religious organizations.

In reality, secular rights advocates in many countries are deeply concerned about threats to human rights from the "opiate of the masses"[2] because of stances taken by some leaders and institutions of organized religion, such as attitudes toward the rights of women and sexual minorities. One commentator in India warned that religiously-motivated laws "favor the interests of powerful (male) groups;"[3] in Nigeria, the country's dominant faith traditions are "known for their unequal treatment of the sexes;"[4] in Mexico, religious conservatives oppose "women's reproductive rights;"[5] and in Morocco, Islamists critique the newly progressive Family Code.[6] Indeed, according to two leading analysts, one of the globe's deepest ideological fault lines is the "sexual clash of civilizations" between world-spanning religious and secular traditions.[7] From this perspective, secular humanist and religious thought are fundamentally at odds in their normative ideologies.

Still others warn that religion, or its cynical manipulation by politicians and movements, pose threats to peace and security (as do other belief systems, such as nationalism).[8] In India, one activist warns, radical Hindu groups are "directly ... responsible for ... violence and terrorist activity;"[9] in Nigeria, Islamist Boko Haram insurgents "exemplify the most extreme religious fanaticism and fundamentalism;"[10] in Morocco, Islamist radicals, including possible al-Qaeda affiliates, have been repeatedly responsible for terrorist outrages.[11] Across world regions, it appears all too easy to manipulate faith in the service of violence. Some even argue that religion per se is antithetical to the universal humanism of which human rights is a major component. Several best-selling authors, many with training in the natural sciences, have given support to the notion that religion is little more than an irrational belief system inevitably leading to violence, oppression, and other social ills.[12] Practitioners sometimes espoused these views, and many seemed concerned about a perceived irreconcilable conflict between religion and human rights.

On the other hand, many believe just as strongly that human rights and religion can be and often are mutually supportive. Larry Cox, former head of Amnesty-USA and a long-time proponent of combining faith and human rights, argues that the global "human rights movement's real power comes from its inherent religious dimensions."[13] International relations scholar Jack Snyder similarly suggests that rights activists require a "leg up from progressive religion to gain organizational and emotional traction."[14] Some experts even claim that secular bias has led researchers to ignore the faith community's massive contributions to transnational human rights efforts.[15]

A quick look at the empirical record suggests that faith-rights linkages do in fact abound. In the United States, for example, religious groups often inspire civil and human rights activism at home and abroad.[16] In Mexico (and Latin America more broadly), liberation theologians have historically advocated for basic rights for the poor;[17] in India, some Hindu orders have worked hard to reject caste-based discrimination;[18] in Nigeria, the Catholic Church has often been a voice for democratization, social justice, and human rights;[19] and in Morocco, the Islamist and feminist movements have influenced and shaped one another in important ways.[20] For every skeptic concerned with religion's adverse human rights impacts, an equal number claim the opposite and cite examples of productive collaboration.

Our research team recorded similarly split perspectives among the practitioners we interviewed: some saw religion as an ally, whereas others saw the opposite. Most emphatically agreed, however, that religious leaders, ideas, and organizations play a central role in their societies; few were indifferent to the powerful influence of organized religion over the cultural, social, and political lives of their countries. Even those who perceived religion as a potential or actual ally, however, often found their organizations facing confusion or frustrations about how to best engage with religious ideas or collaborate with religious actors.

Our evidence suggests that among global South publics, religion is neither inherently inimical to, nor propitious for, human rights. As scholar Reza Aslan argues, all religions contain elements that are supportive of and critical of contemporary conceptions of human rights. People of faith do not so much "derive their values primarily from their Scriptures ... [but rather] insert their values into their Scriptures, reading them from the lens of their own cultural, ethnic, nationalistic and even political perspectives."[21] Our data suggest that some aspects of organized religion sustain rights whereas others stifle them; the task for human rights practitioners remains trying to find an appropriate and productive balance.

Measuring Religiosity

We use multiple dimensions to measure religiosity—an incredibly complex social phenomenon—among survey respondents.[22] As a starting point, we distinguish between religious identities, such as "Catholic" or "Muslim." We also include measures of: personal or private religiosity (salience of religion in daily life, frequency of prayer); social religiosity and behavior (participation in religious organizations, frequency of attendance); and institutional religiosity (trust in religious institutions, asked as part of the trust series explored in Chapter 3).

Our *Human Rights Perceptions Polls* unequivocally confirm the centrality of all aspects of religiosity among publics in Mexico, Rabat/Casablanca, Mumbai, and Lagos. As Table 5.1 indicates, the public's average *Trust in Religious Institutions* was 25 percent higher than their *Trust in Local Human Rights Organizations*.[23] Indeed, most respondents regarded religious institutions as the *most* trusted of over a dozen actors, institutions, and organizations we asked about.[24]

Our other questions also revealed deep religiosity among publics in these countries: an average *Personal Religious Importance* score of 8.6 on a 0–10 scale,[25] 85 percent reported *Prayer* at least once per day,[26] 74 percent reported *Religious Attendance* at least once a week,[27] 34 percent reported *Religious Participation* in a faith-based organization of some kind,[28] and at least 47 percent reported a *Donation to Religious Organizations* at some point in their life.[29]

On the other hand, the rights practitioners we interviewed were generally less religious than the surrounding public, except in Lagos. As Figure 5.1 indicates, 56 percent of the LHRO leaders we interviewed as part of the representative LHRO leader samples reported they were "practicing members" of their faith, as did 71 percent of the 60-country key informant sample.[30]

Compare this to the 78 percent of the general public who selected a response of 8 or more to the question, "*How important is religion in your life?*" (0–10 scale, 10 = "extremely important").[31] Our bar for practitioners—simply to identify as "practicing members" of a religion—is even lower than the comparison we are making with the public—to rate religion as *highly* important in their lives. Even despite this, there is a gap between rights practitioners and the general public (in all samples except Lagos, where the human rights community may be even more religious than the surrounding public). Although publics are highly religious, human rights practitioners are much less so, immediately suggesting a baseline disconnect between the human rights movement and highly religious potential constituents.

Trends in the public opinion data are context- and issue-specific, suggesting great complexity and fruitful potential for future research. By some indicators or in some countries, religiosity is associated with *more* support for rights groups, but in others it is associated with *less*. We found that religious factors are strongly associated with human rights attitudes and behaviors, but in often contradictory ways. Our statistical findings thus confirm both sides of the broader debate; religion and human rights are intensely linked, but the relationship is complex, multidirectional, and hard to summarize in broad strokes. The seemingly contradictory ways that human rights scholars, activists, and practitioners evaluate religion is in fact an accurate reflection of a complex reality. Rather than revealing which side of the debate is "right," our evidence suggests that *both* perspectives are rooted in empirical reality, depending on the vantage point. Rather than "either/or," our conclusion is "both/and"—less tidy, but more faithful to the facts. We first explore practitioners' views before turning to our survey findings in depth.

Practitioners' Evaluation of Religion

Regardless of whether they thought religion was ultimately "good" or "bad" for human rights, many practitioners believed faith-based groups did a better job than LHROs at reaching ordinary people. We asked, *"In [your country], are there political or religious organizations that are* **more effective** *than human rights organizations at reaching the grassroots?"*[32] Most practitioners

TABLE 5.1 Religiosity Across Publics in Four Case Studies

	Mexico (N = 2,400)	Rabat and Casablanca (N = 1,100)	Mumbai (N = 1,680)	Lagos (N = 1,000)	Pooled (N = 6,180)
Identity or affiliation	80% Catholic, 11% non-Catholic Christian, 8% none	100% Muslim	77% Hindu, 8% Muslim, 5% Buddhist 9% Christian	56% non-Catholic Christian, 34% Muslim, 9% Catholic	N/A
Trust How much more does the public trust religious institutions than LHROs?	14%	30%	24%	32%	25%
Personal Religiosity Religious importance in daily life (mean, 0–10 scale)	7.7	9.9	7.6	9.0	8.6
Prayer (% at least once a day)	N/A	85%	81%	88%	85%

Social Religiosity					
Attendance (% at least once a week)	N/A	46%	79%	96%	74%
Participate in religious organizations (% yes)	21%	2%	24%	87%	34%
Donations to religious organizations (% yes)	60%	0%	38%	88%	47%

Figures are based on valid percentages, include country-specific weights, and weight countries equally for pooled figures. Number of respondents indicate total sample size. We oversampled Buddhists and Christians in Mumbai; see the Appendix for details.

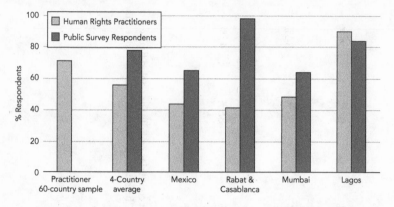

For practitioners, these figures include those who said they are a "practicing member of their faith." For public respondents, figures indicate those who selected 8 or above (0–10 scale) when asked how important religion is in daily life. Four-country average weights the four countries equally. 60-country sample is purposive. Response rates for public samples are 95–99% and practitioner samples are 67–93%.

FIGURE 5.1 Human Rights Practitioners Are Less Religious than Publics

(77 percent) said there *were* groups better than LHROs at grassroots mobilization; of these, most (61 percent) cited faith-based organizations. Most rights practitioners realized that religious groups were more socially embedded than rights groups and concluded that rights practitioners should seriously consider how best to build collaborative bridges.

Religious groups have multiple advantages when seeking to recruit followers, practitioners explained. For starters, they are better equipped to engage simultaneously in promoting ideals and offering goods and services, a potent combination. In Chapter 4, we learned that faith-based groups are leading *recipients* of philanthropy, but our interviews also suggest they are often leading *distributors* of charity. Bolstered by donations from the public, governments, and international sources, faith groups distribute money, goods, and services through volunteers working in strategically situated venues, such as temples, mosques, and churches, and aided by a broad array of mass communication tools, including radio, newsletters, and websites. As a result, faith groups are far more effective than LHROs at making a direct difference in ordinary peoples' lives. One practitioner from Burkina Faso explained that LHROs can only "explain" to citizens about their right to education, whereas faith groups do that *and* offer free reading classes.[33]

In Mexico, several practitioners told us the Church has a particularly powerful presence in areas sparsely administered by local governments,[34] where its long history of "living with the people" puts it in touch with the public's "daily concerns."[35] In Morocco, another said religious groups "offer concrete benefits to underprivileged communities"[36] and engage in "very active social work with the underprivileged,"[37] including "daily ... charity-based work," which LHROs rarely do.[38] A rights worker in Mumbai explained that members of the public attend meetings only when there are material gains to be had, and faith-based groups are far more likely to offer concrete goods and services than LHROs.[39]

This combination of service and advocacy is dynamic. Political scientist Samuel Popkin found this combination bolstered the strength of Vietnamese guerrillas fighting the French and US military,[40] and others have noted similarly powerful outreach by Islamic groups in the Middle East.[41] This combination of advocacy and service lies at the heart of the "collective action and advocacy organization" approach articulated by leading NGO scholars.[42] Public goods, including human rights, are in the interests of many, but as each individual's contribution is small, people are reluctant to sacrifice scarce time and money to provide general goods that can be claimed by anyone, regardless of their contribution to the cause. To overcome this classic collective action problem, organizers offer selective incentives to those who attend meetings and participate in activities.[43]

Although the rights-based approach to development recognizes the importance of this combination, the practice is still new, and neither development nor rights groups have fully internalized its implications.[44] Development agencies have long focused on service provision while avoiding advocacy, whereas human rights activists have done the opposite. Combining the two successfully is not easy, but faith-based groups have spent decades, if not centuries, honing their capacities.

A second crucial advantage enjoyed by faith-based groups, practitioners told us, is their practical or structural ability to regularly bring people together at predesignated times and places. Even the most grassroots-oriented rights groups lack established routines of this sort, but organized faith communities have such mechanisms in abundance. As noted above, 74 percent of the publics we surveyed reported attending a religious place of worship at least once a week, providing faith-based organizers a steady institutionalized forum to access constituents. This kind of long-standing and geographically diffuse spread, often constructed over hundreds of years, is something even the most energetic or well-funded LHRO could never hope to match.

Practitioners also referred to public trust when explaining religious groups' comparative strength. One practitioner from the Philippines noted, "Most of the people really respect the priest, so they would follow whatever the parish priest would tell them. Because they feel that the priest has a certain moral ascendency over them."[45] In Ecuador, similarly, the Catholic Church has "a lot of credibility with the people,"[46] and in the Gambia, the "Islamic Council . . . has influence in terms of commanding . . . attention from the general public."[47] In Lebanon, human rights workers must first "visit the [Islamic] sheik" or the "priest . . . [to] gain all the trust of the population."[48] *Trust in Religious Institutions* is very high.

Frame resonance is a fourth explanation of religion's mobilizing power. Social movements mobilize much more effectively when their message resonates or is compatible with existing worldviews, and religious ideas are among the most widely known, popular, and legitimate. Two prominent scholars of African religion and politics note that most political engagement on the continent is expressed through religious idiom, making it hard to imagine participating in public life in ways entirely removed from a religious worldview.[49] As one Moroccan practitioner explained, "Religious discourse is generally very easily welcome in a Muslim society," and religious actors can "use a religious discourse and mosques to diffuse their political messages," deeply "touch[ing] upon people's faith and emotions."[50] In Uganda, "Preachers have mastered the art of persuasion, using techniques that make rights advocates appear like novices. Religious leaders can gather a street congregation faster than it takes human rights workers to travel to a local workshop."[51]

Some of the practitioners we interviewed negatively evaluated faith leaders' power of persuasion. In Mumbai, one told us, "The religious people promise the moon and deliver nothing [but] people never recognize that." Religious figures "promise [people] that if you change your name ... or do this *puja* [religious ceremony] or that *puja* ... you will change your current life's karma," and although this never works, "it's like an opiate" for many.[52]

Still, many practitioners have tried to work with religious groups. In Mumbai, one practitioner explained that her organization often asks religious leaders to preach acceptance of LGBT populations, and when they do so, "it matters."[53] In Mexico, another said parishes and churches often allow rights activists to "occupy the facilities of their atrium or their community centers" so that they can conduct human rights activities,[54] and in other instances, an LHRO's "initial link [to a new area] is with the priest or a group of religious [individuals or organizations] who know the community."[55] In Lagos, a third explained that some rights groups invite churches to participate in their programs and are invited to some religious events in return.[56]

Nearly half our Montreal sample of 128 respondents from 60 countries reported witnessing successful instances of human rights collaboration with faith-based entities. A Kenyan practitioner explained, "There are quite a number of [human rights] organizations that forge partnerships with religious institutions . . . because they have more muscle, more resources than most NGOs."[57] Another noted that in parts of Kenya that are heavily Muslim, ordinary people ignore human rights messages until announced in local mosques, at which point public support grows exponentially. As a result, she said, collaborations with friendly imams in that part of the country have proven "really useful."[58] In Senegal, one simply "cannot have a successful campaign on AIDS . . . without being in contact with religious leaders."[59]

Human rights practitioners thus ignore religious ideas and representatives at their peril. Most of the people LHROs seek to represent are deeply religious, and to overlook a significant portion of their worldview is unwise. Even though rights practitioners may be more secular on average than the general public, many LHRO workers *are* religious and should perhaps more consciously leverage these commonalities. They can identify issues where tactical alliances are likely to be successful, including opposition to corrupt elites. Though LHROs cannot match religious organizations' power to mobilize, they do bring expertise that religious groups may not have, such as legal representation and research. And of course, social change messages framed in religious idiom may be more successful than those framed in purely secular terms.

What the Polls Show

This assessment of religion's power and influence will not surprise most social scientists; particularly after 9/11, few deny or ignore faith's role in local or global politics and its potential for mobilization, for whichever cause or purpose. However, relatively few scholars have directly explored the links between religiosity and human rights attitudes and behaviors, particularly using representative data from large-scale survey research. Our polls can begin to shed light on these connections.

Drawing on data from publics in Mexico, Rabat/Casablanca, Mumbai, and Lagos, we examine the associations between religiosity and human rights attitudes and ideas. We measure several aspects of "religiosity" and find complicated relationships with human rights. We discuss three areas of findings: first, the relationship between *Trust in Religious Institutions* and *Trust in Local Human Rights Organizations*; second, links between *Religious Identity* and *Human Rights Associations*; and third, the relationship between *Social Religiosity* and *Human Rights Participation*.

Religious Institutions and the Anti-Power Constituencies

In Chapter 3 we identified statistical determinants of *Trust in Local Human Rights Organizations* and found greater mistrust in the US government, multinational corporations, and domestic political institutions was associated with more trust in LHROs (controlling for many other factors). In other words, pro-LHRO constituencies were skeptical of concentrated economic and political power at both the national and international level. We extend this analysis to investigate whether *Trust in Local Human Rights Organizations* is similarly (inversely) related to *Trust in Religious*

Institutions. Do people who are skeptical of established religious institutions also trust local rights organizations more? Are the anti-religious counted among the anti-power constituents?

Our statistical analysis reveals that this is indeed the case; the more people *mis*trust religious institutions, the more likely they are to *trust* local rights groups. We replicated our earlier analysis predicting *Trust in Local Human Rights Organizations* (Table 3.2), but added a number of faith-related explanatory variables and controls, including *Trust in Religious Institutions;*[60] *Religious Identity* (Catholic, non-Catholic Christian, Muslim, Buddhist, or Hindu); a *Personal Religiosity Index* score (average of *Prayer Frequency* and *Personal Religious Importance*, after converting both to a common scale);[61] and a *Social Religiosity Index* (average of *Religious Attendance Frequency* and *Religious Participation*, converted to a common scale).[62]

Table 5.2 presents our regression results in summary form, and Table B.4 in Appendix B presents the full pooled and country-specific models, along with the relevant statistical controls. *Trust in Local Human Rights Organizations* is the dependent variable in these models, and religious indicators are the explanatory variables of interest.[63]

As Table 5.2 shows, *Trust in Religious Institutions* is generally associated with less *Trust in Local Human Rights Organizations*, mirroring the relationship with trust in the US government, multinational corporations, and domestic authorities. In the pooled, Mexico, and Lagos models, the more respondents *mistrust* religious institutions, the more they *trust* their country's local rights groups. This inverse relationship bolsters the claims of those arguing that religion and rights are antithetical; people who trust churches, mosques, and temples are more likely to mistrust their local rights groups. This suggests that any attempt to create a LHRO-religious group alliance, as suggested above, could face a dubious public. Organized religion

TABLE 5.2 Religiosity and Trust in LHROs

	Pooled (N = 3,825)	Mexico (N = 1,843)	Rabat and Casablanca (N = 403)	Mumbai (N = 763)	Lagos (N = 759)
Specific religious identity	n.f.	n.f.	N/A	n.f.	n.f.
Greater trust in religious institutions	LESS trust in LHROs	LESS trust in LHROs	n.f.	n.f.	LESS trust in LHROs
Greater personal religiosity*	n.f.	n.f.	n.f.	n.f.	n.f.
Greater social religiosity**	n.f.	MORE trust in LHROs	n.f.	n.f.	n.f.

The dependent variable, Trust in LHROs, is scaled 0 to 1 (1 = a lot of trust). All models are OLS regressions. All models include **Mistrust in Powerful Actors** (mistrust in the US government, MNCs, and domestic political authorities), **HR Contact, Politics** (support for the ruling party, voting), **SES** (education, subjective income squared, rural/urban residence, internet use), **Average Trust**, and **Controls** (age, gender). The pooled model controls for country and weights countries equally.

n.f. = "No finding."

* Personal religiosity is: frequency of prayer in Rabat and Casablanca, importance of religion in daily life in other countries, index of both variables in pooled model.

** Social religiosity is: participation in activities of a religious organization in Mexico, frequency of religious service attendance in other countries, index of both variables in pooled model.

is important, but any attempt by rights practitioners to build bridges and reach new supporters could alienate their core constituents, who do tend to be skeptical of faith institutions.

Yet as Table 5.2 also demonstrates, other measures of religiosity, including *Personal Religiosity* or *Religious Identity*, are *not* systematically associated with *Trust in Local Human Rights Organizations*. In Mexico, *Social Religiosity* is associated with greater *Trust in Local Human Rights Organizations*. Taken together, these findings suggest that once again, the faith-rights nexus is complex: not all religious indicators are statistically significant, some are positively associated with *Trust in Local Human Rights Organizations*, and others are negatively associated.

For our purposes, the takeaway is that mistrust in religious institutions has the same relationship with trust in local rights groups as did multinational corporations, domestic political authorities, and the US government. This suggests that human rights supporters may view the religious hierarchy similarly to political and economic hierarchies, with an underlying skepticism of authority extending to religious institutions. The domestic human rights community's local constituencies, in other words, may be found among people opposed to hierarchy, power, and elites of all kinds—people who lean against institutionalized power in any form, including religious manifestations. These anti-institutionalists are not libertarian in the classic US sense; as we saw in Chapter 3, there is a positive statistical association between *Trust in Local Human Rights Organizations* and associating "human rights" with "promoting social and economic justice." The pro-LHRO constituency tilts against what social historian Michael Mann calls the "sources of social power."[64] Popular trust in local human rights organizations can be a tool in the arsenal of the powerless, a "weapon of the weak."[65]

We in no way mean to suggest that religiosity is either *uniformly* or *intrinsically* opposed to human rights. Rather, with the help of more nuanced measurements of respondents' engagement with different aspects of faith, we show that other, less institutionalized, aspects of religiosity are in fact positively related to pro-human rights attitudes. It seems religiously-originating skepticism toward LHROs is rooted in anti-institutional attitudes more broadly, rather than in elements or content of the faith itself.

Religious Identities and Conceptualizing "Human Rights"

As Chapter 3 demonstrated, publics hold varied definitions of "human rights," ranging from positive-sounding phrases such as "promoting social and economic justice," "protecting people from torture and murder," and "promoting free and fair elections," to phrases that evoke the specter of foreign meddling, such as "promoting foreign values and ideas" or "promoting US interests," to strongly negative-sounding phrases, such as "protecting terrorists" or "protecting criminals." Across samples, however, positive associations with human rights strongly outweigh the negative.

What impact might religious identity have on these associations? Are Muslims more likely to associate human rights with US interests, as many experts expect? Do Catholics see human rights in more socioeconomic terms? To learn more, we examined the statistical association between *Religious Identity,* our independent variable, and associations with "human rights," our dependent variables.

We start with Catholics, where both scholarship and the daily news suggest the association with rights could go either way. On the one hand, elements of the Catholic Church have supported human rights ideas and activists for almost a century across the world, especially (but not exclusively) in Latin America. Worldwide and cross-nationally, higher concentrations of Catholic populations are often associated with stronger support for human rights-related ideas, such as liberal democracy.[66] Many of the practitioners we spoke with reinforced this message; we even interviewed some in "human rights" offices located on the premises of the local Catholic diocese. On the other hand, some conservative Catholic leaders have supported repressive right-wing governments, such as Argentina's during the Dirty War; criticized liberation theology as a form of radical Marxism; fought against women's reproductive rights and gender equality; refused to recognize or punish their own staff's abuse and predatory sexual behavior; and undermined the equality and rights of LGBT populations.[67] In our countries of interest, which of these two tendencies has the strongest impact overall on Catholics' views of human rights?

To investigate, we created an index of *Positive Human Rights Associations*, averaging respondents' associations with human rights (on the 1 to 7 scale) as "promoting social and economic justice," "protecting people from torture and murder," and "promoting free and fair elections." As discussed in Chapter 3, correlations and factor analysis demonstrate that these three associations are strongly interrelated, suggesting it makes both statistical and logical sense to combine these three into an index. An individual's *Positive Human Rights Associations* index score could range from 1 to 7; by averaging these three positive associations, we retain the information of respondents who did not respond to one (or even two) of these questions, giving us more statistical leverage.

First we compare *Catholics'* score on *Positive Human Rights Associations* to all others, including any other religious affiliation and the (few) who self-identify as secular. Self-identified Catholics comprise 80 percent of our Mexican sample, 9 percent of our Lagos sample, 1 percent of our Mumbai sample (in weighted terms), and are absent from our Morocco sample. We use OLS regression and control for socio-demographic, political, and religious factors mentioned in previous chapters and above.[68] This simple statistical technique allows us to investigate whether self-identification as "Catholic" is related to respondents' associations with "human rights," beyond all the other variables we are accounting for. Recall that our analysis controls for country, meaning that significant findings are specifically related to identification as *Catholic* over and above the fact that the respondent lives in a particular country (including Mexico, where most of the Catholics in our samples reside).

We find that Catholics have more positive associations with "human rights" than members of other religions; Figure 5.2 shows that Catholics score 4 percent higher on the *Positive Human Rights Association* index than non-Catholics.[69] This difference may seem small, but recall that it represents a statistically significant finding above and beyond the effects of all other controls. Given the extensive controls and the complexity of the outcome we seek to explain—an index of individuals' positive conceptualizations of "human rights"—any statistically significant difference at all is meaningful.

To investigate further, we disaggregated "non-Catholics" into Hindu, Muslim, Buddhist, non-Catholic Christian, or "other." The results indicate that the Catholic appreciation for human rights comes chiefly in comparing Catholics to Hindus and non-Catholic Christians. There is no statistically significant difference between Catholics and Muslims on positive human rights associations, with both groups having roughly similar (and comparatively high) levels of human rights appreciation.

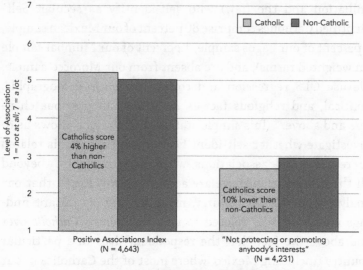

Associations with "Human Rights"

OLS regressions pooling the four countries together (weighted equally), controlling for the *Personal Religiosity Index; Social Religiosity Index; Trust in Religious Institutions; Trust in Local Human Rights Organizations;* the *Human Rights Contact Index;* socioeconomic factors; political preference and voting; age, gender, and country.

FIGURE 5.2 Catholics Modestly Associated with More Positive Human Rights Ideas

There is other evidence that Catholics view human rights more positively than members of other faiths. We ran similar regressions to predict responses to the negative association of "human rights" with *Not Protecting or Promoting Anyone's Interests.* As Figure 5.2 demonstrates, Catholics were 10 percent *less* likely to report this association than members of all other religions, taken both together as a "non-Catholic" group, as well as with each religion considered separately.[70] Once again, this suggests that in our locales of interest, Catholics define human rights more positively than the members of other faith communities.[71] Although it is hard to know for sure why this is so, it seems logical that the Church's legacy of liberation theology— still alive at the parish level, notwithstanding a conservative hierarchy in many instances—orients Catholics more favorably toward human rights and related notions of liberal democracy.

This finding should prove encouraging for those concerned about the human rights impacts and orientation of the contemporary Catholic Church. Despite fraught relations between the clergy and rights activists on issues of sexuality, gender, and reproductive rights, the overall human rights/Church relationship—assessed here in terms of individual Catholics' associations with "human rights" in Mumbai, Lagos, and Mexico—is positive.

Next, we similarly explore the unique associations that Muslim respondents (in these locations) have with "human rights." Once again, we found it hard to anticipate the relationship a priori, as both scholarship and current events point in contradictory directions. Some commentators argue that Islam or Muslims are fundamentally opposed to human rights ideas, a position that gained currency after 9/11 and was infused with even greater vigor following Islamic State attacks in the Middle East and elsewhere. Suspicion about Muslims' allegedly negative views of human rights predates these events, however. In the early 1990s, political scientist Samuel Huntington's work on the "clash of civilizations" argued that there was an essential Western-Christian conflict with Islam (and other world civilizations, determined in part by religion) over the content of liberal norms, including human rights. Western attempts to "propagate these [liberal] ideas" worldwide, Huntington wrote, inspired cries of "human rights imperialism" among Muslims and were largely counterproductive.[72]

Other scholars, activists, and commentators have supported elements of Huntington's argument regarding Islam and human rights. For example, in 1991 Kevin Dwyer, the former head of Amnesty International's Middle Eastern section, argued that "human rights" are too "closely associated with the West" in the Middle East. As a result, he said, "The notion of 'human rights'

[by Middle Easterners] in good faith."[73] In 2001, Michael Ignatieff warned that a "resurgent Islam" was becoming increasingly aggressive toward rights promoters.[74] That same year, Neil Hicks, Middle East coordinator for the New York-based NGO Human Rights First (formerly, the Lawyers Committee for Human Rights), wrote that Islamists fear that "human rights activists [are] 'working to a Western agenda.'"[75] In 2003, global public opinion analysts Ronald Inglehart and Pippa Norris confirmed a profound Western/Islamic attitudinal cleavage. They attributed this gap in large part to tensions between liberal Western ideas of "gender equality and sexual liberalization" and Muslim traditionalism.[76] In 2014, international relations scholar Stephen Walt warned that US efforts to promote liberal values always produced global backlash.[77] Similar concern over Islam's oppositional stance toward human rights ideas and actors persist, including among liberal Muslims.[78]

Others maintain that Islamic theology and practice can and often do complement human rights principles. The 1990 Cairo Declaration on Human Rights in Islam, for example, was adopted by the 45 member states of the Organization of the Islamic Conference; its creators said they had crafted a uniquely Muslim human rights interpretation.[79] In 2004, human rights scholar and activist Susan Waltz recalled that many Muslim political leaders had been "active participants" in drafting the Universal Declaration of Human Rights.[80] In 2008, the WorldOpinion. org poll of over 47,000 people in 28 countries and territories found little evidence that Muslims were particularly opposed to human rights. Instead, they discovered that "*national differences* between predominantly Muslim countries [were] more illuminating."[81] In 2014, three leading members of Islamic Relief publicly claimed that the global human rights framework fully conformed with Islam's own commitments to morality, compassion, and social justice.[82] Overall, scholars such as Abdullah an-Naim, Zakia Salime, and Rachel Rinaldo have all argued that the alleged contradictions between Islam and human rights can and often are reconciled.[83]

Until now, few scholars have probed cross-country Muslim opinion on human rights while controlling for country-level effects and other relevant factors, such as socio-demographics and political views. The 2008 WorldOpinion.org poll analyzed Muslim responses *within* each country, but published only country-level frequencies, rather than cross-national multivariate analyses. Our analysis uses separate country models, but our pooled models—in which all respondents are placed together in the same statistical model, with a wide range of relevant controls—can help us discern what Muslims think, on average, holding constant a wide range of other factors, including the effects of residing in a specific country.

Our data include Muslims in only three countries—India, Morocco, and Nigeria. Given political sensitivities, the Moroccan survey company we worked with was reluctant to ask directly about religious identity; official statistics and our survey company agree that the Moroccan population is overwhelmingly Muslim, leading us to code all Moroccan respondents as such.[84] In weighted terms, 34 percent of our Lagos sample self-identified as Muslim, as did 8 percent of our Mumbai sample (not weighted, in this case, because religion was part of our sampling criteria for this locale).

In investigating Muslims' associations with "human rights," we found that like Catholics, they tended to be *more* kindly disposed than the members of other religions. As Figure 5.3 indicates, self-identified Muslims evaluated "human rights" 4 percent more positively than non-Muslims, just as did the self-identified Catholics.

What this means is that contrary to those who disparage the connection between Islam and human rights, we find no

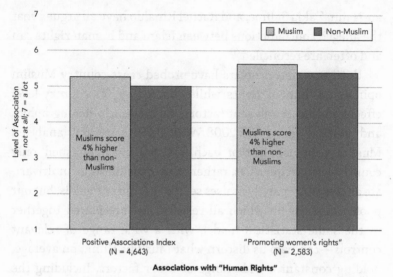

Associations with "Human Rights"

OLS regressions pooling the four countries together (weighted equally), controlling for the
Personal Religiosity Index; Social Religiosity Index; Trust in Religious Institutions;
Trust in Local Human Rights Organizations; the Human Rights Contact Index;
socioeconomic factors; political preference and voting; age, gender, and country.
"Promoting women's rights" was not asked in Mexico.

FIGURE 5.3 Muslims Are Moderately More Positive Toward Human
Rights and Have Stronger Associations with "Promoting Women's
Rights"

evidence, *in our geographic areas of investigation*, that Muslim
identity is antithetical to human rights. Instead, the opposite
is true, controlling for other factors, across Rabat/Casablanca,
Mumbai, and Lagos. Further statistical analysis suggests this
pro-human rights attitude is driven by the gap between Muslim
and Hindu attitudes in Mumbai and between Muslim and non-
Catholic Christians in Lagos. Moroccan Muslims have lower positive associations with human rights than Muslims elsewhere.
This suggests that when Muslims are a minority group, as they
are in Mumbai and Lagos, they may be likely to regard "human
rights" more positively, perhaps as a form of protection against

majoritarian domination. In this sense, "Islam" may function just like other minority categories.

Many analysts believe gender is the biggest part of the contentious Islam/human rights interface, so we explore the relationship between Muslim identity and respondents' association of "human rights" with *Promoting Women's Rights*. Running a regression and controlling for a wide variety of additional factors, we found that Muslims are slightly more likely than non-Muslims to associate "human rights" with *Promoting Women's Rights,* although this effect may not be statistically significant in Nigeria. As Inglehart and Norris would expect, the "sexual clash of civilizations" does weigh more heavily on Muslim minds than on those of members of other religions. This association's implications, however, are not straightforward. As we saw in Chapter 3, respondents who associated human rights with *Promoting Women's Rights* in Morocco and Nigeria tended to trust local rights groups *more,* whereas respondents who did the same in Mumbai trusted rights groups *less.*

Does the association of human rights with *Promoting Women's Rights* mean that Muslims in fact support women's rights more than assumed? Or does it simply mean that, for Muslims, the association with women's rights simply reflects the prominence of gender in the Western rights agendas, although not indicating agreement with that agenda?

To find out, we reran the regression predicting *Trust in Local Human Rights Organizations.* This time our independent variable of interest was an interaction term between *Muslim* and associating "human rights" with *Promoting Women's Rights.* This statistical procedure allows us to explore whether Muslims who associate "human rights" with "women's rights" are more or less trusting of LHROs than non-Muslims with similar associations.

As Figure 5.4 demonstrates, the more strongly Muslims associate "human rights" with women's rights, the more they *Trust Local Human Rights Organizations*. For non-Muslims, associating "human rights" with women's rights may actually have a negative relationship with trust in rights groups. Among those who do not associate human rights with *Promoting Women's Rights* (the left side of the figure), Muslims (the solid line) are .12 points less trusting of LHROs than non-Muslims (the dotted line). Among those who most strongly associate human rights with *Promoting Women's Rights*, however (the right side of the figure), there is no significant difference between Muslims and non-Muslims. In other words, when Muslims strongly associate "human rights" with women's rights, their trust in local rights groups equals that of non-Muslims. The conflation of human and women's rights

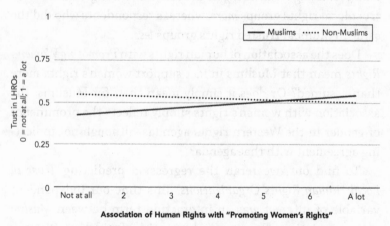

Association of Human Rights with "Promoting Women's Rights"

OLS regression model in three countries (not asked in Mexico) controls for other religious variables (personal religiosity, social religiosity, trust in religious institutions), socioeconomic factors, political preference and voting; other controls; average trust, gender, age, country; and mistrust in powerful actors (mistrust in US, MNCs, and domestic political authorities) (N = 1,901).

FIGURE 5.4 For Muslims, Associating Human Rights with "Promoting Women's Rights" Is Associated with Increased Trust in LHROs

is a net positive for Muslim trust in LHROs, controlling for other relevant factors.

Interestingly, Muslims in the countries we studied do not link women's rights with a US or Western agenda. Associating human rights with *Promoting Women's Rights* is *negatively* correlated with *Promoting US Interests* and with *Promoting Foreign Values and Ideas* in small but statistically significant correlations.

Additional statistical regressions also suggest that among surveyed Muslims, the tendency to associate human rights with women's rights is a primarily urban, secular, and perhaps middle class phenomenon. Rural residents and people who attended mosque frequently were less likely to make this association, as were Nigerians, men, and to some extent respondents in the middle of our subjective income scale.

It is difficult to square these results with scholars' criticisms of the treatment of women in Muslim countries. Of course, none of the countries we surveyed with significant Muslim populations (India, Morocco, and Nigeria) is in the Middle East; there may be a regional effect that we cannot account for here. India and Nigeria are democracies (troubled, perhaps, but democracies nonetheless), and Morocco is a liberalizing monarchy. Conditions may be different for Muslims in highly authoritarian contexts. In the last few years, moreover, India has seen both grave violations of women's rights as well as massive street protests against those attacks. Like everyone else, Muslims assimilate the values of the societies they live in and combine these values with their religious beliefs, and our results reflect this process. At the very least, our findings underscore the historically and culturally contingent nature of rights recognition, suggesting there is nothing inherently "Islamic" about denying women their rights.

Personal versus Social Religiosity

Our multidimensional religiosity variables allow us to further nuance these findings. Muslim religious identity does have a general positive impact on respondents' attitudes towards human rights, but disaggregating components of religious practice shows religious publics are not monolithic.

Above, we found *Trust in Religious Institutions* was negatively associated with *Trust in Local Human Rights Organizations* overall, and this relationship is consistent for both Muslims and non-Muslims.[85] When we distinguish between the social and personal manifestations of religiosity, however, we find different effects.[86] In the all-Muslim Rabat/Casablanca sample, most respondents reported that religion was of great importance to them personally; 96 percent told us that religion was "very important" (selecting 10 on the 0 to 10 scale) in their daily lives, and 85 percent reported praying at least once a day. As a result, their average *Personal Religiosity Index* score was a high 9.3 on the 0–10 scale. The Rabat/Casablanca respondents' average *Social Religiosity* scores were much more moderate; only 46 percent reported attending mosque once or more per week, only 2 percent reported "participating in the activities of a religious organization," and 57 percent trusted their country's religious institutions "some" or "a lot." In Rabat and Casablanca, *personal* piety was intense and pervasive, but social religiosity was less so. Lower levels of social religiosity were not driven by less frequent female attendance in mosques.[87]

Personal and social religiosity had very different relationships with conceptualizations of "human rights" in Rabat/Casablanca. We ran three sets of Morocco-specific regressions and summarize the results in Figure 5.5.

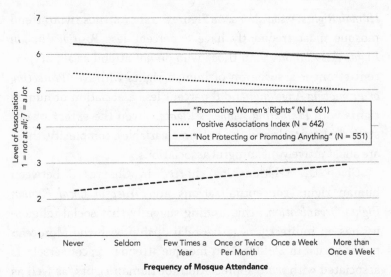

OLS regression of Moroccan sample, controlling for *Frequency of Prayer*; *Trust in Religious Institutions*; *Trust in Local Human Rights Organizations*; the *Human Rights Contact Index*; socioeconomic factors; political preference and voting; age and gender.

FIGURE 5.5 In Rabat and Casablanca, Mosque Attendance Is Associated with Less Support for Human Rights

Our three dependent or outcome variables are the *Positive Human Rights Associations* index, the critical association of *Not Protecting or Promoting Anything*, and the association with *Promoting Women's Rights*. *Frequency of Mosque Attendance* is our explanatory variable of interest, with a full set of statistical controls, including trust in religious institutions and frequency of prayer. We use *Frequency of Mosque Attendance* rather than the full *Social Religiosity Index* because so few Moroccan respondents reported participating in religious organizations, perhaps because those groups are identified with militants or the political opposition.

In Rabat, Casablanca, and their rural surroundings, mosque attendance has a strong and *negative* relationship with *Positive*

Human Rights Associations. As Figure 5.5 shows, those who attend mosque most frequently have 8 percent less *Positive Human Rights Associations* than those who do *not* attend at all; 30 percent stronger association of human rights with *Not Protecting or Promoting Anything*; and 6 percent less association of human rights with *Promoting Women's Rights*. Given the extent of our statistical controls and the outcome variable's complexity, these are substantively meaningful associations.

Given the relationships charted in Chapter 3 between human rights conceptualizations and *Trust in Local Human Rights Organizations,* this finding suggests that social religiosity has an indirectly negative relationship with the Moroccan public's trust in LHROs. Non-mosque attendance, conversely, is associated with *more* appreciation for human rights, as well as (indirectly) more *Trust in Local Human Rights Groups.* In Rabat, Casablanca, and their rural surroundings, it seems to be the *collective practice of Islam,* rather than personal expressions of Islamic faith, which pose the greatest challenge to contemporary human rights practitioners.

Survey data analysis cannot explain these associations, but other methodologies, including ethnography and focus groups, could tease out the causal mechanisms linking more frequent mosque attendance with more negative human rights views. We can only offer speculation. In 2004, the Moroccan government initiated a religious reform to counter Islamic extremism, advocating an interpretation that awarded the king a unique role as Commander of the Faithful. Moroccan mosques are in theory government-supervised, and all of them should *technically* be advocating for this government-friendly interpretation. In practice, however, some mosques (often in poorer neighborhoods) have escaped strict government control, and their religious leaders often denounce US government policy—despite the king's ties with Washington—or criticize the monarch's religious pretensions.[88] The government has launched a counteroffensive, transforming Morocco's mosques into a political and ideological battleground. Our *Human Rights Perceptions Polls* did not ask respondents what *type* of mosque they attended, nor did we investigate the distribution of "radical" or "pro-government" imams in Rabat and Casablanca. Our findings, however, do suggest either that many mosque-goers are attending more radical mosques where they are exposed to anti-human rights messaging, or that many of the pro-monarchy mosques are countering the radicals' influence by stealing their (human rights-skeptical) thunder.

Regardless of the precise causal mechanism, the main point for our purposes is this: in Rabat, Casablanca, and their rural surroundings, it is the way in which Islam is collectively practiced in mosques, not Muslim identity *per se* or personal religious beliefs, that challenges human rights ideas and organizations.

Suggesting a broader pattern, this negative association between social religiosity and human rights is true for other faith traditions in Mumbai and Lagos. When we pooled respondents from Rabat/Casablanca, Lagos, and Mumbai into a single statistical model in which *Positive Human Rights Association* was the dependent variable and *Religious Attendance* was the independent variable of interest, we found those who regularly attend a place of worship—be it a Hindu temple, a Muslim mosque, or any kind of Christian church—score 10 percent less on the *Positive Human Rights Association* index than those who do not attend weekly, controlling for the usual.

Greater *Personal Religiosity*, on the other hand, is associated with more *Positive Human Rights Associations*; in fact, the most personally observant people in our sample had a 17 percent higher score than the least observant. Social and personal religiosity, in other words, work in diametrically opposed ways. *Personal Religiosity* (frequency of prayer and importance of religion in one's life) is associated with *more* positive human rights conceptualizations. More institutionalized manifestations of religion, by contrast—*Social Religiosity*—are associated with *less* positive conceptualizations. When it comes to human rights attitudes, these two key aspects of religion function at counter-purpose.

Figure 5.6 goes a step further, showing the associations in Lagos, Mumbai, and Rabat/Casablanca between *Religious Attendance* (independent variable) and associating human rights with the negative-sounding *Not Protecting or Promoting Anything* (the dependent variable).[89]

Respondents in Lagos (dashed line) who attended a place of worship more than once a week (located on the right side of the figure) associated human rights with *Not Protecting or Promoting Anything* 51 percent more than those who never attended a place of worship (left side). In Mumbai (solid line), frequent attenders associated human rights with this idea 30 percent more, and in Rabat and Casablanca (dotted line) the association was 31 percent

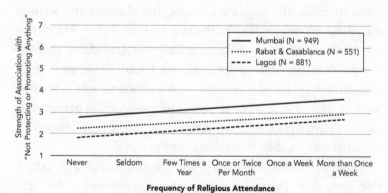

Frequency of Religious Attendance

Country-specific OLS regression models, controlling for *Frequency of Prayer* in Morocco;
Religious Importance in Mumbai and Lagos; *Trust in Religious Institutions; Trust in Local Human Rights
Organizations;* the *Human Rights Contact Index;* political preference
and voting; socioeconomic factors; age and gender.

FIGURE 5.6 In Three Countries, More Religious Attendance Means More Strongly Associating Human Rights with "Not Protecting or Promoting Anything"

higher. The socially religious were much more likely than those who never attended religious services to have a negative view of human rights. Indicators of *personal* religiosity, by contrast, either had no statistically significant association at all, or had contradictory associations with *Not Protecting or Promoting Anything*.

These latter findings reinforce and generalize our discovery from Rabat and Casablanca: some *social* aspects of religion may undermine support for human rights, not the individual or personal aspects of religious identity and affiliation.

Nothing in the faith-human rights relationship is simple, however. In Mexico, we observe the precise *opposite* phenomenon. There, *Religious Participation* (participating in the activities of a religious organization) is associated with more pro-rights attitudes. As Figure 5.7 demonstrates, Mexican respondents who had participated in the activities of religious organizations had weaker associations with the most negative conceptualizations of human rights.

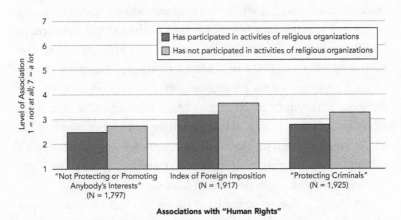

OLS regression model, controlling for *Religious Importance*; *Trust in Religious Institutions*; *Trust in Local Human Rights Organizations*; the *Human Rights Contact Index*; political preference and voting; socioeconomic factors; age and gender.

FIGURE 5.7 In Mexico, Religious Participation Associated with Reduced Human Rights Negativity

In Mexico, religious participants (the darker bars) associated "human rights" 15 percent *less strongly* than non-religious participants (represented by the lighter bars) with *Protecting Criminals*, 13 percent less strongly with *Foreign Imposition* (an average of respondent scores for associating human rights with "promoting US interests" and "promoting foreign values and ideas"), and 10 percent less strongly with *Not Protecting or Promoting Anything*. In another analysis, we also learned that Mexico's religious participants have a predicted 4 percent more *Trust in Local Human Rights Organizations* than the non-participants, controlling for the usual factors.

Once again, without detailed qualitative research, it is difficult to identify *why*, precisely, religious participation in Mexico is associated with less negativity toward human rights. Nor is it easy to know why the Mexico pattern differs so dramatically from that of Lagos, Mumbai, and Rabat/Casablanca. A partial explanation may be methodological. Across all four samples, our question about "participation in the activities of a religious organization" yielded wildly varying responses; as noted above in Table 5.1, rates vary from 2 percent of the sample in Morocco to 87 percent in Nigeria. It is likely that "participation in the activities of a religious organization" meant different things in each context.[90] As a result, we prefer to rely on *Frequency of Religious Attendance* as a measure of social religiosity. The question "how often do you attend a religious place of worship" is less ambiguous and produced more cross-case consistency, with estimates ranging from 46 percent attending at least once per week in Morocco to 96 percent in Lagos.

In Mexico, due to space limitations, we were unable to ask about frequency of religious attendance. The human rights questions in Mexico formed part of a larger survey effort that restricted our ability to add fine-grained questions on religion. As a result, in Mexico we use the less consistent measure,

Religious Participation. Thus, our Mexico measure of social reli-giosity is different than our measure of social religiosity in the three other cases, and at least part of the empirical variation may stem from this.

Yet the Mexican pattern is also likely driven by the regionally specific weight of Latin American liberation theology. The Mexican human rights movement emerged in the early 1980s due in large part to the work of radical Church figures and organizations.[91] Over the next 10 years, Mexican civil society was heavily "influenced by . . . the radical section of the Catholic church."[92] By the 1990s, Mexican human rights NGOs had developed one of the country's "broadest-based" civil society networks, including "many church-oriented groups."[93]

Although more research is needed to unpack the contextual explanations, social religiosity is associated with *greater* suspicion toward human rights in Lagos, Mumbai, and Rabat/Casablanca, but with *less* suspicion in Mexico. Social religiosity, moreover, functions differently than religious affiliation or personal religiosity in shaping human rights ideas and attitudes. Religion's relationship with human rights is powerful but context-specific and at times seemingly contradictory. Religion matters quite a lot for human rights, but in very complex ways.

Reaching the Religious

What should human rights practitioners make of this? How might they best engage with religious communities and religious individuals? In Chapter 3, we found our *Human Rights Contact Index* (combining hearing "human rights" often, meeting a human rights worker, naming a specific LHRO, and participating in HRO activities) was modestly related to greater *Trust in Local Human Rights Organizations*.[94] From a practitioner's perspective, it is crucial to know whether this relationship holds for religious people, to understand whether the contact human rights workers or organizations make with religious people is effective. Does the human rights message and approach resonate? Or does it conflict with a religious worldview and sour the faithful toward LHROs? This is a vitally important question given the extraordinarily high levels of public religiosity we find in these countries. We are especially interested in the effects of human rights contact on the socially religious given the negative association we found between social religiosity and human rights in three of these four countries.

There are two theoretical possibilities. The socially religious are already more skeptical of human rights, and making contact may either mitigate negative perceptions or confirm them. On the one hand, human rights practitioners are less religious than the general public, and this disconnect may make it difficult for them to frame their human rights message in ways that resonate with deeply religious publics. More contact between human rights activists and the socially religious might have *negative* impacts. On the other hand, of course, greater contact between human rights actors and the socially religious might lead to increased understanding and acceptance. As religious publics come into greater contact with human rights discourse, organizations, and activists, perhaps they develop greater appreciation and respect, rather than greater distaste and mistrust. After all, this was the general finding in Chapter 3; the more people have contact with human rights actors and language, the greater their *Trust in Local Human Rights Organizations*. Is this also true for the socially religious, many of whom are human rights skeptics?

To investigate, we ran the pooled model predicting *Trust in Local Human Rights Organizations* with the religious indicators as explanatory variables of interest (as reported in Table 5.2). This time, however, we included an interaction term between our *Human Rights Contact Index* and the *Social Religiosity Index*. This means that we multiply these two variables and run the product as an independent variable in the regression. This allows us to see if the relationship between human rights contact and trust in LHROs is different for the socially religious than it is for the non-socially religious; if the resulting coefficient is statistically significant, the effect of human rights contact on *Trust in Local Human Rights Organizations* is different for those who score high and low on the index of social religiosity.

The results in Figure 5.8 show clear differences: as the socially religious respondents (solid line) move from low to high rates of human rights contact (left to right), their *Trust in Local Human Rights Organizations* increases by 15 percent. For the non-socially religious (dotted line), there is no such effect. Recall

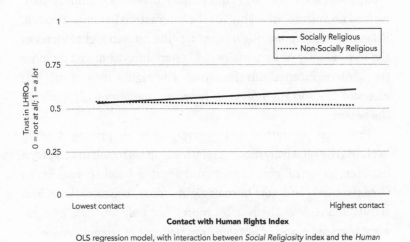

OLS regression model, with interaction between *Social Religiosity* index and the *Human Rights Contact* index. Controls for other religious variables (identity, personal religiosity, trust in religious institutions); socioeconomic factors; political preference and voting; average trust, gender, age, country; mistrust in powerful actors (mistrust in US, MNCs, and domestic political authorities) (N = 3,825).

FIGURE 5.8 For the Socially Religious, More Human Rights Contact Is Associated with Higher Trust in LHROs

that the *Socially Religiosity Index* combines frequency of attendance in a place of worship (church, temple, mosque) and participation in a religious organization. Figure 5.8 plots the expected effects of contact with human rights workers, organizations, and discourse on *Trust in Local Human Rights Organizations* for those who scored 0 on the *Social Religiosity* index (least socially religious) and those who scored 1 (most socially religious). When the socially religious are at their maximum level of human rights contact (all the way to the right), their *Trust in Local Human Rights Organizations* is 18 percent greater than the non-socially religious, *at the same level of human rights contact.*[95]

This is substantial evidence that contact with the human rights movement has profound impacts on the socially religious, but *no perceptible influence* on those who are not socially religious. More intense social practice of religion may increase negative views of human rights, but contact with human rights groups and activists can help mitigate this effect. Importantly, we find no such relationship for the interaction between *Personal Religiosity* and *Human Rights Contact.* The human rights views of the individually or personally pious remain unchanged by more frequent or intense interface with the rights movement; the views of the socially religious, however, meaningfully shift for the better.

From an analytical perspective, this surprising finding explains the relatively modest relationship we found in Chapter 3 between *Human Rights Contact* and *Trust in Local Human Rights Organizations.* To know human rights ideas, organizations, and activists is to love them (a bit more), but *only for those who frequently attend places of worship or participate in religious organizations.* Greater contact has no discernable relationship with trust in LHROs for the non-socially religious, and no association with personal religiosity.

Although our statistical analysis does not allow us to make causal claims, this does not seem to be *purely* about the structural and historical deep-rootedness of religious institutions, a characteristic that can make them effective structural conduits for organizing and mobilizing.[96] On the other hand, it also is not about the content of religious beliefs themselves; we control for personal religiosity and do not find similar relationships with human rights ideas. Our explanation lies somewhere in between. We speculate this finding may be related to specifically *how* religious spaces are *used* (which is related to both their organizational structure and the content of their ideas). Religious spaces are often the places where civic and political life plays out, where various interests are promoted and contested, where people make sense of the world and their place in it. Religious institutions provide space for ideas beyond the confines of the religious; for example, Moroccan mosques have served as ideological battlegrounds, and Mexican churches have been involved in radical politics. As such, these spaces could be particularly fruitful terrains for public engagement with human rights ideas and organizations, though our evidence suggests that currently (everywhere but Mexico) this is not happening, and instead anti-human rights voices may be dominating these spaces.

The implications for practitioners are profound. Although there are all manner of faith-rights tensions, our analysis suggests these difficulties can be and often are moderated by more contact. The more rights practitioners *engage* with religious leaders and believers, the more likely they are to warm toward human rights ideas and organizations. Outreach and dialogue can and do break down suspicion among those most embedded in socially religious contexts.

Nonetheless, bridging the human rights-religion divide can be an uphill struggle. After all, the statistics also demonstrate that in three of our four case studies—Mumbai, Lagos, and Rabat/Casablanca—greater social (but not personal) religiosity is an impediment to public support for human rights ideas and organizations. This effect is minimized but not eliminated by greater human rights contact. We also found lower trust in LHROs among those who more highly trusted religious institutions, suggesting that LHROs might strategically work with religious groups, but do so in a way that engages a religious lens while being cognizant of the tension between hierarchy or power and support for human rights. Even with these difficulties, the numbers clearly suggest that LHROs' outreach efforts can pay off. The qualitative evidence from our practitioner interviews, moreover, suggests there are many instances of successful rights-religion collaborations. Faith-based roads may be steep, rocky, and frustrating for the human rights climber, but they can be successfully traversed. Given the overwhelming predominance of personal piety and organized faith in the lives of most people, human rights activists cannot afford to ignore these findings.

6

Cautious Optimism

By 2011, we had spent several years interviewing human rights activists, professionals, and key informants from 60 countries in the global South. Although the picture they painted was occasionally upbeat, many were concerned about the prospects of their organizations and the human rights sector as a whole. Some were skeptical of their ability to connect with co-citizens, and others worried about their inability to survive without foreign aid. Although the number of local human rights organizations around the world had skyrocketed since the early 1990s, the sector's organizational health and confidence seemed shaky. Many of the practitioners we interviewed were committed professionals overwhelmed by the challenge of diffusing human rights ideas beyond a handful of sympathetic subgroups, many of which were similarly funded or connected to sources in the global North.

These preliminary findings suggested the global nongovernmental human rights infrastructure was in trouble because LHROs had expanded too quickly "from the top," rather than more slowly and organically from below, from local grassroots. As political scientist Kim Reiman argued for NGOs as a whole, "Rather than simply emerging as the result of bottom-up sociological and technological forces ... NGOs have also emerged and grown ... because of top-down processes."[1] Although this top-down process was achieving some results, including fostering the founding and growth of hundreds of domestically based human rights organizations, it seemed increasingly apparent that lack of public support was its fundamental weakness.

The human rights movement *had* begun "from below" in a handful of Latin American and Asian countries during the 1970s and early 1980s.[2] We feared, however, that global development and human rights donors in the 1990s had artificially inflated the number and budgets of all kinds of liberal NGOs, transforming local civil society in the global South into something broader and more globally articulate, but less firmly rooted in local communities. In talking with practitioners and observing contemporary trends and research, LHROs did not appear to enjoy much local citizen support, depended too heavily on foreign aid, and were promoting liberal values that attracted only small numbers of adherents. We feared that LHROs were an example of what development economist William Easterly castigates so brilliantly in *The White Man's Burden*.[3] Northern financial supporters of LHROs based in the global South, in this view, belonged to the community of rich-world bureaucrats who periodically foist new, bright-sounding ideas on developing-world populations who do not necessarily want them. Instead of local rights groups emerging endogenously to meet genuine citizen "demand" from below, Northern donors were generating a "supply" of rights advocates with no discernible local market.[4] As a result, we feared the global LHRO archipelago was a house of cards, a shaky network that could easily collapse once Northern funders pulled out or irritated national governments cracked down on flows of foreign funding to domestic civil society.

As noted earlier, recent events in Ethiopia confirmed these fears.[5] Many Ethiopian LHROs emerged after the 1991 overthrow of Mengistu Haile Mariam, most foreign supported, fueled by the post-dictatorship tsunami of overseas development assistance. When the government resolved in 2010 to drastically curtail foreign aid to domestic NGOs working on politically sensitive issues, most of these "domestic" Ethiopian rights groups promptly shut down. Few Ethiopian citizens protested the closures, and even fewer offered to replace the lost foreign funds with their own money. It seemed that Ethiopian rights groups really were a foreign-inspired product for which there was little genuine local demand. The *real* market for the work of Ethiopian LHROs was overseas—transnational activists and the international development community—rather than within the country itself.

As we mulled over these preliminary findings, a leading British scholar, Stephen Hopgood, published a book on the impending decline of the global human rights movement; the "endtimes" of human rights, he said, were near.[6] The post–Cold War proliferation of human rights discourse and activism had been a geopolitical bubble, Hopgood argued, a short-lived crescendo of diplomatic, legal, and organizational noise built on US political, military, and cultural hegemony. The sands were running out on US global dominance and multipolarity was on the rise, with Brazil, India, Russia, South Africa, Indonesia, Turkey, and others poised to assume greater regional and global roles. In this new geopolitical environment, Hopgood predicted the human rights bubble would soon begin to leak, if not burst entirely.

Others were similarly concerned, highlighting links between the spread of liberal NGOs and global capitalism.[7] The human rights discourse appeared to these critics as an ideological "superstructure" built on the "base" of global capitalism.[8] Some suggested this was the reason that hedge fund magnates such as George Soros were so keen to underwrite Human Rights Watch and other promoters of human rights ideas, using personal fortunes to bankroll private, unaccountable donor agencies such as the ubiquitous Open Society Foundations.[9] Big companies, investors, and the US government were curtailing the most despotic forms of developing world authoritarianism with the help of "human rights" and "democratization" efforts, but these efforts were also helping to create a world safe for the global spread of free markets, private property, and foreign investment.[10] The powers-that-be were domesticating human rights radicalism, just as they had done with other politically oppositional discourses.

What was conspicuously lacking from this conversation, however, was the view of publics in the global South, an understanding of how ordinary people actually perceived human rights ideas and organizations. From 2012 to 2014, we conducted opinion surveys in four contexts where the rise of human rights seemed particularly notable or contentious, and we realized the evidence did not fully support Hopgood's skeptical narrative. Of course, our survey data cannot tell us if critics are correct in linking human rights ideas and organizations to US or capitalist hegemony; to find that out, we would need a different kind of research design. What we can say, however, is that we find little *public* support for these criticisms across very different contexts. Certainly some small segments of global South publics do view human rights as an ideological vehicle for foreign interests and regard human rights organizations with disfavor for this or other reasons. The evidence we present in Chapter 3, however, shows that the number of such skeptics is far smaller than anticipated. In each of our case studies—regardless of region, race, religion, historical trajectory, colonial power, and language—general public opinion holds human rights ideas and organizations with relative favor.

More importantly, we found an inverse relationship between trust in LHROs and trust in the US government and multinational corporations. In our view, this suggests that for most people "human rights" remains a discourse of *opposition* to the global powers-that-be, rather than one of global empire and political or economic co-optation. In the eyes of most ordinary people, human rights are more locally rooted and counter-hegemonic than many critics allege. Our evidence suggests that for many, human rights *are* a discourse of protest, not domination, even in the contemporary geopolitical context and with the global human rights funding structure, described in detail in Chapter 4.[11] Chapter 3 shows that most of this protest is aimed at respondents' own governments, as trust in local human rights organizations is strongly linked with mistrust in domestic authorities, including the executive, legislature, and politicians. Most people do not regard human rights ideas and organizations as agents of Western or Northern neocolonialism. These results should prove encouraging for human rights promoters.

Our picture is not uniformly rosy, and other findings suggest cause for concern within the global human rights sector. Although their reputations may be stronger than assumed, human rights ideas and their local rights organizations suffer from a host of other problems. Chapter 2 demonstrates that ordinary people have very little face-to-face contact with human rights workers and very little concrete knowledge of or engagement with their local rights community. The public's exposure to the words "human rights" is surprisingly high, but most of this exposure is occurring through the national media, not through personal, civic, or professional connections. Social movement scholarship routinely documents the importance of face-to-face contact and on-the-ground networks for building engaged civic communities and actors, and this is one area where LHROs seem to have not made much progress.

The ideas and language of human rights have permeated public discourse in the global South, and their reputation, and those of the NGOs that espouse them, are reasonably strong. The social foundations of global human rights ideas, however, remain shaky. The ideas are present in the public's imagination, but they are *not* deeply rooted in their personal relationships and everyday experiences. People appear to have positive ideas about "human rights" and associate the term with the kinds of ideas that human rights promoters would want, including both socioeconomic and political rights. The vast majority of people, however, have never engaged with the local organizations that many believe are crucial to the meaningful diffusion of international human rights norms. As a result, the actual practice or application of human rights ideas may be underdeveloped, vulnerable, or easily dislodged or manipulated. (This weakness may also exist in the global North, of course; in future research we intend to explore this possibility in greater depth.)

Unfortunately, findings from Chapter 4 further this concern about weak grassroots connections, demonstrating that comparatively few ordinary people in the global South have ever donated to LHROs in their country. And yet, our surveys also show that local *demand* for LHROs' services is stronger than anticipated, with over half of publics evaluating human rights conditions in their country as poor, and 40 percent both trusting local rights groups and having positive associations with "human rights." Despite this potential demand for LHROs' services and support for LHROs themselves, most rights groups are not meeting those who need and want their services. The main reason LHROs do not more actively or effectively pursue this contact, we argue, is because it has become structurally far easier to raise the money they need to survive from private foundations and public donors in the global North. Fundraising in urban neighborhoods and villages of their own country requires new thinking, new strategies, and new personnel. As long as the political economy of the global human rights sector remains Northern-focused, these patterns will not change.

We end our empirical discussions on a more positive note, observing in Chapter 5 that a stronger alliance between LHROs and faith groups offers real potential for success, when pursued strategically and sensitively. The vast majority of publics are personally and socially religious, something that human rights activists cannot afford to ignore. Religious worldviews color motivations and meanings and religious spaces organize social life and public engagement; human rights must operate effectively within both of these dimensions. The evidence suggests when people attend church, temple, or mosque they tend toward greater opposition to human rights ideas and promoters. The religion-human rights nexus is by no means entirely gloomy, however. Some indicators of personal religiosity are positively correlated with attitudes toward human rights, and in Mexico religious participation is associated with *more* support for human rights. And when human rights activists *do* have contact with church/temple/mosque-goers, feelings toward human rights ideas and organizations improve significantly. Our findings suggest that human rights outreach can and does work among those most committed to practicing their faith in collective settings. Of course, much depends on the particular religious interpretations and the particular human rights in question; some rights, such as the right to clean water or freedom from torture, may be easier to promote in church or mosque than others. Still, the general finding in our data is clear; regardless of particular religion or particular right, greater contact between rights activists and the socially religious is associated with substantively meaningful increases in support for human rights organizations.

Future Research

Our findings strongly suggest that human rights research-ers should spend much more time investigating publics' experiences with and opinions about human rights. For the last 20 years, scholars have devoted enormous attention to the construction, diffusion, and reception of international norms, liberal and otherwise, arguing over whether and how states are socialized to new ways of viewing the world. The metrics of "success" have been ratifications of human rights treaties, changes in states' practices, and the formation of domestically-based human rights groups. Few have explored human rights socialization and diffusion among the global South publics, however, and few have explored public attitudes toward international human rights norms and organizations. This dearth of data has not stopped scholars from making claims for and against the universalizing ambitions of liberal ideas, including those of human rights.

This neglect of the public's views toward human rights is a surprising gap in knowledge, given widespread acknowledgment that LHROs and their domestic allies are often crucial players in the human rights reform process. LHRO legitimacy and efficacy depend mightily on the extent to which the general public supports them and their advocacy ideas. For too long, human rights research has focused on states and nongovernmental actors, neglecting the views of ordinary people. This book has addressed this gap with a systematic, cross-national exploration of public attitudes.

Although we are able to suggest some trends based on relationships that seem to hold across these four countries, context-specific variation suggests a need for similar data collection efforts in additional countries and regions. Our findings lend room for optimism, but our arguments are suggestive and preliminary. We are confident that our surveys were well designed and executed, but we and other scholars should replicate these efforts in these and other countries before making strong general claims.[12] For example, we found that public support for LHROs and human rights ideas is often widespread, but how deep and resilient is this sentiment? When faced with painful trade-offs between rights and security, which segments of the public are most likely to jettison their support for human rights ideas? Which types of people or potential constituents are most likely to persevere, and on what issues? Our future work will turn to these and other questions in a rigorous and systematic fashion, again relying on representative public opinion data to provide an empirical basis for claims. Our data suggest that mobilizing more financial support from the general public is a realistic possibility for domestic rights groups. Additional work is needed to investigate who is likely to give, on what issues, and to which types of LHROs. What can groups do to raise the probability of local donations? Once again, we are exploring these questions with new surveys.

In addition, the religion-rights nexus, which has so bedeviled human rights activists for decades, requires significantly more exploration, both in developing cross-country trends and in developing nuanced contextual explanations of findings. We need more and better data on Catholics, Muslims, Hindus, Buddhists, and Jews across world regions to investigate in what ways faith traditions have unique stances vis-a-vis human rights. In this study, most of our Muslim respondents were in Morocco, with some in Nigeria and India; conducting surveys in more Muslim-majority countries in different regions would help disentangle the effects of country, region, and faith tradition. Some of the support we find among Muslims in Nigeria and India for human rights could well be driven by their sociopolitical minority status.

Finally, we need more work on other potential counter-narratives to human rights, including nationalism, patriarchy, economic scarcity, and state security. Under what conditions does patriotism become nationalism, distrust of the "other," and a willingness to abuse that other's human rights? In 2016, the world witnessed a sharp increase in anti-migrant sentiment in the United States and Europe fueled by fears for the host country's physical security, economic well-being, and national identity. Without careful research, we should not assume that these fears are either widespread or limited to a small group. Anger at human rights activists in Europe may be prevalent only in some parts of the media and among the most vocal subgroups, or it may be broadly shared by wide sectors of society. Without collecting data that is representative of broad segments of the population, we simply cannot say.[13]

The empirical, theoretical, and analytical road ahead is long but exciting. This book, we believe, heralds a new way of thinking about both human rights activism and pursuing research on human rights ideas and organizations that can make a real contribution to human rights practice.

Appendix A

Data and Methods

Research for this book occurred in multiple stages from 2006 to 2014. We conducted the first round of research from 2006 to 2010, interviewing 128 key informants and practitioners from 60 countries while attending an annual human rights training program in Montreal, Canada. We discussed this round of interviews in some detail in Chapter 1. Here, we describe our second round of research in greater detail, including the 135 interviews with LHRO leaders that took place from 2010 to 2014 in Mumbai, India; Mexico City and San Cristobal, Mexico; Rabat and Casablanca, Morocco; and Lagos, Nigeria. After reflecting broadly on all the NGOs represented in these 263 practitioner interviews (including those from both the first and second rounds of research), we move to a discussion of our third round of research, the public opinion surveys, which we fielded from 2012 to 2014. Then, we discuss our statistical and modeling choices.

The LHRO Leader Interviews in India, Mexico, Morocco, and Nigeria

Sampling. To build a representative sample of *all* LHROs or LHRO leaders in the global South would be an immensely challenging task. There are no comprehensive lists of country-specific human rights organizations, no authoritative "sampling frames" from which to draw representative organizations. The Union of International Associations (UIA) publishes data on *transnational* nongovernmental groups, but not on groups contained within a single nation-state's borders. Individual government agencies may keep (more or less updated) lists of legally registered NGOs, but they rarely distinguish between those focused on human rights and those dealing with other issues.[1]

As a result of these data challenges, researchers interested in studying the non-profit sector in low or middle-income countries typically have one of three alternatives. The most common is to focus on a single or small handful of groups chosen for some unique quality. Leading examples include Stephen's Hopgood's study of Amnesty International, chosen for its preeminent transnational role, or Harri Englund's ethnography of local rights groups in Malawi, chosen for their size, centrality, and extensive foreign funding.[2] These in-depth case studies provide tremendous insight invaluable to scholarly and practitioner communities, but their goal is not to offer statistically representative findings. A second genre of NGO research does seek generalizable findings, but focuses only on NGOs with formal transnational ties, relying typically on UIA data.[3] The third alternative focuses on NGOs *in general* rather than on issue-specific groups, using lists of domestic registered organizations maintained by government agencies.[4] As a result of these three strategies, there are very few (if any) statistically representative studies of domestic local human rights organizations (LHROs).[5]

From 2010 to 2014, we assembled lists of all current, legally registered, locally headquartered NGOs with the word "rights" in their mission statement, or in a published description of at least one of their major activities. Team members did this by scouring the Internet in multiple languages and searching available NGO lists to distinguish—through careful investigation of individual organizations—those focused on human rights generally or on a particular subset of rights (e.g., women, children, or disability rights). After assembling preliminary LHRO rosters for each city, team members met with knowledgeable key informants and solicited suggestions for inclusion or exclusion. The teams confirmed organizations' human rights focus, official registration status, and headquarters location through additional emails, telephone calls, and in-person office visits.[6] Of course, no sampling frame is immune from "coverage error"—inclusion of irrelevant organizations or exclusion of relevant organizations. We feel confident there is little or no "over-coverage" (false positives)—that is, all the organizations in the frame are rightfully there, and although our process may have excluded a handful of relevant organizations (false negatives), we did our best to guard against this by having local experts repeatedly review our lists. This process was lengthy, costly, and laborious, but necessary, to make generalizable claims about the LHRO communities of entire major cities.

Our team interviewed representatives from 135 LHROs (54 percent of the total 251 groups identified in these six urban areas), using two different selection techniques. In Nigeria, Mexico, and Morocco, we divided each list of LHROs into three strata: (1) groups with websites linked to one another in cyberspace, as identified with the *Issue Crawler* hyperlink tool;[7] (2) groups with websites, but no mutual hyperlinks; and (3) rights-based groups with no discernible Internet presence. We stratified sampling frames in this fashion because we suspected that groups linked to one another online might resemble each other in important ways and also might be more locally influential. To ensure we did not inadvertently oversample like-minded entities, we selected random samples proportional to each strata. In Mumbai, by contrast, we performed simple random sampling on the entire LHRO list, as the city's local rights groups had only a very limited Internet presence and among those that did, very few had links to one another in cyberspace. If we failed to complete an interview with an organization for any reason, we randomly selected a replacement from the list of remaining organizations.

Approach to interview data. Interviews of this sort can be used in several ways. Most commonly, researchers regard such respondents as "key informants" knowledgeable about their immediate organizational, social, and political environments. Investigators ask respondents to recount their activities and worldviews, as well as those of their immediate colleagues, family members, and neighbors. Researchers use that information to build a picture of the inner workings of whatever they are researching, including a specific organization, social sector, or political movement. In these cases, the investigators assume key informants have unique insights due to their geographic, organizational, or social position.

In other instances, researchers rely on respondents of this sort as "data points," asking for bits of information—typically quantitative in nature—about the respondents themselves (demographics, background, education) or about their organizations (size, structure, budget, etc.). Here, researchers are looking not for interpretations and analysis in response to open-ended questions, but rather for short responses to structured questions. In both cases, however, researchers ask respondents for information and perspectives on events, people, and organizations in their immediate vicinity.

A third possibility treats respondents as experts on events and phenomena outside their immediate scope of activity, inviting them to offer interpretations, estimates, and predictions about their broader social, political, or organizational world, often at the national level. In this case, researchers rely on respondents not only as "data points" or interpreters of phenomenon in their immediate vicinity, but also as general experts on the broader state of affairs. Included in this genre are surveys of economists about the state of the national, regional, or global economy; of international relations scholars about the world's most pressing problems; or of businesspeople about the extent of corruption and bureaucracy in a given locale.

Our interviews with LHRO leaders and key informants treated respondents in all three ways. We asked short, quantitative-style questions about the respondents (age, education, religiosity) and their organizations (size, scope, founding dates), using this information as "data points." We also asked them to reflect on their working environments and on national conditions. For example, we asked respondents to comment about what the general public in their country might think of human rights workers; we also asked them to estimate the extent to which rights-based NGOs in their country rely on foreign aid. In these instances, we treated respondents as experts on their country's nongovernmental rights sector, much like the authors of Transparency International's Corruption Perception Index use both "resident and non-resident" experts to estimate national levels of corruption.[8]

Key characteristics of LHROs. Altogether, we interviewed 223 individuals working in LHROs, including people both from the first round of research (the Montreal interviews, from 2006 to 2010), and the second round of research (the case studies, from 2010 to 2014). (Note that not all the Montreal key informants worked in LHROs; some worked for other types of agencies or organizations). Even given different sampling procedures, there are remarkable similarities in these organizations' characteristics. In the Montreal key informant and the representative LHRO leader samples, organizations had median founding dates of 1995 and 1996, respectively.[9] Organizations had similar median staff sizes (20 for the Montreal sample, 15 for LHRO leader sample) and engaged in similar activities at similar rates, including human rights education (31 percent versus 29 percent), formal legal interventions (23 percent versus 26 percent), and public advocacy (21 percent versus 17 percent). LHROs in both samples reported hosting a median of three visits per year from foreign colleagues. The Montreal sample did have higher rates of overseas financial support (87 percent versus 73 percent).

Individual respondents were also strikingly similar across the two samples, suggesting that LHROs worldwide rely on similar human resource pools. Both samples included a majority of full-time workers (75 percent versus 100 percent), and 96 percent had attended university. In fact, respondents in the two samples were so structurally similar that their *parents* also attended university at similar rates. Both groups of interviewees reported modest international travel over the last five years (three trips), reinforcing the notion that they are "rooted cosmopolitans" or global/local "intermediaries."[10] They are not globetrotting elites who adopt human rights as part of a broader "class consciousness of frequent trav-elers."[11] Rather, they are locally rooted inhabitants of major cities in the global South, with significant transnational linkages to the global North, including international funding, contact with col-leagues in the global North, and occasional travel outside their home countries.

Human Rights Perceptions Polls

Our team conducted intensive, on-the-ground work with our sur-vey partners to prepare for and carry out the polls. This included overseeing the translation of questions, helping to train interview-ers, overseeing and developing sampling procedures, piloting and revising the questionnaire after debriefings with interviewers, assessing data quality control in the field and during data entry, and reviewing weighting procedures. This type of engagement is rare among cross-national survey researchers, many of whom intervene in the design phase only at the beginning of the project, and in analysis of the resultant data. What happens in the middle, in the field, and in the offices of the survey company is often a big "black box." Our working in situ helped us lift the lid off this box and get a peek at what lies inside. As a result, we are convinced that survey researchers should be as actively involved as possible in all phases of the research as time and money permit. An important part of this process was building relationships with the principals and field personnel of the firms we worked with. Our physical pres-ence signaled our commitment to the research, and explaining our project helped these colleagues understand and implement our goals better—and, we hope, helped motivate them and increase their own buy-in.

Sampling. Although each country's sampling design differed slightly as a result of unique country conditions, we followed a similar series set of steps. In Mexico, enumerators polled 2,400 people across the country, in Spanish. To build the sample, the survey company randomly selected 240 federal electoral districts, proportional to population size; these were the "primary sampling units." The company then randomly chose 10 households, the "secondary sampling units," within each electoral district, following a systematic sampling scheme in which, after randomly choosing the first household ("random start"), enumerators walked around the block in clockwise fashion, choosing every nth house (where n is a "sampling interval" that varies according to size of electoral district). Finally, enumerators randomly chose individuals within each household, the "tertiary sampling unit," following the "next birthday" method, in which enumerators asked to interview the person in the household with the closest next birthday.[12]

Survey companies in the other locales followed variants on this design (known as "multi-stage cluster" sampling, which draws randomly from successively smaller geographical units). In Morocco, the survey company selected 1,100 people, including 800 living in Rabat and Casablanca and 300 living in rural areas within 70–80 kilometers from either city. All the interviews were conducted in the Moroccan Arabic dialect, Darija. The primary sampling units were "districts," the smallest units for which the company had accurate, government-supplied population figures. Within each district, the survey company used Google Maps-identified permanent landmarks within specific municipalities, including pharmacies, major road crossings, or mosques. Our secondary sampling units were households, which the survey company selected by starting on foot at the landmark, and then selecting households at predefined intervals, moving in predetermined directions. Enumerators used the Kish grid to select individuals in each household for interviews. First, enumerators identify all members of the household who are eligible to take the survey, and then select one according to a table of random numbers.

In India, our survey partner polled 1,080 residents in Mumbai, along with booster samples of roughly 150 Christians, 150 Buddhists, and 300 rural residents in Maharashtra State, of which Mumbai is the capital. Enumerators conducted 51 percent of the interviews in Hindi and 49 percent in Marathi. The primary sampling units were "legislative assembly segments" and the secondary units were "polling booth districts." Instead of tertiary sampling units, the company randomly selected a first potential respondent from each booth's electoral roll (which are considered complete lists of area residents), and then selected additional persons at pre-determined intervals.

Our Nigerian survey partner sampled 800 adults living in Lagos with booster samples from respondents living in rural areas of the surrounding Ogun and Oyo States (100 in each state, for a total rural booster of 200). Enumerators conducted 57 percent of these Nigerian interviews in English, 34 percent in Pidgin, and 9 percent in Yoruba. The primary sampling units were "local government areas" and secondary units were "enumeration areas" within these local government areas, selected proportional to their population size. The tertiary sampling units were dwelling structures selected similarly to the Moroccan method: the company began with a pre-determined permanent landmark in the enumeration area, and then proceeded on foot to select dwelling structures at predetermined intervals. Within each dwelling structure, they randomly selected households and then individuals for interview, also using the Kish grid.

Questionnaire. In developing the questionnaire, we sought to balance the need for cross-national comparability (achieved through uniform questions) with our desire for context-specific resonance (achieved through attention to local nuance). We prioritized maintaining the wording of questions and response categories across countries, forcing us to consider both literal and conceptual translations. As noted above, we conducted the survey in common local languages.

We worked with local partners, conducting and discussing back-translations to ensure accuracy, focusing on translations of key concepts such as "human rights" or "trust." We modified questions and response categories, however, when the local mix of religious identities, political parties, ethnicities, languages, and others necessitated using country-specific options.

In some cases, when a particular text is translated literally, the meaning may shift from context to context. For example, in

TABLE A.1 Human Rights Perceptions Polls Sampling Procedures

	Mexico	Rabat and Casablanca, Morocco	Mumbai, India	Lagos, Nigeria
Sample size	2,400	1,100	1,680	1,000
Rural/Urban sample size	720 rural/1,680 urban	300 rural/800 urban	303 rural/1,377 urban	200 rural/800 urban
Dates	September–October 2012	September–October 2012	December 2012–January 2013	November–December 2014
Representativeness	National, adults	Rabat, Casablanca, and rural areas within 70–80 km of each city, adults	Mumbai and rural Maharashtra State, eligible voters (99% of total adult population)	Lagos, Ogun, and Oyo States, adult citizens
Primary sampling unit	Electoral sections	Local municipalities	Assembly segment	Local government areas
Selection process	Random, proportional to size	Random, proportional to rural/urban population	1 randomly selected per parliamentary constituency	Random

(continued)

TABLE A.1 Continued

	Mexico	Rabat and Casablanca, Morocco	Mumbai, India	Lagos, Nigeria
Secondary sampling unit	Blocks	"Working areas" and landmarks	Polling booth	Enumeration areas / sectors
Selection process	Random (precise method unknown)*	Using Google maps	1 randomly selected per assembly segment	Random, proportional to size
Tertiary sampling unit	Households (individuals randomly selected within)	Household (individuals randomly selected within)	Individuals	Dwellings, then households (individuals randomly selected within)
Selection process	Random (precise method unknown)*	Interval based, beginning on foot from landmark	First individual randomly selected from polling booth list; next individuals selected from list at set intervals	Interval based, beginning on foot from landmark

Response rate	39%	33%	42%	59%
Margin of error, estimated	+/- 2.0%	+/- 3.0%	+/- 2.5%	+/- 3.1%
Over sampling	Northern and Southern regions	Rural areas adjacent to Rabat and Casablanca	Buddhists, Christians, rural resident of Maharashtra State	Rural states of Oyo and Ogun
Weighting procedure	Age, gender, region	Education, age, rural/urban	Education, gender, age, religion	Age, gender
Interview duration mean	35 minutes	21 minutes	48 minutes	44 minutes
Range	Not available	14–41 minutes	33–90 minutes	30–90 minutes

*Our team did not personally supervise and co-construct the sampling procedure in Mexico; as a result, precise methods of random selection remain unclear

Nigeria, when we asked about participation in "environmental organizations," our pilot tests revealed shockingly high participation rates. We discovered that our wording was capturing Nigerian respondents' participation in "environmental sanitation days," a required form of neighborhood cleanup. Because this was not accurately capturing our concept of voluntary civic participation, we revised the question wording to read "not including sanitation days." Another example is our question on the number of light bulbs in a respondent's home, a widely used measure of socioeconomic status in Mexico. In Morocco, however, we discovered that most homes, even those from lower socioeconomic strata, had chandeliers featuring dozens of light bulbs, rendering this particular question useless. This prompted us to add a question about the number of rooms in respondents' homes to capture the desired concept of household socioeconomic status.

Even when we added or modified questions, we strived to maintain the original question meaning across countries. Our ultimate concern was to develop measures that were *valid* in each country—that is, measuring the same thing in each place. This is where our travel to the survey locations and intensive fieldwork with the survey companies and enumerators paid off. By participating in piloting the questionnaires in each country, we were able to revise the survey instrument context-appropriately.

Our record in this area was not perfect, of course. For example, by asking about donations to "religious organizations" in Morocco, our survey may have missed donations through the Islamic charitable practice of *zakat*, a primary mechanism through which Moroccans give to society; we suspect this because other surveys specifically focused on *zakat* in Morocco have found much higher rates of giving than our question revealed. Or, in asking about "participation" in "the activities of religious organizations," our wildly divergent responses between countries—from 2 percent in Rabat and Casablanca to 87 percent in Lagos—indicate that we likely captured different local interpretations or understandings of this question across countries.

Another issue complicating cross-country comparisons was variation in the number of questions we were able to ask. In

Mexico, we added human rights questions to a major existing survey, limiting the number of human rights items we could ask about. In Morocco and India, we carried out our own independent surveys and were able to include additional questions. In Nigeria, the last location we surveyed for this project, we included the most complete range of questions—many informed by suggestions and constructive criticism we received when we presented preliminary results from India and Morocco—again conducting our own independent survey. As a result, the Nigerian questionnaire, available in full online at www.jamesron.com, included more human rights-related questions and more questions about respondent characteristics than were in the other surveys.

Fieldwork. As discussed above, we worked with local survey experts and companies in each country. Our Mexican collaboration was with *The Americas and the World* project at CIDE, a public research center in Mexico City.[13] This project has conducted biannual, multi-country surveys on foreign policy and public opinion in Mexico and other Latin American countries since 2004. Their surveys are national and cover a wide range of topics, including political knowledge and interest, contact with the broader world, trust and security, national and regional identity, foreign policy, international laws and norms, and international relations. The Mexican survey was administered by Data-Opinión Pública y Mercados in 2012 and 2014; we generally utilize the 2012 data in this book.[14] We also contracted local survey research firms to carry out data collection in the other three countries: LMS-CSA[15] in Rabat and Casablanca,[16] in Mumbai, and Practical Sampling International (PSI)[17] in Lagos.

In all four cases, our survey partners administered paper questionnaires in person, typically in respondents' homes or nearby areas. This allowed us to conduct longer and, hopefully, more valid and reliable interviews than the telephone or computer-based surveys common in the developed world. In India, Morocco, and Nigeria, interviews lasted an average of 39 minutes. Survey firms maintained a staff of interviewers and field supervisors, who were local residents who spoke the dominant language(s). Most had significant prior experience carrying out other social surveys.

Fieldwork of this magnitude necessitates flexibility, adaptability, and constant attention to reliability and consistency. For example, our Lagos survey was initially scheduled for September 2014, but threat of an Ebola outbreak caused the public to fear contact with strangers. As a result, we postponed fieldwork until later that year. After completing fieldwork, moreover, data-entry problems in Lagos led to confusion with the resultant dataset. As a result, the local survey company sent all 1,000 paper questionnaires to Minneapolis, where a team of research assistants carefully reviewed them and worked painstakingly with the survey firm to correct errors. In each country, we believe that our face-to-face collaboration with local survey companies boosted the data's validity and reliability.

Data analysis. We write this book with a non-statistical audience in mind.[18] One of our aims is to make the types of statistical analyses often isolated behind the paywalls of academic journals accessible to a broader public audience, including those who may have little or no statistical experience. We hope our analytical strategies and reporting styles are digestible to these readers. Our hope is to bring large-scale comparative public opinion data more squarely into public conversations about human rights, helping to guide the thinking of practitioners, donors, and students, as well as that of professional scholars.

To analyze the *Human Rights Perceptions Polls* data, we use descriptive statistics and multivariate inferential statistical models. Descriptive statistics include measures such as averages (means), medians, frequency distributions, or percentages, and because our samples were representative, we know the sample characteristics closely resemble those of the broader population, within a set margin of error. For example, 256 people of the 2,400 people surveyed in Mexico (11 percent) said they had "met a human rights worker" at least once in their life. If we were to go back in time to 2012 in Mexico and use the same techniques to randomly select another 2,400 people, the precise number reporting having met a human rights worker would likely not be 256, but should be reasonably close. With appropriately randomized sample design, descriptive statistics give us a reasonable sense of what we would find if we had the time and resources to conduct a census of the *entire* population, such as all Mexican adults, or all adult residents of Rabat and Casablanca, Mumbai, and Lagos (and their rural environs).

When we describe our data throughout the book, we take several steps to ensure the information we report is as accurate as possible. Unless otherwise noted, we use the following procedures. First, we report **valid percentages**. For example, in Mumbai, 1,425 people (out of the entire sample of 1,680) answered our question about how much they trust LHROs. This means that the 254 people who said they trust LHROs "a lot" represent a valid percentage of 18 percent (254 out of 1,425, not out of 1,680).

Second, we use **weighting** to account for our sampling procedures and adjust the samples to population figures. In Mexico, we adjust to national population figures for sex and age and add a "design weight" to correct for oversampling of northern and southern regions.[19] In Morocco, we adjust to government-issued population figures in Rabat and Casablanca on education, age, and urban/rural residence, with appropriate adjustments for rural areas. In India, we used a "raking" procedure to adjust the Mumbai sample proportions to Mumbai population figures on education, gender, age, and religion.[20] For rural respondents, we adjust to rural population figures for all of Maharashtra State. In Nigeria, we adjust to the respective age and gender distribution of the three states where we gathered data: Lagos, Ogun, and Oyo. In reporting descriptive findings, we use weighted data, except for the variables used to create the weights: for gender, age, rural/urban, education (in Morocco and India), and religion (in India), we report unweighted data.

Third, we use the **average across countries** when reporting pooled descriptive findings; this is a simple mean of the values for the four countries. For example, across the four countries, if each respondent is counted once in the calculation, 9 percent of respondents reported never hearing the phrase "human rights." However, because there were more respondents in Mexico than in the other three countries, Mexico would have a greater impact on this combined percentage. To correct for this, we take the average of the four countries' totals: 6 percent in Mexico, 1 percent in Morocco, 24 percent in India, and 1 percent in Nigeria, and report that 8 percent of respondents in the pooled data said that they never hear "human rights." That is, for cross-country samples, we weight each country equally so that it contributes one-quarter to the pooled average. The differences between the weighted and unweighted samples are usually small in both the descriptive and multivariate analyses. Nevertheless, we employ this additional weighting procedure in pooled analyses for the sake of thoroughness and to forestall the possibility that, on occasion, the larger samples could seriously distort our estimates.

In most chapters, we go beyond description of respondents in the samples and use inferential statistics to make predictions, based on the samples, about the relationships between various characteristics in the larger population. Much of this analysis relies on multivariate regressions, which allow us to simultaneously analyze associations between multiple factors. For example, we created statistical models to predict respondents' levels of trust in LHROs and include multiple explanatory variables, including demographics and trust in other actors, such as the US government. Our models thus *control for* a range of alternative explanations of what might affect respondent trust in LHROs. Any significant relationships that emerge between variables in the model are *above and beyond* the effects of other variables in the model. Thus, if we think women may trust LHROs more than men, our inclusion of gender as a statistical control suggests that any other relationships we find are true even *after* accounting for gender's unique impact.

When we find a relationship between an explanatory factor (an "independent variable") and an outcome ("dependent variable"), it is important to know whether this relationship is statistically significant. If it is, this means we are reasonably certain that the relationship is true for the population at large, and not just due to random error or chance. The term "statistical significance" indicates our confidence that the finding would hold, even if we drew a completely new sample from the same population. We use a standard level of significance of 0.10 or lower, meaning there is a 10 percent or less chance that the relationship observed is a "false positive"—that is, a relatively low probability of detecting a relationship in the sample when none in fact exists within the broader population. Put another way, we are 90 percent confident that the relationship we observe in the samples holds true for the broader population—in other words, this statistical relationship would appear in 9 of every 10 samples hypothetically drawn from the same population.

More important than statistical significance, however, is practical significance: Are these estimated relationships substantively important as well as statistically significant? After all, it is entirely possible to have statistically significant relationships that are trivial in terms of actual impact. For this reason, we also try to characterize effect sizes ("small," "modest," "large," etc.), in addition to reporting statistical significance. Furthermore, we sometimes assess effect sizes using predicted values—the average value or probability of the outcome variable for a given combination of explanatory variables. The essence of this technique consists in defining a respondent profile and calculating the average outcome for all people sharing those characteristics. Suppose, hypothetically, that of all rural women, 30 years old, who live in Oyo state, 50 percent donate to religious organizations. We manipulate one element of the profile (e.g., age) without changing the other elements—holding all else constant—and calculate the new predicted value. In this example, of rural women from Oyo who are 40 (instead of 30), 60 percent give to religious organizations. The difference between the first and the second predicted value is 10 percentage points, and this gives us an estimate of the influence age has on religious donations.

When we conduct multivariate analyses, we perform checks to ensure our models are appropriate for the data and that our findings are robust. One of our primary concerns was the appropriateness of using "pooled" models that combine data from all four of our samples. As these countries differ from one another in both observable and less observable ways, we feared it could be statistically inappropriate to lump Mexican, Indian, Moroccan, and Nigerian respondents together in the same statistical models. To

TABLE A.2. Human Rights Perceptions Polls Respondent Characteristics

	Mexico (N = 2,400)	Rabat and Casablanca (N = 1,100)	Mumbai (N = 1,680)	Lagos (N = 1,000)	Pooled (N = 6,180)
Women	51%*	52%	44%*	50%*	49%
Age (mean years)	41*	39*	44*	33*	39
Primary activity last week					
Work inside home (excluding students, unemployed, retired)	31%	47%	34%	12%	31%
Work outside home	53%	37%	61%	68%	55%
Income					
Mean monthly household income (2014 USD, PPP-adjusted)	$464	$1,100	$1,420	$523	$877
Feel income covers household expenses ("can just cover expenses" or "can cover expenses and save")	41%	38%	37%	53%	42%

	9	7*	9*	11	9
Education					
Mean years	9	7*	9*	11	9
No formal education	4%	26%*	7%*	3%	10%
Completed secondary	36%	29%*	57%*	28%	38%
Connectivity					
Have a cell phone	56%	88%	75%	91%	78%
Use the Internet	33%	25%	8%	48%	29%
Have traveled abroad	24%	10%	2%	16%	13%
Religion					
Catholic	80%	0%	8%*	9%	24%
Non-Catholic Christian	12%	0%	3%*	56%	18%
Muslim	0%	100%	8%*	34%	36%
Hindu	0%	0%	62%*	0%	15%

(continued)

TABLE A.2. Continued

	Mexico (N = 2,400)	Rabat and Casablanca (N = 1,100)	Mumbai (N = 1,680)	Lagos (N = 1,000)	Pooled (N = 6,180)
Buddhist	0%	0%	16%*	0%	4%
Attend place of worship once a week	NA	46%	79%	97%	74%
Religion "important" in life					
(6 or above on 0–10 scale)	78%	99%	81%	96%	89%
Politics					
Does not support a political party	39%	62%	7%	48%	39%
Supports ruling party	18%	27%	20%	19%	21%
Voted in last election	76%	47%	93%	65%	70%

Figures are valid percentages. Country figures apply sampling and population weights where appropriate; asterisks indicate unweighted data. Pooled total figures weight all four country samples equally.

address this concern, we first include **country dummy variables** (binary variables coded 0 if the respondent does not live in the country and 1 if they do) in all pooled models. These so-called country "fixed effects" help control for unobserved or unmeasured country characteristics. We also include a **country weight**, which allows each country to contribute equally to the model. This is the same as taking the average across countries for descriptive statistics, described above. Third, we **run country-specific models** and in most chapters report these findings in addition to the pooled models. We do this to test for variables that might operate differently in different countries. For example, gender might have a different effect on trust in LHROs in Morocco than in Mexico.[21]

We checked the robustness of our results by including more **stringent standard error** calculations using robust standard errors or bootstrap estimations of errors.[22] Although we typically report models without these extra methods, we did perform the checks. We also test a few different types of models. Thus, when we run ordinary least squares (OLS) regressions, the most simple and widely used technique, we also check the findings with **ordinal logistic regression**. We do this because many of our dependent variables are ordinal, meaning that there is a clear ordering to their categories, but the distance between any two adjacent categories is not necessarily the same. For example, we asked respondents whether they had "a lot," "some," "a little," or "no" trust in certain institutions, such as LHROs. OLS regression is most typically used to predict continuous variables, but can also be used to predict ordinal variables, such as ours, if certain assumptions are met. We prefer to report OLS in most cases because the coefficients are easier to interpret, but also run ordinal logistic regressions to ensure the findings are consistent.

Characteristics of respondents. The following table describes the public survey respondents in detail. Our samples include a roughly equal gender split, with respondents ranging from 18 to 95 years old, with an average age of 39. Socioeconomically, over half of respondents work outside the home, and just under a third engage in home-based activities. On average, 42 percent reported that their household income either met or exceeded their monthly expenses, but the majority struggle to make ends meet. Across the four samples, respondents' mean monthly household income in PPP-adjusted 2014 US dollars is $877.[23] On average, respondents reported nine years of formal education, but 10 percent had no formal education whatsoever. Morocco was a clear outlier in this respect, with over a quarter of respondents reporting no formal education, even though our polls focused on the country's two major urban areas. Most respondents in all four locales (78 percent) had cell phones, but less than one-third (29 percent) reported using the Internet, and only 13 percent reported having ever traveled abroad. In all statistical models, we use socioeconomic and demographic factors as control variables.

Across countries, respondents were highly religious: 89 percent reported that religion was "important in their daily life," and 74 percent reported attending a religious place of worship weekly. Most Mexican respondents were Catholic, and Moroccan respondents were Muslim.[24] India and Nigeria had greater religious heterogeneity: Hindus, Muslims, Buddhists, and Christians in Mumbai, and (mostly) non-Catholic Christians and Muslims in Lagos. Many respondents were politically active, with 70 percent reporting voting in the last national election. The vast majority did not support the ruling party, however, and many reported no party affiliation at all, suggesting that many may vote along non-party lines or be disconnected from institutional party politics.

Appendix B

Regression Tables

This appendix presents full regression tables for the key models discussed in the preceding chapters. The models in Table B.1 are discussed in Chapter 2. Table B.1 presents pooled models from Mexico, Mumbai, Rabat/Casablanca, and Lagos. Model 1 uses ordinal logistic regression, which predicts the relationship between SES indicators and hearing "human rights," a dependent variable with ordered categories. Interpret Model 1's coefficients as the association between an increase in one unit of the independent variable, and the log odds of moving from one category of "hear human rights" to another, with all other variables in the model held constant. In Models 2, 3, and 4, the dependent variables are dichotomous "yes" or "no" responses, so we use binary logistic regressions. Here, interpret coefficients as the effect of a one-unit change in the independent variable (or, in the case of independent dummy variables, the presence of an attribute) on the percentage change in the odds of a respondent having met a "human rights worker," being able to name a specific human rights group in the respondent's country, or having participated at least once in the respondent's life in a "human rights organization activity." A common way of interpreting the effects of logit regression is calculating and reporting the probabilities of the outcome at different values of a given independent variable.

TABLE B.1 Socioeconomic Factors Predicting Human Rights Exposure and Engagement

	(1) Hear HR discourse	(2) Met HR worker	(3) Name Specific HRO	(4) Participated in HRO	(5) Participated in HRO: Expanded Model
Education	0.0386** (0.00631)	0.0928** (0.0137)	0.115** (0.0160)	0.0557** (0.0177)	0.0476* (0.0218)
Subjective income	−0.549** (0.135)	−0.387 (0.283)	−0.126 (0.355)	−0.366 (0.359)	−0.389 (0.447)
Subjective income squared	0.103** (0.0276)	0.104+ (0.0570)	0.0285 (0.0714)	0.0827 (0.0709)	0.0822 (0.0870)
Rural residence	−0.468** (0.0584)	−0.621** (0.147)	−0.233 (0.175)	−0.378* (0.175)	−0.481+ (0.258)
Internet user	0.269** (0.0619)	0.358** (0.128)	0.207 (0.163)	0.404* (0.172)	0.374+ (0.213)
Female	−0.196** (0.0482)	−0.294** (0.103)	−0.0772 (0.125)	−0.195 (0.132)	−0.202 (0.169)

Age	0.00428*	0.0134**	0.0209**	0.0120**	0.00901
	(0.00182)	(0.00353)	(0.00479)	(0.00441)	(0.00584)
Country: Morocco (Mexico is omitted category)	0.732**	-0.189		-0.851**	
	(0.0688)	(0.133)		(0.276)	
Country: India	-0.928**	-1.408**	-4.167**	0.830**	1.916**
	(0.0716)	(0.166)	(0.342)	(0.152)	(0.278)
Country: Nigeria	-0.219**	-0.280*	-1.248**	0.524**	1.410**
	(0.0670)	(0.127)	(0.143)	(0.168)	(0.290)
Constant cut1	-3.249**				
	(0.200)				
Constant cut2	-1.365**				
	(0.194)				

(continued)

TABLE B.1 Continued

	(1) Hear HR discourse	(2) Met HR worker	(3) Name Specific HRO	(4) Participated in HRO	(5) Participated in HRO: Expanded Model
Constant cut3	0.241 (0.193)				
Constant cut4	1.711** (0.195)				
Frequency of hearing "human rights"					0.198* (0.0907)
Met human rights worker					1.059** (0.228)
Name at least one HRO in country					−0.255 (0.297)
Constant		−3.074** (0.412)	−2.858** (0.495)	−3.885** (0.493)	−5.325** (0.732)
Observations	5,829	5,730	3,543	5,621	3,155

Standard errors in parentheses.
** p<0.01, * p<0.05, + p<0.1.

Table B.2 presents the full models predicting *Trust in LHROs*, discussed in Chapter 3. The models are ordinary least squares (OLS) regressions. The dependent variable, *Trust in LHROs*, is a 0–1 scale that standardizes the 7-point scale used for half of the Mexico sample and the 4-point scale used everywhere else. The coefficients can be interpreted as the multipliers that indicate the size of the effects of the independent variables on the dependent variable. For example, in the pooled model, when *Mistrust of Multinationals* goes up by one unit (for example, from "a little trust" to "no trust at all"), we predict that *Trust in LHROs* will increase by 0.176 on the 0–1 scale.

The models in Table B.3 are mentioned, though not fully discussed, in Chapter 3. These models use socioeconomic indicators, contact with human rights discourse and actors, political variables, and standard controls to predict the three *Anti-Power Worldviews* shaping public trust in local rights groups (0–1 scale, 1 = "no trust at all"). Table B.3 presents findings for OLS regressions for pooled, all-country samples. The left side of the table lists the independent variables, applied to models with different dependent variables: *Mistrust in the US Government* (1), *Mistrust in Multinationals* (2), and *Mistrust in Domestic Political Authorities* (3).

Table B.4 is discussed in Chapter 5. The models replicate the analysis reported in Table B.2, but add religiosity variables: religious identity, trust in religious institutions, personal religiosity (depending on the country, this analysis includes the index, frequency of prayer, or personal religious importance), and social religiosity (depending on the country, the index, frequency of attendance, or participation in religious organizations).

TABLE B.2 The Anti-Power Worldviews Predicting Public Trust in LHROs

	(1) Pooled	(2) Mexico	(3) R&C	(4) Mumbai	(5) Lagos
Anti-Power Worldviews					
Mistrust of US Government	0.0973** (0.0149)	0.177** (0.0221)	0.123* (0.0496)	0.0766* (0.0322)	0.0281 (0.0326)
Mistrust of Multinationals	0.176** (0.0159)	0.217** (0.0233)	0.196** (0.0546)	0.0663+ (0.0359)	0.212** (0.0330)
Mistrust of Domestic Political Authorities	0.271** (0.0256)	0.471** (0.0390)	0.0880 (0.0855)	0.196** (0.0557)	0.279** (0.0561)
Contact and Socioeconomic					
Contact with Human Rights	0.0446* (0.0182)	-0.000160 (0.0210)	0.0784 (0.0568)	0.0823 (0.0607)	0.0678 (0.0415)
Education	-0.000961 (0.000992)	-0.00108 (0.00133)	-0.000252 (0.00304)	-0.00205 (0.00240)	0.000375 (0.00224)
Rural residence	-0.00377 (0.00921)	-0.00149 (0.0113)	-0.0176 (0.0344)	-0.00475 (0.0253)	-0.00365 (0.0212)
Subjective income	-0.0298 (0.0207)	-0.0411 (0.0284)	0.0975 (0.0666)	-0.0862+ (0.0494)	-0.00829 (0.0482)

192

		(1)	(2)	(3)	(4)	(5)
	Subjective income squared	0.00553 (0.00417)	0.00634 (0.00597)	-0.0220 (0.0138)	0.0186+ (0.0101)	0.00275 (0.00905)
	Internet user	-0.00584 (0.00919)	-0.0114 (0.0120)	-0.0357 (0.0309)	0.00862 (0.0269)	-0.00591 (0.0188)
Politics	Supports the ruling political party	-0.000643 (0.00228)	-0.00150 (0.00182)	0.00778 (0.0266)	0.00260 (0.0235)	-0.0118 (0.0189)
	Voted in last election	-6.91e-06 (0.00892)	-0.0154 (0.0117)	-0.00435 (0.0256)	0.0181 (0.0436)	0.00772 (0.0171)
Controls	Woman	0.0165* (0.00741)	0.00820 (0.00975)	0.00255 (0.0243)	0.0265 (0.0195)	0.0204 (0.0153)
	Respondent's age	-0.000138 (0.000291)	-2.57e-05 (0.000350)	-0.000740 (0.000989)	-0.000600 (0.000669)	-0.000260 (0.000798)
	Average trust	1.592** (0.0437)	1.907** (0.0593)	1.490** (0.137)	1.279** (0.113)	1.596** (0.100)
	Country: Morocco (Mexico is omitted category)	-0.0203 (0.0132)				

(continued)

TABLE B.2 Continued

	(1) Pooled	(2) Mexico	(3) R&C	(4) Mumbai	(5) Lagos
Country: India	-0.0580** (0.0118)				
Country: Nigeria	-0.00416 (0.0113)				
Constant	-0.489** (0.0505)	-0.784** (0.0679)	-0.481** (0.162)	-0.221+ (0.121)	-0.543** (0.117)
Observations	3,956	1,909	416	863	768
Adjusted R-squared	0.400	0.489	0.443	0.168	0.388

Standard errors in parentheses.
** p < 0.01, * p < 0.05, + p < 0.1.

TABLE B.3 The Socioeconomic Factors Predicting Anti-Power Worldviews

	(1) Mistrust in US Government	(2) Mistrust in Multinationals	(3) Mistrust in Domestic Government Authorities
Contact with human rights	−0.0586** (0.0188)	0.0201 (0.0180)	−0.00642 (0.0110)
Education	−0.000572 (0.000996)	−0.000329 (0.000962)	0.000862 (0.000569)
Rural residence	0.0246** (0.00939)	0.0186* (0.00899)	−0.0221** (0.00529)
Subjective income	−0.0152 (0.0210)	−0.0195 (0.0200)	0.0248* (0.0119)
Subjective income squared	0.00573 (0.00425)	0.00348 (0.00405)	−0.00725** (0.00245)
Internet user	−0.00562 (0.00937)	−0.0133 (0.00900)	−0.00116 (0.00553)
Supports the ruling political party	0.00438+ (0.00240)	−0.000789 (0.00229)	−0.000541 (0.00145)
Voted in last election	0.00546 (0.00905)	0.00408 (0.00886)	−0.0153** (0.00523)
Woman	0.00940 (0.00752)	0.0133+ (0.00721)	−0.00950* (0.00433)
Respondent's age	0.000218 (0.000295)	−0.000285 (0.000281)	−0.000327+ (0.000167)
Average trust	−1.024** (0.0230)	−1.044** (0.0221)	−1.008** (0.0129)

(continued)

TABLE B.3 Continued

	(1) Mistrust in US Government	(2) Mistrust in Multinationals	(3) Mistrust in Domestic Government Authorities
Country: Morocco (*Mexico is omitted category*)	0.112** (0.0126)	0.0163 (0.0129)	-0.0555** (0.00712)
Country: India	0.0546** (0.0121)	0.0230* (0.0112)	-0.0270** (0.00703)
Country: Nigeria	-0.157** (0.0115)	-0.0778** (0.0109)	0.0714** (0.00694)
Constant	1.047** (0.0323)	1.106** (0.0307)	1.109** (0.0184)
Observations	4,762	4,341	5,493
Adjusted R-squared	0.392	0.375	0.571

Standard errors in parentheses.
** $p < 0.01$, * $p < 0.05$, + $p < 0.1$.

TABLE B.4 Religiosity Predicting Trust in LHROs

		(1) Pooled	(2) Mexico	(3) R&C	(4) Mumbai	(5) Lagos
Anti-power Frames	Mistrust of US Government	0.105** (0.0153)	0.196** (0.0226)	0.129** (0.0511)	0.0567 (0.0345)	0.0468 (0.0332)
	Mistrust of Multinational Corporations	0.189** (0.0164)	0.258** (0.0240)	0.185** (0.0562)	0.0436 (0.0385)	0.230** (0.0339)
	Mistrust of Domestic Political Authority	0.293** (0.0271)	0.514** (0.0399)	0.115** (0.0893)	0.171** (0.0647)	0.301** (0.0582)
Religiosity	Religious Identity (*Catholic omitted*)					
	Non-Catholic Christian	-0.000530 (0.0140)	-0.000552 (0.0145)		0.0459 (0.0776)	-0.00956 (0.0275)
	Hindu	0.0305 (0.0231)			0.0271 (0.0380)	
	Muslim	-0.00114 (0.0173)	0.0642 (0.210)		0.00631 (0.0518)	-0.00987 (0.0294)
	Buddhist	0.00920 (0.0317)			0.0478 (0.0465)	
	Trust in Religious Institutions	-0.0588** (0.0140)	-0.127** (0.0194)	-0.0422 (0.0458)	0.0234 (0.0363)	-0.0658* (0.0291)

(continued)

TABLE B.4 Continued

	(1) Pooled	(2) Mexico	(3) R&C	(4) Mumbai	(5) Lagos
Personal Religiosity Index	0.00126 (0.00211)				-0.00724 (0.00501)
Personal religious importance		0.00111 (0.00221)		0.00394 (0.00448)	
Prayer Religiosity frequency			0.00287 (0.00768)		
Social Religiosity Index	0.00998 (0.0127)				
Religious organization participation		0.0284* (0.0121)			
Religious attendance frequency			0.00452 (0.00770)	-0.00346 (0.00898)	0.00675 (0.0124)
Contact and Socioeconomic High contact with HR	0.0336+ (0.0185)	-0.0158 (0.0213)	0.0490 (0.0609)	0.0481 (0.0667)	0.0830* (0.0406)
Education	-0.000554 (0.00101)	-0.00201 (0.00134)	0.000401 (0.00312)	0.000350 (0.00257)	0.000302 (0.00227)
Rural residence	-0.00293 (0.00933)	0.00523 (0.0114)	-0.0154 (0.0353)	-0.0116 (0.0269)	-0.00383 (0.0216)

	Subjective income	-0.0346	-0.0390	0.0889	-0.0933+	0.000933
		(0.0211)	(0.0287)	(0.0683)	(0.0526)	(0.0489)
	Subjective income squared	0.00664	0.00614	-0.0199	0.0207+	0.000668
		(0.00423)	(0.00601)	(0.0141)	(0.0106)	(0.00919)
	Internet user	-0.00794	-0.0118	-0.0343	0.00622	-0.0110
		(0.00933)	(0.0122)	(0.0314)	(0.0288)	(0.0192)
Politics	Supports the ruling political party	-0.000615	0.00207	0.0255	0.00602	-0.00374
		(0.00904)	(0.0124)	(0.0271)	(0.0249)	(0.0194)
	Voted in last election	-0.00172	-0.0142	-0.0177	0.0526	0.00170
		(0.00902)	(0.01 17)	(0.0261)	(0.0448)	(0.0173)
Controls	Female	0.0171*	0.0104	0.00778	0.0231	0.0212
		(0.00752)	(0.00997)	(0.0298)	(0.0205)	(0.0156)
	Respondent's age	-0.000224	-0.000131	-0.000792	-0.000661	-0.000313
		(0.000296)	(0.000355)	(0.00102)	(0.000711)	(0.000811)
	Average trust	1.683**	2.117**	1.553**	1.149**	1.691**
		(0.0502)	(0.0669)	(0.164)	(0.139)	(0.111)
	Country: Morocco (Mexico is omitted category)	-0.0217				
		(0.0206)				

(continued)

TABLE B.4 Continued

	(1) Pooled	(2) Mexico	(3) R&C	(4) Mumbai	(5) Lagos
Country: India	-0.0859** (0.0220)				
Country: Nigeria	-0.00804 (0.0171)				
Constant	-0.525** (0.0540)	-0.874** (0.0713)	-0.515** (0.169)	-0.214 (0.144)	-0.535** (0.137)
Observations	3,825	1,843	403	763	759
R-squared	0.408	0.505	0.463	0.189	0.406

Standard errors in parentheses.
** p < 0.01, * p < 0.05, + p < 0.1.

Notes

Preface

1. For the link between poverty, authoritarianism, inequality, and abuse of civil and political rights, see Poe, S. C., Tate, C. N., and Keith, L. C. (1999). Repression of the Human Right to Personal Integrity Revisited: A Global Cross-National Study Covering the Years 1976–1993. *International Studies Quarterly*, 43(2), 291–313; Landman, T. and Larizza, M. (2009). Inequality and Human Rights: Who Controls What, When, and How. *International Studies Quarterly*, 53(3), 715–736; and Khan, I. and Petrasek, D. (2009). *The Unheard Truth: Poverty and Human Rights*. New York: Norton; and Thoms, O. N. T. and Ron, J. (2007). "Do Human Rights Violations Cause Internal Conflict?" *Human Rights Quarterly* 29(3): 674–739.

2. For claims of human rights imposition from the global North, see Englund, H. (2006). *Prisoners of Freedom: Human Rights and the African Poor*. Berkeley: University of California Press; Hopgood, S. (2013). *The Endtimes of Human Rights*. Ithaca: Cornell University Press; and Mutua, M. (2001). Savages, Victims and Saviors: The Metaphor of Human Rights. *Harvard International Law Journal*, 42(1), 201–245.

3. A key anthropological text in this genre is Merry, S. E. (2006). *Human Rights and Gender Violence: Translating International Law into Local Justice*. Chicago: Chicago University Press.

Chapter 1

1. Moyn, S. (2010). *The Last Utopia: Human Rights in History*. Cambridge, MA: Belknap Press; Cmiel, K. (2004). The Recent History of Human Rights. *The American Historical Review*, 109(1): 117–135.

2. For human rights as policy justification, see Chandler, D. (2002). *Rethinking Human Rights: Critical Approaches to International Politics*. Basingstoke: Palgrave Macmillan; Perugini, N. and Gordon, N. (2015). *The Human Right to Dominate*. New York: Oxford University Press; and Rajagopal, B. (2003). *International Law from Below: Development, Social Movements, and Third World Resistance*. New York: Cambridge University Press.

3. Moyn (2010).

4. For the political science of human rights, see Cardenas, S. (2009). Mainstreaming Human Rights: Publishing Trends in Political Science. *PS: Political Science and Politics*, 42(1): 161–166; and Hafner-Burton, E. M. (2014). A Social Science of Human Rights. *Journal of Peace Research*, 51(2): 139–144.

5. For general scholarship on international norm-creation, diffusion and reception, see Barnett, M. and Finnemore, M. (1999). The Politics, Power, and Pathologies of International Organizations. *International Organization*, 53(4): 699–732; Carpenter, C. (2014). *Lost Causes: Agenda-Setting and Agenda-Vetting in Global Issue Networks*. Ithaca, NY: Cornell University Press; Finnemore, M. and Sikkink, K. (1998). International Norm Dynamics and Political Change. *International Organization*, 52(4): 887–917.

6. Multiple scholars stress the importance of domestic civil society for human rights reform, including Bob, C. (2005). *The Marketing of Rebellion: Insurgents, Media, and International Activism*. New York: Cambridge University Press; Hafner-Burton, E. M. (2013). *Making Human Rights a Reality*. Princeton, NJ: Princeton University Press; Keck, M. E. and Sikkink, K. (1998). *Activists beyond Borders: Advocacy Networks in International Politics*. Ithaca, NY: Cornell University Press; Murdie, A. (2014). *Help or Harm: The Human Security Effects of International NGOs*. Palo Alto, CA: Stanford University Press; Simmons, B. (2009). *Mobilizing for Human Rights: International Law in Domestic Politics*. New York: Cambridge University Press; and Wong, W. (2012). *Internal Affairs: How the Structure of NGOs Creates International Human Rights*. Ithaca, NY: Cornell University Press.

7. The classic study of interaction between social movements and professional organizations is Staggenborg, S. (1988). The Consequences of Professionalization and Formalization in the Pro-Choice Movement. *American Sociological Review*, 53(4): 585–605.

8. Merry (2006).

9. Bob, C. (2005) and Hertel, S. (2006). *Unexpected Power: Conflict and Change among Transnational Activists*. Ithaca, NY: Cornell University Press.

10. Prakash, A. and Gugerty, M. K., eds. (2010). *Rethinking Advocacy Organizations: A Collective Action Perspective*. New York: Cambridge University Press.

11. For the organizational-material interests of principled NGOs, see Cooley, A. and Ron, J. (2002). NGO Scramble: Organizational Insecurity and the Political Economy of Transnational Action. *International Security* 27(1): 5–39.

12. Carothers, T. and Brechenmacher, S. (2014). *Closing Space: Democracy and Human Rights Support under Fire*. Washington, DC: Carnegie Endowment for International Peace; Dupuy, K., Ron, J., and Prakash, A. (2016). Hands off My Regime! Government Restrictions on Foreign Aid to Non-governmental Organizations in Poor and Middle-Income Countries. *World Development*, 84: 299–311.

13. Scheindlin, D. (2016). Why Some Human Rights Groups Avoid Public Opinion Research—and Why They're Wrong. *openGlobalRights/openDemocracy*. London.

14. Dicklitch, S. and Lwanga, D. (2003). The Politics of Being Non-political: Human Rights Organizations and the Creation of a Positive Human Rights Culture in Uganda. *Human Rights Quarterly*, 25(2): 482–509.

15. Dicklitch, Susan and Doreen Lwanga. (2003). The Politics of Being Non-Political: Human Rights Organizations and the Creation of a Positive Human Rights Culture in Uganda. *Human Rights Quarterly* 25: 482–509, 485.

16. Roth, K. (2015, September 16). For Human Rights, Majority Opinion Isn't Always Important. *openGlobalRights/openDemocracy*. London.

17. González-Ocantos, E. (2013, November 20). Speaking with an Elite Accent: Human Rights and the "Masses." *openGlobalRights/openDemocracy*. London.

18. Pruce, J. (2015, October 13). Myth-Busting Human Rights Awareness. *openGlobalRights/openDemocracy*. London.

19. Many scholars use this "most different" strategy for case selection. See George, A. L. and Bennett, A. (2005). *Case Studies and Theory Development in the Social Sciences*. Cambridge, MA: MIT Press; Gerring, J. (2007). *Case Study Research: Principles and Practices*. New York: Cambridge University Press.

20. Human rights scholarship highlighting the importance of world region includes Cole, W. M. (2006). When All Else Fails: International Adjudication of Human Rights Abuse Claims, 1976–1999. *Social Forces*, 84(4): 1909–1935; Hafner-Burton, E. M. and Ron, J. (2013). The Latin Bias: Regions, the Anglo-American Media, and Human Rights. *International Studies Quarterly*, 57: 474–491. The more general international relations research on the importance of world region includes Katzenstein, P. J. (2005). *A World of Regions: Asia and Europe in the American Imperium*. Ithaca, NY: Cornell University Press. Comparative political scientists, by contrast, often *assume* that regions have unique effects, and thus speak of themselves as "Africanists," "Latin Americanists," "Europeanists," or "East" or "South Asianists."

21. The scholarship on religion and politics or human rights is vast; almost all of it shares the assumption that religious traditions and interpretations are meaningful causal factors. As one expert notes, "religion molds the nation in which it thrives," and political scholars ignore religion's effects at their peril; see Atran, S. (2012, August 6). God and the Ivory Tower. *Foreign Policy*, 1–9. Religion's purported impacts on human rights practices are contested, as discussed in Chapter 5.

22. The colonial experience's impact on subsequent political developments is established in the comparative historical literature. See, for example, Englebert, P. (2002). *State Legitimacy and Development in Africa*. Boulder, CO: Lynne Rienner; Mahoney, J. (2010). *Colonialism and Post-colonial Development: Spanish America in Comparative Perspective*. New York: Cambridge University Press. For a study on the impact of colonialism and religion on political development via missionaries, see Woodberry, R. D. (2012). The Missionary Roots of Liberal Democracy. *American Political Science Review*, 106(02): 244–274.

23. The notion of a unique "civilization" stretching across national boundaries and exerting independent causal effects comes from Huntington, S. P. (2011). *The Clash of Civilizations and the Remaking of World Order*. New York: Simon and Schuster.

24. The importance of language and linguistic conventions is emphasized by virtually every social scientist working in the constructivist tradition. For a recent example, see Wendt, A. (2015). *Quantum Mind and Social Sciences*. New York: Cambridge University Press.

25. These data on charitable giving come from a series of Gallup polls discussed in Chapter 4, as reported by the Charities Aid Foundation.

26. For argument and evidence that individual country conditions shape national NGO sectors, see Stroup, S. (2012). *Borders among Activists: International NGOs in the United States, Britain and France*. Ithaca, NY: Cornell University Press.

27. This sample combines elements of "convenience" and "purpose." It was "convenient" in that a leading Canadian NGO gathered hundreds of human rights-oriented NGO workers and key informants from all over the world each year on Ron's doorstep, in Montreal, Quebec. It was "purposive" in that Ron chose to work with this population because of its unique characteristics, and selected 128 men and women to interview from among some 600 possible respondents so as to achieve a balance of regions and perspectives.

28. For details, see Kindornay, S., Ron, J., and Carpenter, R. C. (2012). The Rights-Based Approach to Development: Implications for NGOs. *Human Rights Quarterly*, 34(2): 472–506.

29. Kumar, R. (2005). *Research Methodology: A Step-by-Step Guide for Beginners*. Thousand Oaks, CA: Sage.

30. For an overview of human rights movements in India, Mexico, Morocco, Israel, and Nigeria, see Anaya Muñoz, A. (2009). Transnational and Domestic Processes in the Definition of Human Rights Policies in Mexico. *Human Rights Quarterly*, 31(1): 35–58; Gordon, N. and Berkovitch, N. (2007). Human Rights Discourse in Domestic Settings: How Does It Emerge? *Political Studies*, 55(1): 243–266; Gudavarthy, A. (2008). Human Rights Movements in India: State, Civil Society and Beyond. *Contributions to Indian Sociology*, 42(1): 29–57; Okafor, O. C. (2006). *Legitimizing Human Rights NGOs: Lessons from Nigeria*. Trenton, NJ: Africa World Press; Slyomovics, S. (2005).

The Performance of Human Rights in Morocco. Philadelphia: University of Pennsylvania Press. For a list of LHROs identified in each city, see Ron, J. and Crow, D. (2015). Who Trusts Local Human Rights Organizations? Evidence from Three World Regions. *Human Rights Quarterly*, 37(1): 188–239.

31. In Lagos, due to time and budget constraints, we conducted 20 interviews via written questionnaire or online survey. These respondents completed a modified, condensed version of the in-person interview.

32. Summaries of our findings can be found in country-specific reports, available at www.jamesron.com.

33. For NGO classification, see Vakil, A. C. (1997). Confronting the Classification Problem: Toward a Taxonomy of NGOs. *World Development*, 25(12): 2057–2070. For the merging of "development" and "human rights," see Cornwall, A. and Nyamu-Musembi, C. (2004). Putting the "Rights-Based Approach" to Development in Perspective. *Third World Quarterly*, 25(8): 1415–1437; Kindornay, Ron and Carpenter (2012); Schmitz, H. P. (2012). A Human Rights-Based Approach (HRBA) in Practice: Evaluating NGO Development Efforts. *Polity*, 44(4): 523–541; and Uvin, P. (2007). From the Right to Development to the Rights-Based Approach: How "Human Rights" Entered Development. *Development in Practice*, 17 (4/5): 597–606.

34. We conducted the national Mexican survey in August–October 2012, and then again in October 2014–January 2015; the Moroccan, September–October 2012; the Indian, December 2012–January 2013; and the Nigerian, November–December 2014. We conducted the additional Mexico City survey in July 2016.

35. The *Americas and the World* survey is coordinated by CIDE in Mexico City (www.lasamericasyelmundo.cide.edu).

36. Crow lives in Mexico; Ron and Crow traveled to Casablanca for the enumerator training and survey pilot, Pandya and Crow traveled to Mumbai, and Golden and Crow traveled to Lagos.

Chapter 2

1. Hafner-Burton (2013), 93.

2. Possible responses: *Daily, Frequently, Sometimes, Rarely,* or *Never.* We translated "human rights" into Moroccan Arabic (Darija), French, Hindi, Marathi, Spanish, Yoruba, and Pidgin.

3. Meyer, J. W., Boli, J., Thomas, G. M., and Ramirez, F. O. (1997). World Society and the Nation-State. *American Journal of Sociology*, 103(1): 144–181.

4. For the rivalry between cosmopolitan and national identities, see Soysal, Y. (1995). *Limits of Citizenship*. Chicago: Chicago University Press.

5. Possible responses: *Yes, No*.

6. We thank Barbara Frey for this insight.

7. Possible responses: *Yes, No*. We did not specify any organizational names. We did not ask this question in Mexico.

8. Survey team recorded responses verbatim. Unfortunately, we did not ask this question in Mexico.

9. Lubell, M. (2007). Familiarity Breeds Trust: Collective Action in a Policy Domain. *Journal of Politics*, 69(1): 237–250.

10. McCarthy, J. D. and Zald, M. N. (1977). Resource Mobilization and Social Movements: A Partial Theory. *American Journal of Sociology*, 82(6): 1212–1241.

11. Collins, R. (1998). *The Sociology of Philosophies: A Global Theory of Intellectual Change*. Cambridge, MA: Belknap Press of Harvard University Press.

12. Brunnee, J. and Toope, S. (2010). *Legitimacy and Legality in International Law: An Interactionist Approach*. New York: Cambridge University Press.

13. McAdam, D. (1990). *Freedom Summer*. New York: Oxford University Press.

14. Possible responses: *Yes, No*.

15. Mancur Olsen, J. (1971). *The Logic of Collective Action*. Cambridge, MA: Harvard University Press.

16. Drury, J. and Reicher, S. (2005). Explaining Enduring Empowerment: A Comparative Study of Collective Action and Psychological Outcomes. *European Journal of Social Psychology*, 35(1): 35–58.

17. Bob (2005).

18. Interviews 192-Morocco and 205-Morocco.

19. For a description of this sample and our methodology, see Ron, J., Crow, D., and Golden, S. (2014). Human Rights Familiarity and

Socio-Economic Status: A Four-Country Study. *Sur: International Journal on Human Rights*, 11(20): 335–351.

20. El Haitami, M., Golden, S., and Ron, J. (2015, July 7). In Morocco, Human Rights and Islam Are Not Necessarily at Odds. *openGlobalRights/openDemocracy*. London.

21. Touchtou, R., Ron, J., and Golden, S. (2015, July 28). For Moroccan Rights Groups, Good Reputations Aren't Enough. *openGlobalRights/openDemocracy*. London.

22. For a theoretical and empirical discussion of which issues do, and do not, get framed by the media in explicit "human rights" terms, see Gordon, N. and Berkovitch, N. (2007).

23. For Figure 2.2: **Met HR Worker**: Mexico N = 2,366; Rabat and Casablanca N = 1,094; Mumbai N = 1,554; Lagos N = 1,000; **Named Specific HRO**: only asked of respondents who reported hearing about specific HROs working in their country (Rabat and Casablanca N = 257; Mumbai N = 56; Lagos N = 105), but Figure 2.2 reports the percent of the entire samples who could name an HRO; **Participated in HRO**: Mexico N = 2,397; Rabat and Casablanca N = 1,079; Mumbai N = 1,388; Lagos N = 997.

24. Of course, it is also possible that the reverse occurred—that is, respondents misclassified a human rights worker as something else, and said they had not met one. In any case, the rate of contact and participation are low.

25. All four questions were asked in Morocco, Nigeria, and India, but one was not asked in Mexico. Hence, the total possible pool of respondents in this case is 3,780, rather than 6,180.

26. For this approach, see Prakash and Gugerty (2010).

27. Khan and Petrasek (2009).

28. Pandya, S. S. (2010). Labor Markets and the Demand for Foreign Direct Investment. *International Organization*, 64(03): 389–409.

29. Mutua, M. (2001) and Razack, S. H. (2004). *Dark Threats and White Knights*. Toronto: University of Toronto Press. For an application to Israel, see Mizrachi, N. (2016). Sociology in the Garden: Beyond the Liberal Grammar of Contemporary Sociology. *Israel Studies Review*, 31(1): 36–65.

30. We adapted this question to the peculiarities of each country's educational system. The average number of years of formal education, across all

four samples, was 9.1. Each sample contributes 25 percent of the pooled averages reported here; descriptive statistics also have sampling weights applied, unless the variable was used in constructing the weights.

31. Possible categories: *Rural, Urban.* 30 percent of respondents were rural, 70 percent urban. The Mexico survey was nationally representative, and the Lagos, Mumbai, and Rabat/Casablanca urban surveys included supplementary rural over-samples.

32. Possible responses: *My income allows me to cover expenses and save; My income can just cover expenses, without major difficulties; My income cannot cover expenses, and I have difficulties; My income cannot cover expenses and I have major difficulties.* Across all four samples, 58 percent reported they could not cover monthly expenses, and had either "major" or "some" difficulties. We also collected monetary income measures, but these are notoriously error-prone and result in lower response rates than subjective income measures.

33. Possible responses: *Yes, No.* Across all four samples, 29 percent, on average, reported using the Internet.

34. The average respondent age was 39, and 49 percent were women.

35. The models presented here use standard estimations of standard errors. Results are unchanged if we estimate robust standard errors or use bootstrap estimations of standard errors. In these pooled models, we weight all countries equally. Results are also consistent if we run country-specific models, though not every variable is significant in every country model.

36. Again, we present the full statistical model in Appendix B at the end of the book.

Chapter 3

1. Human rights professionals distinguish between rights listed in the International Covenant on Civil and Political Rights and the International Covenant on Economic, Social and Cultural Rights. Although both appear in the Universal Declaration of Human Rights, the covenants elaborate on each in greater detail. During the Cold War, policymakers and scholars often considered the two in isolation. Since the 1993 United Nations World Conference on Human Rights, however, many practitioners insist that all human rights are indivisible and mutually supporting.

2. For the argument that human rights promote the foreign policy of the United States and its allies, see Chandler, D. (2005). *From Kosovo to Kabul and Beyond: Human Rights and International Intervention.* London: Pluto Press; Hopgood (2013); Laurienti, J. M. (2007). *The U.S. Military and Human Rights Promotion: Lessons from Latin America.* Westport, CT: Praeger Security International; and Peck, J. (2011). *Ideal Illusions: How the US Government Coopted Human Rights.* New York: Metropolitan Books. For human rights as support for other illiberal agendas, see Bob, C. (2012). *The Global Right Wing and the Clash of World Politics.* New York: Oxford University Press; and Perugini and Gordon (2015).

3. For potential links between human rights and a rising global middle class, see Hopgood (2013); Petrasek, David. (2014). "New Powers, New Approaches? Human Rights Diplomacy in the 21st Century." *Sur: International Journal on Human Rights,* 19, available online. For the general connection between the middle class and liberal democracy, see Lipset, S. M. (1994). The Social Requisites of Democracy Revisited. *American Sociological Review,* 59(1): 1–22.

4. Interview 85-Bolivia.

5. Interview 118-Philippines.

6. Pruce, J. R. (2015, June 23). Human Rights Are Revolutionary in Principle—Not Practice. *openGlobalRights/openDemocracy.* London.

7. Interview 62-Cameroon.

8. Interview 38-Pakistan.

9. Interview 57-Yemen.

10. Interview149-Mexico.

11. Montalvo, T. L. (2012, February 9). Los Personajes Polemicos Cercanos a Pena Nieto. *CNN Mexico.*

12. Miliband, R. (1989). Reflections on the Crisis of Communist Regimes. *New Left Review,* I(177): 27–36.

13. Frey, B. (2014, February 2). Doing Orwell Proud: "Human Rights" Slogans in Mexico. *openGlobalRights/openDemocracy.* London.

14. Mondak, J. J., Carmines, E. G., Huckfeldt, R., Mitchell, D. G., and Schraufnagel, S. (2007). Does Familiarity Breed Contempt? The Impact of Information on Mass Attitudes toward Congress. *American Journal of Political Science,* 51(1): 34–48.

15. Englund, H. (2006). *Prisoners of Freedom: Human Rights and the African Poor.* Berkeley: University of California Press.

16. Mutua (2001).

17. We developed this list of phrases based on common definitions discussed in the scholarly literature, but also based on our practitioner interviews; we wanted to directly test the ways that practitioners hoped or feared the public saw "human rights."

18. We unfortunately did not have space in the Mexico version of our survey to ask about "protecting terrorists" or "protecting women's rights."

19. Factor analysis showed a lone positive eigenvalue of 1.27 with factor loadings tightly grouped between .62 and .69; Chronbach's alpha = .73.

20. Zoglin, K. (2009). Morocco's Family Code: Improving Equality for Women. *Human Rights Quarterly*, 31(4): 964–984.

21. Belli, R. F., Traugott, M. W., Young, M., and Mcgonagle, K. A. (2010). Reducing Vote Overreporting in Surveys: Social Desirability, Memory Failure, and Source Monitoring. *Public Opinion Quarterly*, 63(1): 90–108; Crowne, D. P. and Marlowe, D. (1960). A New Scale of Social Desirability Independent of Psychopathology. *Journal of Consulting Psychology*, 24(4): 349–354.

22. WorldPublicOpinion.org. (2008). World Public Opinion and the Universal Declaration of Human Rights. International Affairs. College Park. Retrieved fromhttps://wpo.hkpop.hk/pipa/articles/home_page/resources/20081210/WPO_UDHR_Dec08_rpt.pdf.

23. Koo, J., Cheong, B. E., and Ramirez, F. O. (2015). Who Thinks and Behaves According to Human Rights? Evidence from the Korean National Human Rights Survey. *Korea Observer*, 46(1): 53–87, 67.

24. Gerber, T. P. (2017). Public Opinion on Human Rights in Putin-Era Russia: Continuities, Changes, and Sources of Variation. *Journal of Human Rights*, 16(3): forthcoming.

25. We asked about trust in domestic institutions—the executive, legislature, general population, police, army, domestic banks, religious institutions, businesses, domestic NGOs, and LHROs—and in international institutions, including the United Nations, the dominant regional organization, European Union, multinational corporations,

US government, international NGOs, and international HROs. We omitted some of these in some surveys, and added others, such as Nigeria's anti-corruption office. In Morocco, we were not permitted to ask about the king.

26. Anderson, C. J. and Guillory, C. A. (1997). Political Institutions and Satisfaction with Democracy: A Cross-National Analysis of Consensus and Majoritarian Systems. *The American Political Science Review*, 91(1): 66–81; Canache, D., Mondak, J. J., and Seligson, M. A. (2001). Meaning and Measurement in Cross-National Research on Satisfaction with Democracy. *The Public Opinion Quarterly*, 65(4): 506–528; and Crow, D. (2010). The Party's Over: Citizen Concepts of Democracy and Political Dissatisfaction in Mexico. *Comparative Political Studies*, 43(1): 41–61.

27. Clarke, H. D., Dutt, N., and Kornberg, A. (1993). The Political Economy of Attitudes toward Polity and Society in Western European Democracies. *The Journal of Politics*, 55(04): 998–1021.

28. Cohen, J. E. (2000). "The Polls": The Components of Presidential Favorability. *Presidential Studies Quarterly*, 30(1): 169–177; Gronke, P. and Newman, B. (2003). FDR to Clinton, Mueller to?: A Field Essay on Presidential Approval. *Political Research Quarterly*, 56(4): 501–512; Iyengar, S. (1980). Subjective Political Efficacy as a Measure of Diffuse Support. *The Public Opinion Quarterly*, 44(2): 249–256; Nelson, S. C. (2008). Feeling Thermometers. In *Sage Encyclopedia of Survey Research Methods*. Sage Publications; Wilcox, C., Sigelman, L., and Cook, E. (1989). Some Like It Hot: Individual Differences in Responses to Group Feeling Thermometers. *Public Opinion Quarterly*, 53(2): 246–257.

29. Factor analysis shows that correlations between trust items are positive, with a relatively high Cronbach's alpha (0.86); the trust questions all tap into an underlying construct, "the propensity to trust." The factor analysis supports a one-factor model, indicating that people are either likely to trust across the board, or not.

30. Paired-sample t-tests on each country individually and on the pooled data set reveal statistically significant differences between *Trust in LHROs* and trust in domestic NGOs more generally.

31. For popular sentiments toward the United States and its government, see Blaydes, L. and Linzer, D. A. (2012). Elite Competition, Religiosity, and Anti-Americanism in the Islamic World. *American Political Science Review*, 106(02): 225–243; Chiozza, G. (2009).

Anti-Americanism and the American World Order. Baltimore, MD: Johns Hopkins University Press; Katzenstein, P. J. and Keohane, R. O. (2007). *Anti-Americanisms in World Politics.* Ithaca, NY: Cornell University Press; McPherson, A. (2006). *Anti-Americanism in Latin America and the Caribbean.* New York: Berghan. For sentiments toward multinationals, see Pandya (2010).

32. All differences are statistically significant. However, this descriptive picture does not account for the effects of *Average Trust*, as our later multivariate analysis will do. This illustrates that, though the Morocco sample trusts LHROs the least, they also trust all other institutions less than respondents in other countries. Moroccan respondents, on average, are simply less trusting than the other publics surveyed. It is, thus, important to control for this sample-specific "average trust" in multivariate statistical analyses.

33. The dependent variable in these regressions is *Trust in LHROs* on the 0 (no trust)–1 (most trust) scale. The independent variables are the associations (taken singly), with *Average Trust* as a control. The pooled models include country dummy variables and weight each country equally.

34. We calculated *Human Rights Inclined* using data from the Mexico survey we conducted in 2014, rather than 2012, to match analysis we conduct in Chapter 4 using *Human Rights Inclined*. The *Human Rights Inclined* in the Mexico 2012 data are even higher: 59 percent. We also calculated *Human Rights Inclined* using a more strict definition, in which a respondent needed to trust LHROs above the midpoint *and* strongly associate human rights with *all three* positive definitions. Across the pooled samples, an average of 24 percent of respondents fit this definition.

35. A third possibility, not explored here, is the importance of genetic-psychological traits. See Jost, J. T., Federico, C. M., and Napier, J. L. (2009). Political Ideology: Its Structure, Function, and Elective Affinities. *Annual Review of Psychology*, 60: 307–337.

36. Hurwitz, J. and Peffley, M. (1987). How Are Foreign Policy Attitudes Structured? A Hierarchical Model. *The American Political Science Review*, 81(4): 1099–1120.

37. Kertzer, J. D., Powers, K. E., Rathbun, B. C., and Iyer, R. (2014). Moral Support: How Moral Values Shape Foreign Policy Attitudes. *The Journal of Politics*, 76(3): 825–840.

38. Chiozza (2009); Katzenstein and Keohane (2007); McPherson (2006). For details, see below.

39. Edwards, M. S. (2006). Public Opinion Regarding Economic and Cultural Globalization: Evidence from a Cross-National Survey. *Review of International Political Economy*, 13(4): 587–608.

40. When attitudes are only loosely linked to material interests, opinion leaders can more easily convince people to support positions that go against economic self-interest.

41. This could be viewed as a form of what neo-realists call "soft balancing" in international affairs. For the notion of soft balancing, see Pape, R. A. (2005). Soft Balancing against the United States. *International Security*, 30(1): 7–45.

42. For Chávez, see the Associated Press (2010, December 22). Venezuelan National Assembly Bars Foreign Funding for NGOs. *The Guardian*. Manchester. For Correa, see Carothers and Brechenmacher (2014).

43. For Russia, see Herszenhorn, D. M. and Barry, E. (2012, September 18). Russia Demands US End Support of Democracy Groups. *New York Times*; for Egypt, Hubbard, B. (2013, June 4). Egypt Convicts Workers at Foreign Nonprofit Groups, Including 16 Americans. *New York Times*; for Pakistan, Haider, I. (2014, October 16). Imran Accuses HRCP of Promoting Foreign Agenda. *Dawn:* Islamabad; for Hungary, Donors: Keep Out. (2014, September). *The Economist*; and for India, Aurora, B. V. (2015, September 16). India to Counter Accusations About Its Human Rights Records. *Economic Times*. Delhi; and Najar, N. (2015, April 23). Indian Authorities Put Restrictions on Ford Foundation. *New York Times*.

44. Open letter to HRW executive director Kenneth Roth, dated May 12, 2014, signed by Nobel laureates Adolfo Pérez Esquivel and Mairead Maguire; the former United Nations (UN) Assistant Secretary General, Hans von Sponeck; current UN Special Rapporteur on Human Rights in the Palestinian Territories, Richard Falk; and others, available online at *Nobel Peace Laureates to Human Rights Watch: Close Your Revolving Door to U.S. Government.* For an application to HRW's work on Latin America, see Bhatt, K. (2013). The Hypocrisy of Human Rights Watch. *NACLA Report on the Americas*, 46(4): 55–58.

45. For earlier allegations that HRW's Latin American reporting is overly close to the position of "official Washington," see Naiman, R. (2009, September 21). Latin American Scholars Urge Human Rights Watch to Speak Up on Honduras Coup. *Huffington Post.*

46. For HRW's response, see Roth, Kenneth. Letter to Nobel Laureates, undated. Retrieved from http://www.hrw.org/node/126019. For an acknowledgment of the problem of Western imposition, see Levine, I. (2014, April 1). Internationalizing the Human Rights Movement: Creating a North-South Bridge? *openGlobalRights/openDemocracy.* London.

47. Hopgood (2013), 99–102.

48. Chandler (2005); Chomsky, N. (2011). *The Umbrella of US Power: The Universal Declaration of Human Rights and the Contradictions of US Policy.* New York: Seven Stories Press; Peck (2011); and Rajagopal, Balakrishnan (2006). Counter-Hegemonic International Law: Rethinking Rights and Development as a Third World Strategy. *Third World Quarterly,* 27(5): 767–783.

49. Hafner-Burton (2013), 138.

50. Carothers, T. and Ottaway, M. (2000). The Burgeoning World of Civil Society Aid. In M. Ottawa and T. Carothers (Eds.), *Funding Virtue: Civil Society Aid and Democracy Promotion.* Washington, DC: Carnegie Endowment for International Peace; Carothers, T. (2009). *Revitalizing U.S. Democracy Assistance: The Challenge of USAID.* Washington DC: Carnegie Endowment for International Peace.

51. Website of the State Department's *Bureau of Democracy, Human Rights and Labor.* Retrieved from http://www.state.gov/j/drl/, last accessed March 7, 2016.

52. In most cases (except for half the Mexico sample, who were asked the question on the 7-point scale), this criterion includes those who said they trust the US government "not at all" or "a little."

53. The notion of hegemonic versus counter-hegemonic human rights discourse is explored in Rajagopal (2006) and Santos, Boaventura de Sousa, and Cesar A. Rodriguez-Garavito. (2006). Law, Politics, and the Subaltern in Counter-Hegemonic Globalization. In Boaventura de Sousa Santos and Cesar A. Rodriguez-Garavito (Eds.), *Law and Globalization from Below: Towards a Cosmopolitan Legality,* 1–26. New York: Cambridge University Press.

54. For general discussion see Brody, R., Narula, S., Ganesan, A., Stork, J., Buttigieg, J., Swanson, J., and Gordon, N. (2001). Human Rights and Global Capitalism: A Roundtable Discussion with Human Rights Watch. *Rethinking Marxism*, 13(2): 52–71. For discussion of liberation theology, Marxism, and human rights, see Engler, M. (2000). Toward the "Rights of the Poor": Human Rights in Liberation Theology. *Journal of Religious Ethics*, 28(3): 339–365. For the intersections between leftist and human rights thought in Europe, see Hopgood (2006) and Moyn (2010). For broader discussion of the link between NGOs and global capitalism, see Petras, J. (1999). NGOs: In the Service of Imperialism. *Journal of Contemporary Asia*, 29(4): 429–440.

55. Cartalucci, T. (2012). Soros Leverages "Human Rights" for Personal Gain, as Does His Global NGO Empire. Retrieved from http://landdestroyer.blogspot.com/2012/03/surpise-soros-is-convicted-criminal.html.

56. N.A. (2014, December). NGOs—Do They Help? *New Internationalist*. Retrieved from http://newint.org/features/2014/12/01/ngos-keynote/.

57. The question is: "*Please tell me how much trust you would place in the following institutions, groups or persons ... multinational corporations.*" Possible responses include "a lot," "some," "a little," "none," and "don't know."

58. Norris, P. (2011). *Democratic Deficit: Critical Citizens Revisited.* New York: Cambridge University Press.

59. Pew Research Center. (2014). Crime and Corruption Top Problems in Emerging and Developing Countries. Retrieved from http://www.pewglobal.org/2014/11/06/crime-and-corruption-top-problems-in-emerging-and-developing-countries/.

60. See Nader, L. (2014). Solid Organizations in a Liquid World. *Sur: International Journal on Human Rights*, 11(20): 483–490.

61. According to Cronbach Alpha tests, these three variables are modestly related (0.57). When we run each variable separately but simultaneously in the multivariate regressions, each one is individually significant, in the same direction. Hence, we combine all three here into the index, *Mistrust in Domestic Political Authorities*.

62. We also ran logistic regression models using the same set of explanatory variables, but predicting the dichotomous variable *Human Rights*

Inclined, rather than *Trust in LHROs*. The findings between these two sets of models are generally consistent, particularly in showing the positive relationship between mistrust in powerful actors and positive feelings toward human rights (whether operationalized as *Trust in LHROs* or *Human Rights Inclined*).

63. The pooled model weights each of the four country samples equally. These models predict *Trust in LHROs* on a 0 to 1 scale. We report results of an ordinary least squares (OLS) regression, but these results are consistent when we use ordinal logistic regression. To test our findings more stringently, we also calculated robust standard errors and used bootstrap estimation of standard errors; results are consistent.

64. In the *Contact Human Rights* index, "maximum contact" (1 on the 0–1 scale) would be a respondent who hears "human rights" daily or frequently, has met a human rights worker, can name a specific human rights organization in his or her country, and has participated in the activities of a human rights organization.

65. *Average Trust* is the mean of trust scores given by each respondent to the 15 or more domestic and international institutions we asked about.

66. For the most recent data on public attitudes toward the United States worldwide, see either Globescan or the Pew Global Attitudes Project. For theoretical approaches to anti-Americanisms, see Katzenstein and Keohane (2007); for global trends and statistical analysis, Chiozza (2009); for Latin America, Baker, A. and Cupery, D. (2013). Anti-Americanism in Latin America: Economic Exchange, Foreign Policy Legacies, and Mass Attitudes toward the Colossus of the North. *Latin American Research Review*, 48(2): 106–130; and for the Middle East, Blaydes and Linzer (2012).

67. Anti-Americanism may be best conceived as a family of distinct sub-perspectives, including variants such as "liberal anti-Americanism," which takes America to task for not living up to its own ideals; "social anti-Americanism," which dislikes the country's tolerance and production of economic injustices; "sovereign-nationalist" anti-Americanism, which resents perceived US threats to their country's political, economic and cultural autonomy; and "radical anti-Americanism," which views the very essence of the United States, as currently configured, as a threat to global security and socioeconomic

justice. See Katzenstein and Keohane (2007), 28–34. Our data do not allow us to carefully distinguish among these four variants.

68. Median favorability rating for the United States, based on representative samples from 39 countries. Pew Research Center (2015). Global Publics Back U.S. on Fighting ISIS, but Are Critical of Post-9/11 Torture. Retrieved from http://www.pewglobal.org/2015/06/23/global-publics-back-u-s-on-fighting-isis-but-are-critical-of-post-911-torture/.

69. O'Neil, S. K. (2013). *Two Nations, Indivisible.* New York: Oxford University Press. Quotation from p. 165.

70. International Crisis Group. (2013). *Peña Nieto's Challenge: Criminal Cartels and Rule of Law in Mexico.* Brussells: International Crisis Group, 19.

71. Mohan, C. R. (2006). India and the Balance of Power. *Foreign Affairs* (July/August), 1–10.

72. Chacko, P. (2014). A New "Special Relationship"?: Power Transitions, Ontological Security, and India-US Relations. *International Studies Perspectives*, 15(3): 329–346; Kapur, D. (2009). Public Opinion and Indian Foreign Policy. *India Review*, 8(3): 286–305; Kapur, S. P. and Ganguly, S. (2007). The Transformation of U.S.-India Relations: An Explanation for the Rapprochement and Prospects for the Future. *Asian Survey*, 47(4): 642–656.

73. Zoubir, Y. H. and Benabdallah-Gambier, K. (2005). The United States and the North African Imbroglio: Balancing Interests in Algeria, Morocco, and the Western Sahara. *Mediterranean Politics*, 10(2): 181–202.

74. For classic treatments of globalization's dark side, see Rodrik, D. (1997). *Has Globalization Gone Too Far.* Washington DC: Pearson Institute for International Economics, and Stiglitz, J. E. (2003). *Globalization and Its Discontents.* New York: Norton.

75. For an overview of the various antiglobalization movements, see Green, D. and Griffith, M. (2002), Globalization and Its Discontents. *International Affairs*, 78(1): 49–68. For concerns over foreign direct investment, see Pandya (2010). For accountability in international financial institutions, see Woods, N. (2001). Making the IMF and the World Bank More Accountable. *International Affairs*, 77(1): 83–100. Properly speaking, this movement is not opposed to globalization per

se, as many of its leaders are resolutely transnational; the main concern is with globalization's current style.

76. Pew Research Center. (2014, September 16). Faith and Skepticism about Trade, Foreign Investment. Retrieved from http://www.pewglobal.org/2014/09/16/faith-and-skepticism-about-trade-foreign-investment/.

77. Edwards (2006).

78. Katzenstein and Keohane (2007) also discuss "radical anti-Americanism," which combines elements of both.

79. Rajagopal (2006); Santos and Rodríguez Garavito (2006).

80. Paul Nelson and Elizabeth Dorsey call this the "New Rights Advocacy," and differentiate it from the "older" rights advocacy for civil and political rights. The new rights advocacy is an anti-capitalist, antiglobalization, and anti-privatization struggle for economic and social rights by Southern activists, best exemplified by struggles for public control over water resources and life-saving drugs. The older advocacy, by contrast, relies more heavily on support from Northern rights advocates and on diplomatic and economic pressure from Western capitals. Nelson, P. and Dorsey, E. (2007). New Rights Advocacy in a Global Public Domain. *European Journal of International Relations*, 13(2): 187–216.

Chapter 4

1. Our findings dovetail with those of two others conducted in Israel and Nigeria: Berkovitch and Gordon (2008) and Okafor (2006).

2. Dupuy, Ron and Prakash (2016).

3. Baoumi, H. (2016, June 27). Local Funding Is Not Always the Answer. *openGlobalRights/openDemocracy*. London.

4. Amnesty raises most of its money through individual membership dues in the United States, Canada, Europe, and Australia. Human Rights Watch raises more funds from wealthy individuals in those countries, as well as from foundations in the global North. Neither raises funds in the global South, and neither accepts government money.

5. For the 60-country sample, we counted responses only from practitioners working in local NGOs, excluding those working for government agencies or international organizations.

6. This 2016 study involved 34 in-person interviews with LHRO leaders in Mexico City.

7. Dupuy, Ron and Prakash (2015).

8. Percentage of persons aged 15 or older who told Gallup pollsters they had donated money to "a charity" in the last 30 days. Charities Aid Foundation. (2014). *World Giving Index 2014: A Global View of Giving Trends*. London, 34. We do not know how many, if any, donated to a formally and legally constituted "NGO," as Gallup did not ask the question in this way.

9. According to five-year averages reported in the World Giving Index 2014, of the 15 countries that say their index score rose at least 5 percent above their five-year average, only one was a high-income country. Retrieved from https://www.cafonline.org/docs/default-source/about-us-publications/worldgivingindex2012web.pdf, last accessed July 31, 2016.

10. Human Rights Watch. (1995). *Human Rights in Morocco*. New York; Human Rights Watch. (2013). *"Just Sign Here": Unfair Trials Based on Confessions to the Police in Morocco*. New York.

11. Najar (2015).

12. Jalali, R. (2008). International Funding of NGOs in India: Bringing the State Back In. *VOLUNTAS: International Journal of Voluntary and Nonprofit Organizations*, 19(2): 161–188.

13. Interview with key informant in Lagos, Nigeria, November 2014.

14. Interview with key informant in Lagos, Nigeria, November 2014.

15. See Chapter 3 for the definition of *Human Rights Inclined*.

16. This is a replication of a *World Values Survey* question. Response options were: *"There is no respect at all for individual rights," "there is not much respect," "there is some respect,"* and *"there is a lot of respect."* In Mexico, we asked this question in a 2014 follow-up survey, rather than in the original 2012 poll.

17. Unfortunately, we did not ask respondents to rank human rights problems in comparison to other social, political, or economic problems in their country. This would have provided a stronger test.

18. See the World Bank's *World Development Indicators*' GNI per capita based on purchasing power parity (PPP), available here: The World Bank. *GNI Per Capita, PPP (current international $)*. Retrieved

from http://data.worldbank.org/indicator/NY.GNP.PCAP.PP.CD, last accessed on March 7, 2016. Considering their non-PPP adjusted GDP per capita, both India and Nigeria are just over the World Bank's "low income economy" line.

19. $6,670 for Morocco compared to $5,000 for India and $5,130 for Nigeria. All figures from 2012, available here: http://data.worldbank. org/indicator/NY.GNP.PCAP.PP.CD, last accessed March 7, 2016.

20. Mexico's PPP-adjusted GNI per capita for 2012 was $15,960, as of August 11, 2015.

21. We tested a simple correlation for the 60-country sample practitioners, and also ran regressions on the entire sample of 263 practitioners, controlling for a wide range of factors. In no case was per capita country income significantly related to practitioners' estimate of how many LHROs in their country relied on foreign aid.

22. Themudo, N. S. (2013). *Nonprofits in Crisis: Economic Development, Risk, and the Philanthropic Kuznets Curve.* Bloomington: Indiana University Press, argues for a U-shaped relationship between per capita income and philanthropy.

23. All data cited here are from the 2013 full report (which cites 2012 data), pp. 33–34. The Charities Aid Foundation reports are available online at: *World Giving Index 2014-donating money.* Retrieved from https://www.cafonline.org/about-us/publications/2014-publications/world-giving-index-2014/donating-money.aspx.

24. In 2010, the Charities Aid Foundation (CAF) report said Gallup's Morocco surveys revealed that 72 percent of polled adults had donated money to "an organization," including religious institutions, in the previous 30 days. From 2011 onward, CAF says Gallup asked respondents if they had donated to "a charity," rather than to "an organization." It is not clear from either question wording if *zakat* is or is not included.

25. Pew Center. (2012). The World's Muslims: Unity and Diversity. Retrieved from www.pewforum.org/2012/08/09/the-worlds-musl.

26. The other two options were "*My income cannot cover expenses, and I have difficulties*" and "*My income cannot cover expenses, and I have major difficulties.*"

27. Egan, B. (2001). *The Widow's Might: How Charities Depend on the Poor.* London: Social Market Foundation; Piff, P. K., Kraus, M. W., Côté,

S., Cheng, B. H., and Keltner, D. (2010). Having Less, Giving More: The Influence of Social Class on Prosocial Behavior. *Journal of Personality and Social Psychology*, 99(5): 771–784.

28. Based on Charities Aid Foundation reporting of Gallup polls.

29. The World Bank does not offer PPP-adjusted per capita GNI figures for Myanmar; Thailand's 2013 PPP-adjusted per capita GNI was $13,340.

30. As the Mexican polling firm asked about donating to HROs only of people who had reported *participating* in HROs, we do not know the true percentage of either all respondents or of *High Probability Rights Donors* who reported donating in Mexico. Combining the available data with reasoned assumptions, we estimate that an upper bound of 11 percent of all respondents donate, and that an upper bound of 12 percent of *High Probability Donors* actually donate. Even these figures, which are almost certainly too generous, show low donation rates. Many Mexicans who *could* be giving are not.

31. Ilchman, W. F., Katz, S. N., and Queen, E. L. (1998). *Philanthropy in the World's Traditions*. Bloomington: Indiana University Press.

32. Bornstein (2009); Dulany, P. and Winder, D. (2001). *The Status of and Trends in Private Philanthropy in the Southern Hemisphere*. New York: Synergos Institute.

33. Pew Center (2012).

34. Telushkin, J. (2008). *Jewish Literacy*. New York: William and Morrow.

35. Dulany and Winder (2001).

36. Asia Pacific Philanthropy Consortium. (2002). *Investing in Ourselves: Giving and Fund Raising in Asia*. Manila: Asian Development Bank.

37. Challand, B. (2008). A Nahda of Charitable Organizations? Health Service Provision and the Politics of Aid in Palestine. *International Journal of Middle East Studies*, 40(2): 227–247

38. 240-Nigeria.

39. Beckerlegge, G. (1990). Human Rights in the Ramakrishna Math and Mission: "For Liberation and the Good of the World." *Religion*, 20(2): 119–137.

40. Bornstein, Erica. (2009). "The Impulse of Philanthropy." *Cultural Anthropology* 24(4): 622–651; Juergensmeyer, M. and McMahon, D. M. (1998). Hindu Philanthropy and Civil Society. In Ilchman, W. F., Katz, S. N., and Queen, E. L. (Eds.), *Philanthropy in the World's Traditions*, 263–278. Bloomington: Indiana University Press.

41. Candland, C. (2000). Faith as Social Capital: Religion and Community Development in Southern Asia. *Policy Sciences*, 33: 355–374; Kozlowsky, G. C. (1998). Religious Authority, Reform, and Philanthropy in the Contemporary Muslim World. In Ilchman, Katz, and Queen (1998).

42. Lawrence, S. and Dobson, C. (2013). *Advancing Human Rights: The State of Global Foundation Grantmaking.* New York: The Foundation Center and The International Human Rights Funders Group.

43. Hopgood, S. (2006). *Keepers of the Flame: Understanding Amnesty International.* Ithaca, NY: Cornell University Press.

44. Cognizant of this North-South divergence, human rights-oriented foundations in the global North are increasingly keen to encourage Southern human rights philanthropy.

45. Easterly, W. R. (2006). *The White Man's Burden: Why the West's Efforts to Aid the Rest Have Done So Much Ill and So Little Good.* New York: Penguin Press. Swidler, A. and Watkins, S. C. (2009). "Teach a Man to Fish": The Sustainability Doctrine and Its Social Consequences. *World Development*, 37(7): 1182–1196; Swiss, L. (2011). Security Sector Reform and Development Assistance: Explaining the Diffusion of Policy Priorities among Donor Agencies. *Qualitative Sociology*, 34(2): 371–393.

46. Easterly, W. (2007). The Ideology of Development. *Foreign Policy*, 31–35.

47. Sano, H. O. (2000). Development and Human Rights: The Necessary, but Partial Integration of Human Rights and Development. *Human Rights Quarterly*, 22(3): 734–752.

48. The Organization for Economic Cooperation and Development (OECD) monitors the flow of development assistance from its members to less developed countries and classifies these as Overseas Development Assistance (ODA).

49. Uvin (1998).

50. HRBA Portal. (n.d.) *The Human Rights Based Approach to Development Cooperation: Towards a Common Understanding among UN Agencies.* Retrieved from http://hrbaportal.org/the-human-rights-based-approach-to-development-cooperation-towards-a-common-understanding-among-un-agencies, last accessed January 28, 2017.

51. Organization for Economic Cooperation and Development (2015, August 4). *Development Aid Stable in 2014.* Retrieved from http://www.oecd.org/dac/stats/development-aid-stable-in-2014-but-flows-to-poorest-countries-still-falling.htm.

52. Atwood, B. (2013, November 11). Human Rights, Democracy and Development: Partners at Last. *openGlobalRights/openDemocracy.* London.

53. Pierson, P. (2000). Increasing Returns, Path Dependence, and the Study of Politics. *American Political Science Review,* 94(2): 251–267.

54. Henderson, S. L. (2002). Selling Civil Society: Western Aid and the Nongovernmental Organization Sector in Russia. *Comparative Political Studies,* 35(2): 139–167.

55. In Rabat and Casablanca, these questions about donations likely do not account for *zakat,* the practice of religious tithing. According to Pew 2012 data, 92 percent of Moroccans reported giving *zakat.* According to the Charities Aid Foundation from 2010, 72 percent of Moroccans donated "to an organization," which likely included *zakat*-eligible entities.

56. As noted above, the Mexican survey company asked about donations only of respondents who first reported having participated in the activities of that organization. In Mexico, India, and Morocco, the survey did not ask specifically about religious tithing, and did not distinguish between voluntary and compulsory donations. Our Nigerian survey was the most comprehensive on this question, asking about a broader array of organizations, asking specifically about religious tithing, and differentiating between voluntary and compulsory donations.

57. In Mexico, 37 percent of those who reported participating in HRO activities also reported having given money to HROs. As 3.8 percent claimed to have participated in an HRO, the 37 percent who said they donated (given they had participated) represents 1.4 percent of the total sample (.038 × .37 = .014). Of course, the true donation rate may

be somewhat higher, as people may donate to LHROs even though they have not participated in their activities. We calculate that, at most, 11 percent could have donated to LHROs.

58. Interview 121-India.

59. Interview 139-Mexico.

60. Interview 215-Morocco.

61. In 2014, the GNI per capital based on purchasing power parity (PPP) was $5,680 in Nigeria ($473/month) and $55,860 in the United States ($4,655/month), in current international dollars. Data are from the World Bank, International Comparison Program database, using World Development Indicators. Available here: The World Bank. *Explore. Create. Share: Development Data.* Retrieved from http://databank.worldbank.org/data/, last accessed March 7, 2016.

62. As a way to test if a hypothetical "willingness to give" corresponds to actual patterns of behavior, we used simple logistic regression to analyze the relationship between willingness to give and actual donations to HROs. We found no statistically significant relationship when comparing any of the three lower hypothetical donation amounts to actual donations. However, there is a statistically significant and positive relationship between being willing to give 5,000 naira (the largest amount) and actual HRO donations. Thus, asking about this high level of donation seems to be a somewhat reliable test of a respondent's actual proclivity to donate; we can support the conclusion that the 51 percent of respondents who said yes to this hypothetical high level of donation might actually make a donation, if an HRO solicited their contribution.

63. We fielded this survey in Mexico City in July 2016 with funding from the Open Society Foundations. Our goal was to explore the potential for local fundraising for Mexican rights groups. The survey was supervised by CIDE, and carried out by the survey company, DATA-OPM, which we used for our 2012 and 2014 *Human Rights Perceptions Polls*.

64. Shetty, S. (2015, January 20). Moving Amnesty Closer to the Ground Is Necessary, Not Simple. *openGlobalRights/openDemocracy*. London.

65. Discussions with Salil Shetty, Amnesty Secretary General, in Marrakech, Morocco, April 1–5, 2014.

66. Campolina, A. (2015, April 2). Decentralizing Can Make Global Human Rights Groups Stronger. *OpenGlobalRights/openDemocracy*: London.

67. Barnett, M. (2011). *Empire of Humanity*. Ithaca, NY: Cornell University Press.

68. Muguongo, W. (2015, January 19). To Truly Internationalize Human Rights, Funding Must Make Sense. *openGlobalRights/openDemocracy*. London.

69. Interview 2-Nigeria.

70. Interview 105-Indonesia.

71. Interview 92-Bangladesh.

72. Interview 191-India.

73. Interview 130-Mexico.

74. Interview 192-Morocco.

75. These were the findings of a logistic regression of willingness to donate (N=876). We found positive and statistically significant associations with *Human Rights Inclined, Contact Human Rights, Subjective Income, Age*, and *Gender* (male). There was, of course, a negative relationship with the level of hypothetical donation requested. We also controlled for *Education, Residence* (rural/urban), and Web use, all of which were statistically insignificant.

76. Maximum contact are those who hear "human rights" daily or frequently, have met a human rights worker, can name a specific HRO, *and* have participated in the activities of an HRO.

77. For the concept of an NGO "funding scramble," see Cooley and Ron (2002).

Chapter 5

1. *The Economist*. (2014, September 4). Religion and Human Rights: Awkward, but Necessary, Bedfellows. London.

2. The term is Karl Marx's, but his views on religion were more complex, as described in Raines, J. C. (2002). *Marx on Religion*. Philadelphia: Temple University Press.

3. Kirmani, N. (2014, April 16). Religion as a Human Rights Liability. *openGlobalRights/openDemocracy*. London.

4. Ezeakile, G. (2014, August 14). Whose Faith Wins? Keeping Religion out of the Law. *openGlobalRights/openDemocracy*. London.

5. Estevez, A. (2014, September 11). Myth and Reality: The Catholic Church and Human Rights in Latin America. *openGlobalRights/openDemocracy*. London.

6. El Haitami, M., Golden, S., and Ron, J. (2015, July 7). Partners in Prayer: Women's Rights and Religion in Morocco. *openGlobalRights/openDemocracy*. London.

7. Inglehart, R. and Norris, P. (2003). The True Clash of Civilizations. *Foreign Policy*, 135 (March–April): 62–70.

8. For general works linking religion and political violence, see Hassner, R. E. (2013). *War on Sacred Grounds*. Ithaca, NY: Cornell University Press; and Juergensmeyer, M. (2003). *Terror in the Mind of God: The Global Rise of Religious Violence*. Berkeley: University of California Press.

9. Prakash, C. (2014, April 30). The Politicization of Hindu Faith in India. *openGlobalRights/openDemocracy*. London.

10. Ezeakile (2014).

11. Souad Mekhenet and Steven Erlanger (2011, April 29). Fatal Bomb in Morocco Shows Signs of al Qaeda. *New York Times*.

12. Dawkins, R. (2006). *The God Delusion*. London: Bantam Press; Harris, S. (2004). *The End of Faith: Religion, Terror, and the Future of Reason*. New York: Norton.

13. Cox, L. (2014, April 14). Human Rights Must Get Religion. *openGlobalRights/openDemocracy*. London.

14. Snyder, J. (2014, April 14). On a Wing and a Prayer: Can Religion Revive the Rights Movement? *openGlobalRights/openDemocracy*. London.

15. Bush, E. L. (2007). Measuring Religion in Global Civil Society. *Social Forces*, 85(4): 1645–1665.

16. Hertzke, A. D. (2006). *Freeing God's Children: The Unlikely Alliance for Global Human Rights*. Lanham, MD: Rowman and Littlefield; Livezey, L. W. (1989). US Religious Organizations and the International Human Rights Movement. *Human Rights Quarterly*, 11(1): 14–81; Morris, A. D. (1986). *Origins of the Black Civil Rights Movement*. New York: Free Press; Wood, R. L. and Fulton, B. R. (2015). *A Shared Future: Faith-Based Organizing for Racial Equity and Ethical Democracy*. Chicago: University

of Chicago Press; Wood, R. L. (2002). *Faith in Action.* Chicago: Chicago University Press.

17. For discussion of liberation theology as a broad social movement, see Smith, C. (1991). *The Emergence of Liberation Theology: Radical Religion and Social Movements.* Chicago: University of Chicago Press. Liberation theology and the human rights movement initially differed, but ultimately drew closer, as discussed in Aldunate, J. (1994). Human Rights as the Rights of the Poor: The Perspective from Liberation Theology. *Journal of Moral Education,* 23(3): 297–303 and Engler, M. (2000). Toward the "Rights of the Poor": Human Rights in Liberation Theology. *Journal of Religious Ethics,* 28(3): 339–365.

18. Beckerlegge (1990), 119–137; Khare, R. S. (1998). The Issue of "Right to Food" among the Hindus. *Contributions to Indian Sociology,* 32(2): 253–278; Sharma, A. (2003). *Hinduism and Human Rights: A Conceptual Approach.* Oxford: Oxford University Press; Sharma, A. (2014, April 15). The Rights in Hinduism. *openGlobalRights/openDemocracy.* London.

19. Obadere, E. (2012). A Sacred Duty to Resist Tyranny? Rethinking the Role of the Catholic Church in Nigeria's Struggle for Democracy. *Journal of Church and State,* 55(1): 92–112.

20. Salime, Z. (2011). *Between Feminism and Islam: Human Rights and Sharia Law in Morocco.* Minneapolis: University of Minnesota Press.

21. Aslan, R. (2014, October 8). Bill Maher Isn't the Only One Who Misunderstands Religion. *New York Times.*

22. For a small sample of recent works disaggregating different elements of religiosity, see González, A. L. (2011). Measuring Religiosity in a Majority Muslim Context: Gender, Religious Salience, and Religious Experience among Kuwaiti College Students—A Research Note. *Journal for the Scientific Study of Religion,* 50(2): 339–350; Lima, C. and Putnam, R. D. (2010). Religion, Social Networks, and Life Satisfaction. *American Sociological Review,* 75(6): 914–933; Mockabee, S. T., Monson, J. Q., and Grant, J. T. (2001). Measuring Religious Commitment among Catholics and Protestants: A New Approach. *Journal for the Scientific Study of Religion,* 40(4): 675–690.

23. We calculate these percentages by subtracting *Trust in Local Human Rights Organizations* from *Trust in Religious Institutions,* and dividing the result by *Trust in Local Human Rights Organizations:*

$$\frac{\text{TrustReligInst} - \text{TrustLHRO}}{\text{TrustLHRO}}$$

All other percentages in the text are calculated similarly, as relative to a baseline.

24. On average, respondents *most* trusted "religious institutions" in Mexico and Lagos; *second most* trusted (after "the army") in Morocco; and *third most* trusted (after "banks" and "the army") in Mumbai.

25. To estimate *Personal Religious Importance*, we asked, "How important is religion in your daily life?" The scale was from 0 ("not important at all") to 10 ("extremely important").

26. To estimate *Prayer Frequency*, we asked, "Outside of attending religious services, how often do you pray? Several times a day, once a day, a few times a week, once a week, a few times a month, seldom, or never?" Given space constraints, we did not ask this question in Mexico.

27. To estimate *Religious Attendance Frequency*, we asked, "On average, how often do you attend a religious place of worship such as a temple, mosque, or church? More than once a week, once a week, once or twice a month, a few times a year, seldom, or never?" We were not able to ask this question in Mexico, but did ask about *Religious Participation:* "Could you tell me if you have participated in the activities of any of the following organizations . . . [religious organizations/associations]?"

28. This measure is not as precise as we would like, with wide variation in responses suggesting that respondents were thinking of different types of "participation" or "religious organizations" across countries. We discuss this in the text later in the chapter.

29. To estimate *Donation to Religious Organizations*, as discussed in Chapter 4, we asked, "Have you ever donated money to any of the organizations . . . [religious organizations/associations]?"

30. The practitioners based in Lagos were a notable exception, as 90 percent told us they were "practicing" members of their faith, closely mirroring the general Nigerian population's levels of personal religiosity. This may explain why the Lagos practitioners were more willing than others to collaborate with religious institutions.

31. We realize that these measures are not strictly comparable. Therefore, we choose a high threshold, 8 or above on the 0–10 scale, to define members of the general public as "highly religious." Under a less rigorous standard (6 or above), the differences between practitioners and the general public are even starker.

32. We were interested in any option respondents might mention—asking an open-ended, unstructured question—but some respondents asked for examples of what we meant. In those cases, we proposed a variety of examples, including development organizations, mosques, churches, temples, unions, government agencies, or political parties. If respondents pressed for further clarification, we explained, "Think of it this way: if someone wanted to bring a large number of people out into the streets for a rally of some kind, would other groups be more successful at this than human rights groups?"

33. Interview 10-Burkina Faso.

34. Mexico interviews: 129, 132, 133, 135, 136, 137, 138, 140, 141, 143, 146, 148, 153, 154, 155, 156, 161, 221, 223, 224, 226, 228, 229, 233.

35. Mexico interviews: 129, 132, 133, 137, 138, 149, 153, 154, 156, 157, 224, 229.

36. Interview 185-Morocco.

37. Interview 188-Morocco.

38. Interview 210-Morocco.

39. Interview 167-Mumbai.

40. Popkin, S. L. (1979). *The Rational Peasant: The Political Economy of Rural Society in Vietnam*. Berkeley: University of California Press.

41. Levitt, M. (2007). *Hamas: Politics, Charity, and Terrorism in the Service of Jihad*. New Haven, CT: Yale University Press; Tamimi, A. (2011). *Hamas: A History from Within*. Northampton: Olive Branch Press.

42. Prakash and Gugerty (2011).

43. Material incentives are not the only way to overcome the collective action problem, of course. Governments and other authorities can compel contributions by law, fiat, and force, such as mandatory conscription or taxation. Nongovernmental actors can threaten non-contributors with "negative incentives," such as physical harm; increase each contributor's sense of relative efficacy, including by creating smaller "primary groups" of contributors; engage in ideological conversion and persuasion; or can persuade significant others, such as community leaders, to reward contributors with greater respect, prestige, and social recognition.

44. Kindornay, Ron, and Carpenter (2012).

45. Interview 118-Phillipines.

46. Interview 60-Ecuador.

47. Interview 64-The Gambia.

48. Interview 76-Lebanon.

49. Ellis, S. and Haar, G. (2004). *Worlds of Power: Religious Thought and Political Practice in Africa*. New York: Oxford University Press.

50. Interview 215-Morocco.

51. Lamwaka, B. (2014, October 7). Preaching for Human Rights. *openGlobalRights/openDemocracy*. London.

52. Interview 196-India.

53. Interview 163-India.

54. Interview 132-Mexico.

55. Interview 137-Mexico.

56. Interview 235-Nigeria.

57. Interview 49-Kenya.

58. Interview 107-Kenya.

59. Interview 48-Senegal.

60. Arrayed on a 0–1 scale, with 1 being most trust.

61. Arrayed on a 0–10 scale, with 10 being most personally religious.

62. Arrayed on a 0–10 scale, with 10 being most socially religious.

63. We use *Religious Identity* and *Trust in Religious Institutions* in all models, but vary other variables because we asked slightly different questions across countries. In Mexico, for example, we did not ask about *Prayer Frequency* or *Religious Attendance Frequency*, so our regressions employ *Personal Religious Importance* instead of the *Personal Religiosity Index,* and *Religious Participation* rather than the *Social Religiosity Index.* In Morocco, we use *Prayer Frequency* rather than the *Personal Religiosity Index*, because there was so little variation in *Personal Religious Importance,* and use *Religious Attendance Frequency* rather than the *Social Religiosity Index* because of little variation in *Religious Participation*. In Mumbai and Lagos, we use *Personal Religious Importance,* not *Prayer Frequency*.

64. Mann, M. (2012). *The Sources of Social Power, Volume 1.* New York: Cambridge University Press.

65. Scott, J. C. (1985). *Weapons of the Weak: Everyday Forms of Peasant Resistance*. New Haven, CT: Yale University Press.

66. Casanova, J. (1996). Global Catholicism and the Politics of Civil Society. *Sociological Inquiry*, 66(3): 356–373; Dipboye, C. C. (1982). The Roman Catholic Church and the Political Struggle for Human Rights in Latin America, 1968–1980. *Journal of Church and State*, 24(3): 497–524; Gill, A. (1998). *Rendering unto Caesar: The Catholic Church and the State in Latin America*. Chicago: University of Chicago Press; Huntington, S. P. (1991). *The Third Wave: Democratization in the Late Twentieth Century*. Norman: University of Oklahoma Press; Klaiber, J. (2009). The Catholic Church, Moral Education and Citizenship in Latin America. *Journal of Moral Education*, 38(4): 407–420; Mantilla, L. F. (2010). Mobilizing Religion for Democracy: Explaining Catholic Church Support for Democratization in South America. *Politics and Religion*, 3(03): 553–579; Philpott, D. (2007). Explaining the Political Ambivalence of Religion. *American Political Science Review*, 101(03): 505–525; Trejo, G. (2009). Religious Competition and Ethnic Mobilization in Latin America: Why the Catholic Church Promotes Indigenous Movements in Mexico. *American Political Science Review*, 103(3): 323–342.

67. Estevez (2014); Gill (1998); Green, E. (2013, November). The Vatican's Journey from Anti-Communism to Anti-Capitalism. *The Atlantic*; Smith, B. T. (2012). *The Roots of Conservatism in Mexico*: Albuquerque: University of New Mexico Press; Weaver, M. J. and Appleby, S. R. (1995). *Being Right: Conservative Catholics in America*. Bloomington: Indiana University Press.

68. Controls for this pooled model include *Personal Religiosity; Social Religiosity; Trust in Religious Institutions; Trust in Local Human Rights Organizations; Human Rights Contact*; socioeconomic factors; political preference and voting; age, gender, and country.

69. In the pooled model, Catholics scored 4 percent more highly on the positive index than non-Catholic Christians, and 12 percent higher than Hindus. Again, the formula for calculating this is:

$$\frac{\text{PositiveIndex}_{\text{Catholic}} - \text{PositiveIndex}_{\text{Non-Catholic Christian}}}{\text{PositiveIndex}_{\text{Non-Catholic Christian}}}$$

Catholics do not score higher than Muslims.

70. Catholics scored 14 percent less on this association than Muslims, 13 percent less than Hindus, and 12 percent less than non-Catholic Christians.

71. In country-specific models, we discover a clear Mexico-specific effect. Controlling for the usual factors, Mexican Catholics perceived human rights as "promoting foreign values and interests" 11 percent less than Mexican non-Catholics. See below for discussion.

72. Huntington, S. P. (1993). *The Clash of Civilizations? Foreign Affairs* (Summer): 22–49, 40–41. In general, arguments of this nature suggest that liberal democracy and human rights are specifically Western, rather than universal. For similar arguments about non-Islamic, non-Western civilizations, see Jacques, M. (2009). *When China Rules the World: The End of the Western World and the Birth of a New Global Order.* New York: Penguin; and Kupchan, C. (2013). *No One's World: The West, the Rising Rest, and the Coming Global Turn.* New York: Oxford University Press.

73. Dwyer, K. (1991). *Arab Voices: The Human Rights Debate in the Middle East.* Berkeley: University of California Press, 2.

74. Ignatieff, M. (2001). The Attack on Human Rights. *Foreign Affairs* (November/December): 102–116.

75. Hicks, N. (2002). Does Islamist Human Rights Activism Offer a Remedy to the Crisis of Human Rights Implementation in the Middle East? *Human Rights Quarterly*, 24(2): 361–381. In the 1990s, Hicks directed a project aimed at building bridges between Islamist figures and international human rights promoters.

76. Inglehart, R. and Norris, P. (2003). The True Clash of Civilizations. *Foreign Policy*, 135 (March–April): 62–70, 65.

77. Walt, S. M. (2014, July 1). Democracy, Freedom and Apple Pie Aren't a Foreign Policy. *Foreign Policy.*

78. For example, Ali, A. H. (2007). *Infidel.* New York: Free Press.

79. For the Cairo declaration, see (1990, August 5). *The Cairo Declaration on Human Rights in Islam.* Retrieved from http://hrlibrary.umn.edu/instree/cairodeclaration.html.

80. Waltz, S. E. (2004). Universal Human Rights: The Contribution of Muslim States. *Human Rights Quarterly*, 26(4): 799–844.

81. WorldPublicOpinion.org (2008).

82. Aminu-Kano, M., Ali, A., and Fitzgibbon, A. (2014, April 15). Islamic and UN Bills of Rights: Same Difference. *openGlobalRights/openDemocracy*. London.

83. Abu-Lughod, L. (2013). *Do Muslim Woman Need Saving?* Cambridge, MA: Harvard University Press; Rinaldo, R. (2013). *Mobilizing Piety: Islamic Feminism in Indonesia.* Oxford: Oxford University Press; Salime (2011).

84. Moroccan regulations discourage survey companies from asking about religious identity. The vast majority of Moroccans are Sunni Muslims, however.

85. To determine this, we reran models regressing *Trust in Local Human Rights Organizations* on *Trust in Religious Institutions*, and as our independent variable of interest, interacted *Muslim* with *Trust in Religious Institutions.* The interaction term is not statistically significant, meaning there is no difference between Muslims and non-Muslims on this count.

86. This section was developed in conjunction with a Moroccan scholar of religion and politics, Meriem El Haitami.

87. Moroccan sociologists reach a similar conclusion. See, for example, Ayadi, M. El, Rachik, H., and Tozy, M. (2000). *L'Islam au Quotidien: Enquete sur les Valeurs et les Pratiques Religieuses au Maroc.* Casablanca: Prologues. Note that although mosque attendance is more common among males, some 30 percent of female respondents in Rabat/Casablanca reported attending mosque regularly. In other words, our findings are not an artifact of gender differences.

88. Driss, M. (2009). The Strengths and Limits of Religious Reforms in Morocco. *Mediterranean Politics*, 14(2): 195–211.

89. The controls, once again, are *Trust in Religious Institutions*, income squared, urban/rural residence, Internet use, support for the ruling political party, voted in recent national election, the *Human Rights Contact Index*, *Trust in Local Human Rights Organizations*, age, and gender. In Morocco, we modeled personal religiosity with *Frequency of Prayer*, whereas in Lagos and Mumbai we used *Importance of Religion* in daily life.

90. It is also possible that the translations and phrasing of the question in the local vernacular were not equivalent across countries—though, given the back translations of the question, we do not find

this to be the most probable explanation. The meaning of the word "participation," its dictionary definition, is roughly the same in the different survey languages. However, what *counts as* "participation"—the specific content and forms it assumes—is culturally conditioned. For example, in one context respondents could view simply giving money as participating, whereas in another the threshold might be higher—say, active attendance at religious study sessions. So, the wide-ranging participation figures reflect a mix of real differences in participation rates and differences in cultural constructions of what constitutes participation. Unfortunately, our data do not allow us to determine how much of the cross-country differences in religious participation is "real" and how much owes to "measurement error."

91. Cleary, E. L. (1997). *The Struggle for Human Rights in Latin America.* Westport, CT: Praeger.

92. Blacklock, C. and Macdonald, L. (1998). Human Rights and Citizenship in Guatemala and Mexico: From "Strategic" to "New" Universalism? *Social Politics*, 5(2): 132–157, 142.

93. Fox, J. and Hernández, L. (1995). Mexico's Difficult Democracy: Grassroots Movements, NGOs, and Local Government. In Charles A. Reilly (Ed.), *New Paths to Democratic Development in Latin America: The Rise of NGO-Municipal Collaboration.* Boulder: Lynne Rienner: Boulder, 199.

94. See Table 3.2, which shows that the two have a positive association in the pooled model, but not in the country-specific models.

95. These differences are all statistically significant. The 95 percent confidence intervals for the socially religious with high human rights contact are [.56, .65], whereas those for the non-socially religious with high human rights contact are [.46, .56].

96. McAdam, D. (1982). *Political Process and the Development of Black Insurgency, 1930–1970.* Chicago: University of Chicago Press.

Chapter 6

1. Reimann, K. D. (2006). A View from the Top: International Politics, Norms and the Worldwide Growth of NGOs. *International Studies Quarterly*, 50(1): 45–68.

2. The story of LHRO emergence in Latin America and Eastern Europe, followed by other world regions, is recounted by Ball, P. D. (2000). State Terror, Constitutional Traditions, and National Human Rights Movements: A Cross-National Quantitative Comparison. In J. Guidry, M. Kennedy, and M. Zald (Eds.), *Globalization and Social Movements*, 54–75. Ann Arbor: University of Michigan Press; Brysk, A. (1994). *The Politics of Human Rights in Argentina: Protest, Change and Democratization.* Palo Alto, CA: Stanford University Press; Keck, M. E and Sikkink, K. (1998). *Activists beyond Borders: Advocacy Networks in International Politics.* Ithaca, NY: Cornell University Press; Laber, J. (2002). *The Courage of Strangers: Coming of Age with the Human Rights Movement.* New York: Public Affairs; Thomas, D. C. (2001). *The Helsinki Effect: International Norms, Human Rights, and the Demise of Communism.* Princeton, NJ : Princeton University Press. The LHRO story is of course different than that of *international* human rights NGOs, which is ably recounted in volumes such as Hopgood (2006).

3. Easterly (2006).

4. As noted earlier, this "collective action" approach to studying advocacy NGOs, including human rights groups, was pioneered by Prakash and Gugerty (2010).

5. Dupuy, Ron, and Prakash (2015).

6. Hopgood (2013).

7. Pasha, M. K. and Blaney, D. L. (1998). Elusive Paradise: The Promise and Peril of Global Civil Society. *Alternatives* 23(4): 417–450; Hardt, M. and Negri, A. (2001). *Empire.* Cambridge, MA: Harvard University Press; Petras, J. (1999). NGOs: In the Service of Imperialism. *Journal of Contemporary Asia*, 29(4): 429–440; Reitan, R. (2007). A Global Civil Society in a World Polity, or Angels and Nomads against Empire? *Global Governance*, 13(3): 445–460.

8. The base-superstructure argument in Marxism is complex; see Cohen, G. A. (2000). *Karl Marx's Theory of History.* Princeton, NJ: Princeton University Press.

9. Cartalucci, T. (2012). Soros Leverages "Human Rights" for Personal Gain, as Does His Global NGO Empire. *Land Destroyer Report.* Retrieved from http://landdestroyer.blogspot.com/2012/03/surpise-soros-is-convicted-criminal.html.

10. Robinson, W. I. (1996). *Promoting Polyarchy: Globalization, US Intervention, and Hegemony.* New York: Cambridge University Press.

11. Santos and Garavito (2006).

12. In 2016 and 2017, we replicated these studies in Mexico City and Bogota (and added additional questions) with support from the Open Society Foundations. We have plans to extend this survey effort to other countries, including the US.

13. In 2015–2016, Amnesty International commissioned a GlobeScan poll of 27,000 people in 27 countries, asking how willing respondents were to accept refugees into their country, neighborhood, and home. Roughly 80 percent said they were willing to accept refugees into their country. See Elsayed-Ali, S. (2016, July 14). A Crisis That Shouldn't Be. *openGlobalRights/openDemocracy*. London.

Appendix A

1. Ethiopia is the exception; in 2010, the government recently targeted local human rights groups for extra scrutiny, along with a handful of other politically sensitive organizational categories.

2. Allen, L. (2013). *The Rise and Fall of Human Rights: Cynicism and Politics in Occupied Palestine*. Palo Alto, CA: Stanford University Press; Englund (2006); Hopgood (2006). Other important works in this genre include Clark, A. M. (2001). *Diplomacy of Conscience: Amnesty International and Changing Human Rights Norms*. Princeton, NJ: Princeton University Press; and Gordon, N. (2008). Human Rights, Social Space and Power: Why Do Some NGOs Exert More Influence than Others? *The International Journal of Human Rights*, 12(1): 23–39; Stroup (2012); and Wong (2012). In related work by Shareen Hertel (2006) and Clifford Bob (2005), local rights groups are integral to their analysis.

3. For statistically representative studies of transnational rights groups, see Meernik, J., Aloisi, R., Sowell, M., and Nichols, A. (2012). The Impact of Human Rights Organizations on Naming and Shaming Campaigns. *Journal of Conflict Resolution*, 56(2): 233–256; Smith, J. and Wiest, D. (2005). The Uneven Geography of Global Civil Society. *Social Forces*, 84(2): 621–652; Tsutsui, K. and Wotipka, C. M. (2004). Global Civil Society and the International Human Rights Movement: Citizen Participation in Human Rights International Nongovernmental Organizations. *Social Forces*, 83(2): 587–620.

4. For statistically representative studies of all legally registered NGOs within a given jurisdiction, including, but not limited to, human

rights groups, see Barr, A., Fafchamps, M. and Owens, T. (2005). The Governance of Non-Governmental Organizations in Uganda. *World Development*, 33(4): 657–679; Gauri, V. and Galef, J. (2005). NGOs in Bangladesh: Activities, Resources, and Governance. *World Development*, 33(12): 2045–2065.

5. Two partial exceptions include Berkovitch, N. and Gordon, N. (2008) and Okafor (2006). Both of these studies built comprehensive lists of local human rights organizations in specific jurisdictions (Israel, within the 1967 borders, and Nigeria), but then sampled from those lists in a purposive, rather than a representative, manner.

6. In India, co-author Archana Pandya constructed the Mumbai sampling frame, with supervision from James Ron, and then conducted the LHRO interviews in English and Hindi in 2010–2011; Ron joined her for several of those interviews. In Mexico, Spanish-speaking research assistants Sarah Peek, Laura Sparling, and co-author Archana Pandya constructed the sampling frames, with Ron's supervision, and conducted the interviews in 2010–2012. In Morocco, Moroccan-born research assistant Ghita Bennessahraoui constructed the Rabat and Casablanca sampling frames, under Ron's supervision, and conducted the interviews in French in 2011; in Nigeria; co-author Shannon Golden constructed the Lagos sampling frame and conducted 10 face-to-face and 20 written or online interviews in 2014.

7. Issue-Crawler analyzes virtual connections between websites. For details, see https://www.issuecrawler.net.

8. *Short Methodological Note* for the Corruption Perceptions Index 2010. Retrieved from http://www.transparency.org/policy_research/surveys_indices/cpi/2010/in_detail#4.

9. Figure pairs ordered so that the numbers from the purposive sample appear first.

10. Merry (2006); Tarrow, S. G. (2005). *The New Transnational Activism*. New York: Cambridge University Press.

11. Calhoun, C. (2002). The Class Consciousness of Frequent Travelers: Toward a Critique of Actually Existing Cosmopolitanism. *South Atlantic Quarterly*, 101(4): 871–897.

12. For details on the Mexican survey methodology, see http://mexicoy-elmundo.cide.edu/home2010english.swf, last accessed March 7, 2016.

13. More information about the project is available at: *Mexico and the World*. Retrieved from http://mexicoyelmundo.cide.edu/home2010english.swf, last accessed on March 7, 2016.

14. Website for Data-OPM, http://www.dataopm.net/, last accessed on March 7, 2016.

15. Website for LMS-CSA, http://www.lms-csa.com/, last accessed on March 7, 2016.

16. Website for CVOTER, http://www.teamcvoter.com/, last accessed on March 7, 2016.

17. Website for PSI, http://www.psi-research.net/nigeria.html, last accessed on March 7, 2016.

18. For the more statistically inclined, replication datasets and syntax files are available online on the project website, www.jamesron.com. We would be happy to provide more detailed information about our data collection and analyses, if requested.

19. Design weights correct for deliberate overrepresentation of specific groups. For example, Christians are about 4.2 percent of Mumbai's population, but constitute nearly 11 percent of our sample. We oversampled Christians (as well as Buddhists) in Mumbai so that we would have sufficient numbers for more precise statistical analysis of religious subpopulations. However, when estimating a descriptive statistic for the *entire* Mumbai population, such as average trust in local human rights organizations (LHROs), the overrepresentation of Christians could unduly pull the estimated average more toward the average for the Christian subpopulation and away from the true overall average.

A "design weight" thus reduces Christians' contribution to overall mean trust in LHROs so that their contribution is proportionate to their percentage in the population.

20. Survey researchers use "raking" techniques when adjusting sample proportions to population proportions for a relatively large number of weighting variables. Suppose that we want to weight the sample based on sex, rural/urban residence, age (four categories), and education (four categories). Combining these variables creates 64 possible categories (2 sex × 2 rural/urban × 4 age × 4 education) into which we could classify each respondent—for example, a rural woman between the ages of 15 and 29 who has completed primary school or less. If we

distribute 1,200 respondents into these 64 categories, each category will have, on average, 18.75 respondents, and conceivably far less for rarer combinations. (A typical raking application might involve many, many more categories.) This is simply too little information on which to calculate reasonable weights. Rather than adjusting sample-to-population proportions *for each possible combination*, "raking" finds a unique, single factor by which to multiply the number of people in each adjustment cell so that sample proportions match population proportions for each weighting variable *considered separately*. That is, the proportion of women in the sample will match the proportion of women in the population, and the proportion of rural residents in the sample will match the same proportion in the population, etc. (The proportion of rural women in the sample may differ from that in the population, though often not by much.) Finding this factor involves a procedure carried out in several passes, "iterative proportional fitting," which evoked a "raking" motion to the algorithm's discoverers. For details, see Deming, W. E. and Stephan, F. F. (1940). On a Least Squares Adjustment of a Sampled Frequency Table When the Expected Marginal Totals Are Known. *Annals of Mathematical Statistics*, 11(4): 427–444; Deville, J. C., Sarndal, C. E., and Sautory, O. (1993). Generalized Raking Procedures in Survey Sampling. *Journal of the American Statistical Association*, 88(423): 1013–1020.

21. There are a few other ways that we could have dealt with country-specific variation. We could have run "interaction effects" for each country-variable combination in the pooled model. To ease interpretation, however, we simply ran the full model on each country. Another technique might have been to adjust our models for "clusters"; however, we did not include cluster-adjusted standard errors, because four countries is too few "clusters" to make this approach appropriate.

22. Robust standard errors use a formula-based approach to correct standard error estimates when the data depart from certain key OLS assumptions, such as "heteroskedacity" (i.e., that the average difference between a model-predicted value and the observed value for a given characteristic is constant for all values of the predictor. "Bootstrapping" is an alternative approach to estimating standard errors for anomalous or complex data. Rather than using a formula, a bootstrap estimate involves "resampling," or using the original sample to draw a large number of additional samples, typically of the same size as the original sample but with "replacement" (meaning the same

respondent can appear more than once, and possibly many times, in the resample). Each resample is used to calculate the average regression coefficient, or other number that interests us, and the variability of this number over many resamples yields an estimate of the standard error.

23. Self-reported household income estimates are typically lower than official per capita GDP for a variety of reasons, the most important of which is that the former do not include corporate earnings, whereas the latter do. Past experience, moreover, demonstrates that polling respondents often underreport household income, whereas official GDP figures are estimated differently and, in some cases, more accurately. For this reason, our surveys asked respondents both for their estimated household income and the perceived relationship between income and expenditures. We typically use the latter in our regression analyses, but double-check our results with the former. In Appendix A, we report mean incomes, instead of the more widely used medians. In countries with heavily skewed income distributions, the **median** household income is often far lower than the **average** household income, which is driven upward by very wealthy households. This makes the median a better measure for estimating the population's central tendency. We were unable to use the median, however, because in each country, we asked respondents to report the *range* their household income fell into rather than estimate the precise number. Reporting income in categories rather than exact amounts allays potential respondent suspicion; furthermore, for economies with large informal sectors, respondents' income may vary widely from month to month. To estimate mean household incomes, we assigned each category the value in the middle of the range (so-called midpoint imputation), converted to 2014 PPP dollars, and with the last, open-ended category simply as 25 percent higher than the lower bound for the category. So, for example, a household income of "$0–$400 dollars" per month would be reckoned as $200, and one of "$5,000 or above" as $6,250. This allowed us to estimate means, but not medians. Even with this "linearized" income measure, income for each country still has only as many values as there are categories (around 10 or 11); that is, the data are still essentially categorical. Estimating a median requires a truly continuous distribution, with many, many different income points; calculating a median with categorical, rather than continuous, data will yield the midpoint of the modal income category

rather than a real median. Nonetheless, we do note that the modal categories of our respondents are roughly similar to those discovered by the relevant country-level Gallup polls in 2013. (For details, see http://www.gallup.com/poll/166211/worldwide-median-household-income-000.aspx.) Gallup, however, specified that the household incomes it was asking about were "pre tax," whereas we did not refer to tax.

Also note that in Morocco, India and Nigeria, our household income figures are for people living in major urban areas, whereas Gallup's estimates are for national populations. Urban household incomes are likely higher than the national median.

24. According to our Casablanca-based survey partners, the Moroccan authorities strongly discourage pollsters from asking directly about religious identity (or about the king). Still, most sources estimate that the overwhelming majority of Moroccans are Muslims.

Index

Note: Page references followed by a "*t*" indicate table; "*f*" indicate figure